Africa in World Politics:

A Pan-African Perspective

GUY MARTIN

Africa World Press, Inc.

P.O. Box 1892
Trenton, NJ 08607

P.O. Box 48
Asmara, ERITREA

Africa World Press, Inc.

P.O. Box 1892
Trenton, NJ 08607

P.O. Box 48
Asmara, ERITREA

Copyright © 2002 Guy Martin

First Printing 2002

Cover Design: Debbie Hird
Book Design: Roger Dormann

Library of Congress Cataloging-in-Publication Data

Martin, Guy, 1945-
    Africa in world politics: a Pan-African perspective/Guy Martin
      p.cm
    Includes bibliographical references (p.) and index
    ISBN 0-86543-857-9--ISBN 0-086543-858-7 (pbk.)
      1. Africa--Politics and government--1960-2. World politics--1945-
      3. Pan-Africanism.
    I. Title

DT30.5.M2752000
  327'.096--dc21   00-030616

Table of Contents

Preface

This volume brings together essays written in the course of twenty-six years of teaching, reflection, and research on Africa at various academic institutions in Africa and the United States. As such, they reflect successive stages of my evolving thinking about Africa's international relations. As the book's subtitle suggests, the common thread that binds these essays together is Pan-Africanism, viewed both as ideology and policy guide. In other words, the theme of the essential political, economic and cultural unity of Africa—as eloquently advocated by Cheikh Anta Diop—undergirds these essays. This book takes a resolutely continental-centered view of Africa's international relations. Such an approach differs significantly from the current literature on the subject, which tends to focus exclusively on sub-Saharan African (excluding north Africa) and to take the African state and its leaders as the main unit of analysis.[1] The essays in this volume show that five centuries of unequal and asymmetrical relations between Africa and Europe characterized by domination and exploitation through the successive historical processes of slavery, mercantilism, imperialism, colonialism, neo-colonialism and globalization have left Africa *un*developed—rather than *under*developed—and politically, economically and culturally dependent on the West as never before. The analysis is supported by detailed case studies of relations between Africa and Europe and Africa and France, as well as of the ideology of EurAfrica that undergirds these relations (chapters 1, 2 , 3 and 4). Thematic case studies of the theory and practice of non-alignment, African cooperation and integration, conflict and conflict resolution in Africa, cooperation in assistance to African refugees, and the crisis of the African nation-state (chapters 5, 6, 7, 8 and 9) complete this analysis. A final chapter (10) summarizes the main findings and takes a fresh look at the crisis of the African nation-state and the possible solutions to this crisis. Two sets of policy prescriptions are presented in the conclusion. The minimalist policy prescription includes the adoption and implementation by the African Union (AU) of the Africa Leadership Forum's 1991 *Kampala Document*, while a maximalist program—which I see as the only way out of the present African predicament—entails the revival and implementation of Kwame Nkrumah's and Cheikh Anta Diop's original Pan-Africanist projects, as updated by Edem Kodjo[2] and recently advocated by Libya's Muammar Qaddafi. In brief, the time has come for an African renaissance based on a thoroughly overhauled African state that would be people-centered and that would reconnect the indigenous/rural and modern/urban sectors, as well as the national, subregional and regional levels in Africa, leading to the eventual realization of continental political, economic and cultural unity. The alternative—the permanent political, geo-strategic, economic and cultural marginalization of Africa in the world system—is too ghastly to contemplate.

Acknowledgments

In the course of a long academic career in three continents, I have incurred too many intellectual debts to mention. During my early university education at *Sciences Po.* Grenoble, Pierre Broué taught me to appreciate the rigors of scientific research in the social sciences from a historical perspective, while Gustave Peiser introduced me to African politics. Donal Cruise O'Brien at the School of Oriental and African Studies, University of London, furthered my understanding of African politics. During my graduate studies at Indiana University-Bloomington in the early 1970s, I benefitted enormously from the teachings, encouragement and advice of Gwendolyn Carter, Sheldon Gellar, Edmond Keller, E. Philip Morgan and Patrick O'Meara. Ed Keller has since become a trusted colleague and friend, as have many scholars and practitioners encountered in my wanderings throughout Africa, Europe and North America. Those who have contributed to shape my thinking on African politics and international relations include: Samir Amin, Albert Bourgi, Michael Chege, Pathé Diagne, Cheik Oumar Diarrah, Yves Gauffriau, Pierre Haffner, Abdul Aziz Jalloh, Mamadou Kanté, Seydou Badian Kouyaté, Max Liniger-Goumaz, Jean-François Médard, Robert Tiéblé N'Daw, Daniel Katete Orwa, Habib Ouane, and William Syad. During and after my tenure on the Board of the African Association of Political Science, I have gained much from intensive intellectual interaction with such exceptional scholars and trusted friends as Claude Ake, Emmanuel Hansen and Sam Nolutshungu (all of whom passed away); and also Peter Anyang' Nyong'o, Abdoulaye Bathily, L. Adele Jinadu, Ibbo Mandaza, Dan Nabudere, and Georges Nzongola-Ntalaja. My stay in South Africa—at the University of the Western Cape,1996-1999—was made more enjoyable by the friendly presence and intellectual companionship of Benoît Antheaume, Jean-Christophe Bélliard, Benny Bunsee, Georges Hérault, Philippe and Muriel Lebreton, Bernard Magubane, Mahmood Mamdani, Johnny Maphunye, Jean-

◆》

Baptiste Meyer, Jacques de Monès, Harry Nengwekhulu, Lungisile Ntsebeza, Xavier Philippe, Kwesi Prah, Lawrence Sakarai, Derrick Swartz, Chris Tapscott, Rex Thakhathi and Peter Vale. Special thanks are due to Ursula Arends (UWC), who expertly typed the first draft of this book while busily engaged on other fronts. In the United States, I owe a particular debt of gratitude to Salih Booker, Herschelle Challenor, Manthia Diawara, Mark DeLancey, Robert Fatton, Jr., Richard Joseph, René Lemarchand, Shelby Lewis, William Minter, Berhanu Mengistu, Amii Omara-Otunnu, Olara Otunnu, Earl Picard, Fatemeh Shafiei, and Barry Schutz for providing intellectual stimulation and encouragement and support at crucial stages of my career. Last—but by no means least—I owe an immense debt of gratitude to my mother Marie-Berthe Martin Castreman (to whom this book is dedicated), and to my wife Mueni Wa Muiu, intellectual *alter ego*, friend and steadfast companion; without her gentle, but constant, prodding, this book might never have seen the light of day. May our wonderful children Yasmina Muthoki and José-Guy Musumbi be able to grow up in a truly independent and prosperous Africa. Needless to say, I am solely responsible for any remaining errors of fact or interpretation.

Endnotes

1. Three recent texts exemplify this perspective: Christopher Clapham, *Africa and the International System: The Politics of State Survival* (New York: Cambridge University Press, 1996); John W. Harbeson & Donald Rothchild (eds.), *Africa in World Politics: The African State System in Flux* (Boulder: Westview Press, 3rd edn., 2000); and Edmond J. Keller & D. Rothchild (eds.), *Africa in the New International Order: Rethinking State Sovereignty and Regional Security* (Boulder: Lynne Rienner, 1996). See also: Jeffrey Herbst, *States and Power in Africa: Comparative Lessons in Authority and Control* (Princeton: Princeton University Press, 2000).

2. These Pan-Africanist blueprints are included in the following: Cheikh Anta Diop, *Les Fondements économiques et culturels d'un État Fédéral d'Afrique noire* (Paris: Présence Africaine, 2nd edn., 1974); translated as *Black Africa: The Economic and Cultural Basis for a Federated State* (Chicago & Trenton: Lawrence Hill Books/Africa World Press, 1987); Edem Kodjo, *Et Demain l'Afrique* (Paris: Éditions Stock, 1985); translated as *Africa Today* (Accra: Ghana Universities Press, 1989); Kwame Nkrumah, *Africa Must Unite* (London: Panaf Books, 1963). See also: Africa Leadership Forum, *The Kampala Document: Towards a Conference on Security, Stability, Development and Cooperation in Africa* (Abeokuta & New York: Africa Leadership Forum, 1991).

INTRODUCTION

This collection of essays offers a Pan-African perspective on Africa's international relations. The theme of the essential political, economic and cultural unity of Africa undergirds these essays, as does a primary focus on African people and people of the African diaspora. Rather than viewing Africa's international relations from a regional and state-centered perspective, this book takes a resolutely continental and people-centered view of the subject. For purposes of this study, Pan-Africanism is defined as a political and cultural movement aimed at uniting African people and people of the African diaspora. Thus, according to Esedebe,

> Pan-Africanism is a political and cultural phenomenon that regards Africa, Africans and African descendants abroad as a unit. It seeks to regenerate and unify Africa and promote a feeling of oneness among the people of the African world. It glorifies the African past and inculcates pride in African values.[1]

The Pan-Africanist movement became institutionalized through the creation of the Organization of African Unity (OAU) in May 1963. The Pan-African definition of "Africa" conforms to the OAU's membership, which includes north Africa and the Indian Ocean islands of Comoros, Madagascar, Mauritius and Seychelles (Réunion and Mayotte remaining French "overseas" territories). Pan-Africanists take exception to the practice of arbitrarily separating the countries of north Africa (Algeria, Egypt, Libya, Morocco and Tunisia) from the rest of the continent under the pretense that they are part of the Arab world, and of focussing exclusively on "sub-Saharan Africa," from which South Africa—seen as "exceptional"—is conveniently excluded. They also denounce the French colonial practice of separating Madagascar and the other Indian Ocean islands from the rest of the continent.

◈

The Three Waves of Independence

The periodization of the international relations of African states closely parallels the decolonization process which unfolded gradually in a series of three successive waves beginning in the 1950s and ending in the 1990s.[2] With the exceptions of Ethiopia and Liberia, which were never colonized—except from the brief Italian occupation of Ethiopia between 1936 and 1941—, and of Egypt—which achieved its independence in 1922—, these three waves of independence were the following.

The first wave of independence began in the1950s and was dominated by the independence of the north African countries (Libya, 1951; Morocco, Tunisia, and Sudan, 1956), and of two West African trail-blazers (Ghana, 1957; Guinea, 1958). In the 1960s, more than 30 African countries peacefully achieved independence, including most former Belgian, British and French colonies in West, East, Central and Southern Africa (the latest being Botswana and Lesotho, 1966; Equatorial Guinea and Swaziland, 1968). This period was characterized by a series of African peoples and states' conferences, mostly initiated and organized by prominent Pan-Africanist leader Kwame Nkrumah of Ghana. These conferences included:
the first All African People's Conference/AAPC (Accra, Ghana, December 1958); the second AAPC (Tunis, Tunisia, January 1960); the third AAPC (Cairo, Egypt, March 1961); the first Conference of Independent African States/CIAS (Accra, April 1958); and the second CIAS (Addis Ababa, Ethiopia, June 1960). This period also saw the creation of two major rival ideological groups of states: The Brazzaville/Monrovia Group, made up of 20 moderate, pro-Western (and predominantly francophone) African states was constituted following the conferences of Brazzaville (December 1960) and Monrovia (May 1961). This group later developed into a moderate francophone political organization, the *Union africaine et malgache*/UAM (September 1961) and the *Organization commune africaine et malgache*/OCAM (1964) (note the arbitrary distinction

◈

made between Africa and Madagascar alluded to above).

The Casablanca Group, seven, predominantly radical nationalist/socialist African states (Algeria, Egypt, Ghana, Guinea, Libya, Mali and Morocco), constituted the other group. From this group emerged first the Ghana-Guinea Union (November 1958), later expanded into the Union of African States/UAS (the previous two, plus Mali: adopted December 1959; effective July 1961), which never actually evolved beyond the planning stage. Both groups eventually merged into the OAU, whose Charter was adopted at Addis Ababa on May 25, 1963.

The second wave of independence began with a military coup d'état in Portugal (April 25. 1974) which brought to power a government intent upon granting immediate independence to the country's five African colonies: Guinea-Bissau (September 1974); Mozambique (June 1975); Cape Verde (July 1975); São Tomé and Principe (July 1975); and Angola (November 1975). Two former French colonies and one former British colony also achieved independence in the mid to late-1970s: Comoros (July 1975); Djibouti (June 1977); and Seychelles (June 1976).

The third wave of independence, which emerged in the 1980s, was led by African liberation movements fighting against white-ruled minority regimes in Southern Africa. It led to the independence of Zimbabwe (April 1980) and Namibia (March 1990) and to the first democratically-elected government in South Africa (May 1994). Eritrea also became independent in May 1993, after a forty-year liberation struggle against Ethiopian imperial rule.

Africa During the Cold War

The first and second waves of independence occurred during the Cold War, a period of intense ideological, political, military and economic rivalry between the two superpowers and their respective allies: the United States and its Western allies within the North Atlantic Treaty Organization/NATO; and the Soviet Union and its

Eastern allies within the Warsaw Pact. Between 1960 and 1975, relations between the superpowers followed a pure "balance of power" logic whereby each side attempted to deny the other access to any supposedly "vacant" space. African states attempted to reduce their dependency and diversify their partners while maximizing diplomatic advantage.

With the 1975 Angolan crisis, relations between the superpowers and Africa changed radically. Soviet-American rivalry was no longer limited to the diplomatic-strategic domain and now extended into the domestic domain of African states as well as to economic dependence. As for the African actors, they were motivated less by a desire to diversify their sources of dependency than by a willingness to take full advantage of East-West divisions.[3] In December 1988, the U.S. and the Soviet Union co-sponsored a tripartite accord between Angola, Cuba and South Africa providing for the total withdrawal of the 50,000 Cuban troops from Angola (by July 1991), as well as for South Africa's withdrawal from Namibia, which was to achieve independence under U.N. supervision. Thus—largely through the diplomatic efforts of U.S. Assistant Secretary of State for Africa Chester Crocker—ended not only the last chapter in Africa's decolonization, but also one of the most serious East-West crises in Africa.[4]

Africa in the Post-Cold War International System

During the third phase of decolonization (late 1980s-early 1990s), the end of the Cold War and the disintegration of the Soviet empire offered both challenges and opportunities for Africa. In the post-Cold War international system, the economic conflict between North and South has replaced the East-West conflict between capitalism and socialism. Sacrosanct principles such as sovereignty, territorial integrity and the sanctity of colonially inherited borders are increasingly being challenged while new ones, such as international humanitarian intervention, regionalism and federalism, are emerging. In Africa as elsewhere, the nation-state is coming under threat from above (regionalism and federalism) and below (ethnicity). Technological innovation is now helping to further undermine the nation-states as capital and information criss-cross the world, unfettered by national boundaries.

The European-centered international system dating back to the Treaty of Westphalia (1648) is progressively giving way to a new, post-Cold War international system characterized by two apparently contradictory (but in fact complementary) trends: the erosion of sovereignty in favor of human rights protection and humanitarian intervention; and the isolationist tendency emerging within the major powers.[5] In the contemporary international system, African states have been characterized by Jackson and Clapham as "quasi-states" endowed with "negative" or "juridical" sovereignty as ascribed to them by other states, but devoid of the "positive sovereignty" that derives from effective control. According to Jackson, quasi-states are states that are recognized as sovereign and independent units by other states within the international system, but which cannot meet the demands of "empirical" statehood, which requires the capacity to exercise effective power within their own territories and to be able to defend themselves against external threat.[6] Such a view is consistent with Zartman's observation that in the post-Cold War world, not only has the bipolar, interstate system of world order dissolved, but in many parts of Africa the state itself has collapsed: "State collapse...refers to a situation where the structure, authority (legitimate power), law, and political order have fallen apart and must be reconstituted in some form, old or new."[7] Even those African states that have not collapsed are "penetrated" as a result of technological progress and the communications revolution that has made the world a truly "global village." As a result, there has been a substantial increase in the number of human activities promoting welfare, development and security across state boundaries in Africa. In particular, aid relief and humanitarian assistance in cases of man-made (war) or natural (earthquake, flood, drought) disasters has dramatically increased over the last five years. Africa is currently devastated by internal conflicts and their catastrophic consequences. Since 1970, more than 30 wars (mostly intra-state) have been fought in Africa. In 1996 alone, 14 of the 53 countries of Africa were afflicted by armed conflict, accounting for more than half of all war-related deaths worldwide and resulting in more than 8 million refugees, returnees and displaced persons. These conflicts have seriously undermined Africa's efforts to ensure long-term security, stability, development and peace for its peoples.[8]

In the post-Cold War international system of the 1990s, sovereignty was further eroded by a host of non-state entities that took an ever larger part in the affairs of Africa. The quasi-universal and compulsory implementation by African states of Structural Adjustment Programs imposed by the World Bank and International Monetary Fund/IMF aimed at liberalizing and privatizing their economies— have made those institutions the most powerful and intrusive intergovernmental organizations in the world. Various specialized agencies of the United Nations—such as the UN Infant & Children's Fund/UNICEF, the UN High Commissioner for Refugees / UNHCR and the World Food Program/WFP—are at the frontline of humanitarian intervention in Africa, along with international humanitarian non-governmental organizations (INGOs)—such as Africare, CARE, Catholic Relief Services, *Médecins sans Frontières*/MSF, the International Committee of the Red Cross/ICRC and World Vision. As a recent article has shown, these agencies are in fact somewhat "governmental" in the sense that they have become major conduits for the provision of governmental development aid and emergency relief, notably in the European Union and the United States. Thus, in 1999, the bulk of U.S. government aid to Africa (amounting to $711 million) was channeled to various INGOs through the U.S. Agency for International Development (U.S.-AID). Indeed, some conflict-resolution INGOs—such as the Carter Center, International Alert and Sant'Egidio—sometimes act as instruments of government foreign policy. Recently, a number of INGOs have come under intense scrutiny and criticism from popular-based local NGOs in Africa and their Western partners. In addition to the usual bureaucratic ills (waste, corruption), INGOs have been accused of posing as the 'secular missionaries' of the 21st century, trying to propagate Western values and impose their ideas on the local populations without debate. Groups that carry out population or birth-control projects—such as the International Planned Parenthood Federation—are particularly controversial; some are paid to carry out sterilization programs in Africa, seen by the West as "overpopulated". Furthermore, INGOs bring in Western living standards, personnel, and purchasing power, which can disrupt local markets and generate deep local resentment. Not only have INGOs diverted funds away from African governments, but they are often seen as directly challenging their sovereignty.[9]

As INGOS progressively take over functions and responsibilities that African states are unable to assume in complex emergencies situations, a new legal doctrine of the 'right' and 'duty' of humanitarian intervention is being shaped to justify such interventions. In an African context characterized by endemic internal conflicts, gross violations of human rights, and massive loss of civilian lives and productive capacity, the international humanitarian agencies are often called upon to step into the moral vacuum left by the state's failure in order to provide necessary protection and assistance. Thus, "The response of the international community has inevitably contributed to an erosion of traditional concepts of sovereignty in order to ensure international access to the affected population within state borders." [10] This new doctrine of the "right" and "duty" of humanitarian intervention is well captured by Deng and Lyons:

> Under exceptional circumstances when governments fail to discharge this responsibility and masses of their citizens become threatened with severe suffering and death, the international community should step in to provide the needed protection and assistance, even if the government of a state has not requested aid. Sovereignty, therefore, should

be understood to have both an internal dimension that requires responsibility by the sovereign authority for the citizens within its jurisdiction and an external dimension that obligates the international community to protect and assist those citizens when the national leaders refuse or fail to act responsibly.[11]

On the international level, sovereignty becomes a pooled function, to be protected when exercised responsibly, and to be shared when help is needed. According to Deng *et. al.*, it is best to think of international operations in terms of layers of assistance. The state exercises sovereignty at home. It can then turn to its neighbors for assistance, then to its regional partners, and finally to the global organization, the UN In the post-Cold War world, the international community is becoming less prone to intervene in internal crises than in the past: "Increasingly, the message to Africa is that even when the international community is prepared to assist, the primary responsibility must fall on the African themselves." Consequently, the sharing of sovereignty begins at the subregional and regional levels. In this regard, the role played by the Economic Community of West African States/ECOWAS in Liberia and Sierra Leone, the Southern African Development Community/SADC in Lesotho and Mozambique, the Inter-Governmental Authority on Development/IGAD in the Sudan, Somalia and Ethiopia/Eritrea, and the Arab Maghreb Union/AMU in Western Sahara are indicative of new attempts to exercise subregional responsibility and accountability within the regional framework.[12]

This book has ten chapters. **Chapter 1** is an inquiry into the major causes of the state of underdevelopment (or rather *un*development) and dependency of Africa in spite of its enormous wealth and tremendous economic potential. It argues that one of the main reasons for this situation lies in the nature of the political, economic, and cultural links which have tied Africa to Europe from the fifteenth century to the present, through successive historical processes of domination and exploitation, namely: slavery, mercantilism, imperialism, colonialism, neo-colonialism and globalization. The ideology of EurAfrica (*L'Eurafrique*), based on the twin concepts of 'complementarity' and 'interdependence', thus appears as a convenient justification for colonialism and for the various neo-colonial contractual arrangements between Africa and Europe, notably the Conventions of Yaoundé I and II (1964 to 1975), the four successive Lomé Conventions (Lomé I, 1975-80 to Lomé IV, 1990-2000) and the Cotonou Agreement (2000-2020). In the final analysis, the ideology of EurAfrica is a mere rationalization of the neo-classical theory of international development and of the contemporary international division of labor. In conclusion, it is argued that only continental economic and political integration can allow Africa to extricate itself from the neo-colonial predicament in which it presently finds itself and attain genuine and complete economic independence.

As a case-study of EurAfrica in action, **Chapter 2** views the conclusion of negotiations for the Lomé V Convention (2000-2010) as an appropriate time to reflect over , and take stock of 25 years of ACP-EU cooperation under the Lomé regime. This chapter explores the potential political and economic impact of the evolving European regionalism on the Lomé regime in general, and on the 47 sub-Saharan African members of the ACP group in particular. Some attention is devoted to an analysis of Franco-African economic relations in the context of the anticipated reform of the franc zone system and associated preferential trade area. The central focus of this chapter is the extent to which the Lomé regime might help mitigate the negative impact of Africa' increasing political and economic marginalization in the context of post-Cold War globalization. The chapter begins with an overview of Euro-African relations between 1958 and 1990. A brief economic evaluation of Lomé I to IV, supplemented by a preview of Lomé V reveals no fundamental change in the traditional pattern of Euro-African relations. Finally, the chapter assesses the short and medium-term economic impact of the Single European Act (SEA) and European Monetary Union (EMU), and the long-term political impact of European integration on the African ACP states.

Taking up the issue of Franco-African relations, **chapter 3** argues that while noticeable signs of change in relations between France and its former colonies in Africa began to appear in the post-Cold War era (particularly since 1990), elements of continuity include their enduring historical and cultural ties; their informal, intimate, and secretive politico-diplomatic relations, typified by the bi-annual Franco-African summit meetings, and the fact that the continent remains of great economic importance to France. As for the gradual process of democratization which has swept throughout francophone Africa in recent years, there is evidence that this has been selectively supported by France according to criteria pertaining more to its core foreign-policy interests than to ideological, legalistic, moral, or humanitarian considerations. This chapter argues that the most profound changes in Franco-African relations have occurred in the economic domain: first the redirection of French trade and capital investment away from francophone states to others on the continent; followed, more ominously, by the 50 per cent devaluation of the CFA franc in January 1994, thereby signaling the demise of the franc zone. This, more than any other single event since independence, might truly mark the dawn of a new era in Franco-African relations.

Taking the analysis one step further, **chapter 4** tries to answer the following question: is France's African policy truly in transition between old-style neo-colonial and patrimonial type of policies characterized by intimate and quasi-familial relations between the French and francophone African elites—variously referred to as *le village franco-africain* or *la Françafrique*—and a new policy in which francophone Africa is subsumed within a broader Third World policy, thus becoming normalized (*normalisée* and *banalisée*)? In other words, is France resolutely moving away from its traditional policy of *domaine réservé* and *chasse gardée* toward a politico-diplomatic, military and economic and financial disengagement from, and redeployment in Africa? In brief, are we truly witnessing a decolonization of

Franco-African relations? After an overview of the historical context and main characteristics of Franco-African relations, this chapter argues that France's African policy is truly at a transitional stage in which clear signs of change and new orientations co-exist with old habits and status quo policies. It concludes that the extent to which real change shall take place in Franco-African relations depends on the political will of the various actors involved, as well as on Africa's 'new leadership' tendency to exclude France and favor purely African solutions to African problems.

Chapter 5 examines the theory and practice of non-alignment in a Cold War context, taking the francophone states of West and Central Africa as a case in point. In a world system that was dominated by the two superpowers (the U.S. and the former Soviet Union), non-alignment was an expression of the resolve of the smaller nations of Africa, Asia, Europe, Latin America and the Pacific to maintain a reasonable degree of political, military, and economic independence in foreign policy decisions and actions. As the former French colonies of West and Central Africa became independent in the early 1960s, they naturally joined the Non-Aligned Movement (NAM). However, while some of these countries retained close political, military, and economic ties with France throughout the following decades, other moved away from France toward closer ties with socialist countries. The purpose of this chapter is to retrace this separate, but unequal historical evolution and to assess the extent to which the francophone African states could still be characterized as 'non-aligned', using such criteria as diplomatic and military alignment, voting in the U.N., and economic relations (trade and aid) with developed countries. This leads us to conclude that by the time of the Eighth Non-Aligned Summit Meeting (Harare, Zimbabwe, August-September 1986), few, if any, francophone African states remained non-aligned in the original sense of the term.

Chapter 6 provides an overview on the subject of African regional cooperation and integration. Part one states a compelling case for regional cooperation and integration in Africa. Thus, of all the developing regions of the world, Africa is, by far, the poorest, least developed, and most foreign-trade and market dependent; it is also the least regionally integrated and the slowest growing in terms of mutual interdependence. Part two reviews contending approaches and perspectives on regional cooperation and integration: *Panafricanists*, who favored political integration as a prerequisite to economic integration, vs. *Gradualists* or *Functionalists*, anxious to preserve their states' sovereignty and favoring a more gradual approach to African integration. Part three surveys the aims and activities of 11 African subregional cooperation and integration schemes, and concludes with an analysis of the continent-wide 1994 *African Economic Community* (AEC) aiming at creating a single *African Common Market* (ACM) by 2025. Part four identifies four main obstacles to the realization of African regional cooperation and integration, namely: (i) the uneven distribution of the benefits and costs of integration; (ii) politico-ideological factors; (iii) external dependence; and (iv) ethno-regional conflct. The chapter concludes with the outline of a strategy for future cooperation and integration in Africa.

Chapter 7 tackles the issue of conflict and conflict resolution in Africa. Over the last forty years, Africa has been (and continues to be) one of the most conflict-ridden regions of the world, resulting in untold human suffering.Thus, it has been estimated that between 1955 and 1995, some 7 to 8 million people died as a result of violent conflict in Africa. In 1996 alone, 14 of the 53 countries of Africa were afflicted by armed conflicts, accounting for more than half of all war-related deaths worldwide and resulting in more than 8 million refugees, returnees and displaced persons. While African conflicts are typically internal rather than inter-state, many of these conflicts take on an increasingly subregional character. Furthermore, 90% of the victims of African conflicts are innocent civilians (mostly women and children). As of March 2000, some form of (latent or open) conflict persists in half of the African countries (26 out of 53). In view of this appalling situation, a number of peace-making, peace-keeping and peace-building measures and policies are advocated to mitigate, resolve and prevent violent conflict in Africa. After a brief overview of the way in which African conflict should be analyzed, this chapter examines the impact of recent changes in the external environment on these conflicts and reviews new conflict management approaches. It concludes that subregional and federal frameworks are best suited for the resolution of conflict in Africa.

The issue of international solidarity and cooperation in assistance to African refugees is anlyzed in **chapter 8**. Taking the exodus into eastern Congo of 2 million Rwandan refugees in the aftermath of the April 1994 genocide as a case in point, this chapter shows how the hesitant, belated and inadequate response of bilateral donor governments (notably the U.S. and France), inter-governmental organizations (notably the U.N. and the OAU) and of certain humanitarian NGOs placed an unbearable burden on the African countries concerned (especially Congo/Zaïre and Tanzania). The Rwanda crisis once again brought into sharp focus the paramount moral duties of the international community in terms of international solidarity and burden-sharing. It also raises the question of the actual commitment of the international community to seeking permanent and durable (i.e. political) solutions to the refugee problem in Africa, and begs the question of whether one is not witnessing a progressive evolution of international humanitarian policies from burden-sharing to what should be more appropriately called 'burden-shifting'.

Chapter 9 focusses on the crisis of the nation-state in Africa. It starts from the observation that the end of the Cold War and the disintegration of the Soviet empire offer both challenges and opportunities for Africa. In the post-Cold War international system, the economic conflict between North and South has replaced the East-West conflict between capitalism and socialism. Sacrosanct principles, such as sovereignty, territorial integrity and the sanctity of existing borders are increasingly being challenged while new ones, such as international humanitarian intervention, regionalism and federalism are emerging. In Africa as elsewhere, the nation-state is coming under threat from above (regionalism and federalism) and below (ethnicity). While Afro-pessimists predict that the African state is in danger of imminent collapse, Afro-optimists caution that it would be unwise to ignore the signs of hope, which could be amplified over time to allow Africa to recover lost ground. After a brief overview of some of the most serious threats to the postcolonial African nation-state's sovereignty and integrity, this chapter examines the opportunities available to these states as they attempt to improve their condition and status in the post-Cold War world through various (subregional, regional or federal) strategies of economic and political development.

Chapter 10 tries to pull together various themes and aspects of African international relations developed in the book and examines the continuing relevance of Pan-Africanism in the twenty-first century. More specifically, this chapter is an enquiry into the root causes, manifestations and possible solutions to the present African predicament. The African state system, I argue, has been shaped by successive exogenous processes of political domination and economic exploitation, namely the trans-Atlantic slave trade, mercantilism, imperialism, colonialism, neo-colonialism, and neo-imperialism (or "globalization"). Recent manifestations of the African predicament include war, ethnic/religious conflict, genocide, disease, famine, and malnutrition. Economically, Africa remains as *un*developed and dependent as ever. Drawing ideological inspiration from various African political thinkers, Mueni Wa Mui and I then sketch the contours of a new paradigm for the study of African politics and international relations named *Fundi Wa Afrika*. This ideal African state builds, on the remnants of African indigenous institutions, a democratic and developmental state which is truly an instrument of people's power. Eventually leading up to the realization of the Pan-African project of a United States of Africa, *Fundi Wa Afrika*, we argue, is a historical necessity if peace and security are to prevail on the continent.

Endnotes

1. P. Olisanwuche Esedebe, *Pan-Africanism: The Idea and Movement, 1776-1991* (Washington, DC: Howard University Press, 2nd edn., 1994), p. 5.

2. Peter Schraeder identifies five successive waves of independence: 1950s, 1960s, 1970s, 1980s-1990s, and 1990s to the present. We prefer to reduce these to three, namely: 1950s-1960s, 1970s, and 1980s to the present. See Peter J. Schraeder, *African Politics and Society: A Mosaic in Transformation* (Boston & New York: Bedford/St.Martin's, 2000), pp. 118-120.

3. See in particular Zaki Laïdi, *The Super-Powers and Africa: The Constraints of a Rivalry, 1960-1990* (Chicago: The University of Chicago Press, 1990).

4. For a first-hand account by one of the key negotiators, see Chester A. Crocker, *High Noon in Southern Africa: Making Peace in a Rough Neighborhood* (New York: W.W. Norton & Co., 1992); see also: Herman J. Cohen, *Intervening in Africa: Superpower Peacemaking in a Troubled Continent* (New York: Palgrave, 2000).

5. See Francis M. Deng, S. Kimaro, T. Lyons, D. Rothchild & I.W. Zartman, *Sovereignty as Responsibility: Conflict Management in Africa* (Washington, DC: The Brookings Institution, 1996), p. xv.

6. Robert H. Jackson, *Quasi-states: Sovereignty, International Relations and the Third World* (New York: Cambridge University Press, 1990); Christopher Clapham, *Africa and the International System: The Politics of State Survival* (New York: Cambridge University Press, 1996), pp. 15-24.

7. I. William Zartman, "Introduction: Posing the Problem of State Collapse," in I.W. Zartman (ed.), *Collapsed States: The Disintegration and Restoration of Legitimate Authority* (Boulder: Lynne Rienner Publishers, 1995), p. 1.

8. *The Causes of conflict and the promotion of durable peace and sustainable development in Africa* (New York: United Nations,

Report of the Secretary-General, 25 February 2000), pp. 2-3.

9. For a comprehensive and well-documented survey of the activities and impact of INGOs in the Third World and Africa, see "Sins of the secular missionaries," *The Economist* (29 January 2000), pp. 25-27. In a recent study on Congo, Colette Braeckman documents how INGOs who had intervened in the Kivu region of eastern Congo in the wake of the 1994 Rwanda genocide seriously contributed to degrading the environment (roads destroyed by their heavy vehicles, destruction of entire forests to provide firewood for the camps); she also shows as the same were party to the indiscriminate slaughtering of 450,000 heads of cattle in North-Kivu by refugees for purposes of providing meat to their camps, thus destroying the means of livelihood of the local peasants (Colette Braeckman, *L'Enjeu Congolais: L'Afrique centrale après Mobutu*. Paris: Fayard, 1999, pp. 134-138).

10. Francis M. Deng *et. al.*, *Sovereignty as Responsibility*, p. xiii.

11. Francis M. Deng & Terrence Lyons, "Promoting Responsible Sovereignty in Africa," in F.M. Deng & T. Lyons (eds.), *African Reckoning: A Quest for Good Governance* (Washington, DC: Brookings Institution Press, 1998), p. 3.

12. F.M. Deng *et. al.*, *Sovereignty as Responsibility*, pp. xvii-xix (the quote is from p. xix).

Chapter 1

Africa and the Ideology of Eurafrica:
Neo-colonialism or Pan-Africanism?

This chapter is an inquiry into the major causes of the continued state of underdevelopment (or *un*development) and dependency of Africa in spite of its enormous mineral wealth and tremendous agricultural potential. It constitutes a follow-up to earlier, historical queries on the present state of African economies:

> In order to understand present economic conditions in Africa, one needs to know why it is that Africa has realised so little of its natural potential, and one also needs to know why so much of its present wealth goes to non-Africans who reside for the most part outside of the continent.[1]

I argue that one of the main reasons for this situation lies in the nature of the political, economic, and cultural links which have tied Africa to Europe ever since the fifteenth century. Trade, based on unequal exchange and specialization, constitutes the mainstay of this relationship, be it the slave trade from the fifteenth to the nineteenth centuries, the "trade economy" of the "colonial pact" from 1900 to 1960, or the unequal neo-colonial trade since then.

The ideology of *L'Eurafrique* (EurAfrica), based on the twin concepts of "complementarity" and "interdependence," appears as a convenient justification for colonialism, and also helps to explain various contractual arrangements between Africa and Europe since independence (Yaoundé and Lomé Conventions, and Cotonou Agreement). In the final analysis, this ideology appears as a mere rationalization of the neo-classical theory of international development, and of the contemporary international division of labour. Ultimately, it seems that continental economic and political integration offers the best prospects for extricating Africa from the neo-colonial predicament in which it presently finds itself, and for the attainment of genuine economic independence.

The ideology of EurAfrica is a body of thought, originating in the colonial period, according to which the fate of Europe and Africa is seen as being naturally and inextricably linked at the political, economic, social, and cultural levels. The two continents are alleged to "complement" each other in almost every way—for example, Europe requires Africa's raw materials, manpower and markets, while Africa needs the capital, technology, and know-how of Europe. This best illustrates their "interdependence"—or rather, their dependence on each other in every respect. Ultimately, the ideology of EurAfrica views the complete integration of the two continents—or the absorption of Africa by Europe—as the ideal solution: "If we do not want to lose Africa as a precious source of raw materials and as an outlet for our products, Europe must participate in the absorption of the black continent."[2]

When placed in its proper historical context—namely, the period of European imperialism and colonialism in Africa during the late nineteenth and early twentieth centuries—the ideology of EurAfrica appears as a justification by the European ruling classes of their polit-

2

ical domination, economic exploitation, and cultural subjugation of the African territories and people. The concepts of "complementarity" and "interdependence" were interpreted in a one-sided manner as serving the interests of the *métropole* rather than those of the colony, which in any case had no say in the matter. Europe needed African resources and manpower for its continued growth, industrialization and development, hence the resort to an ideology to justify Europe's political domination and economic exploitation.

THE IDEOLOGY OF EURAFRICA AS A JUSTIFICATION FOR COLONIALISM

It was through the medium of trade that Europe and Africa first came into contact in the fifteenth century, and this determined their relationship from then onwards.[3] Besides spices, gold, and ivory, the main exports until the end of the nineteenth century were slaves. According to Walter Rodney, "To discuss trade between Africans and Europeans in the four centuries before colonial rule is virtually to discuss slave trade."[4]

This trade was, from the beginning, highly unequal and imposed on a subordinate people. While Africa became progressively, over a period of four centuries, deprived of its most precious economic resource, human capital, "it received in exchange some insignificant hardware, and the means for its cultural, social, and moral destruction. The introduction of alcoholic beverages, guns, and gunpowder served to achieve these aims."[5] Europeans set the rules to benefit themselves, and there is no doubt that their gains were at the expense of the African populations. Thus, to quote Rodney again, "Africa helped to develop Western Europe in the same proportion as Western Europe helped to underdevelop Africa."[6] While the seeds of underdevelopment were being sown on the African continent, the European countries were laying the industrial foundations of their own economic prosperity, which would lead them to compete in Africa to secure sources of raw materials and markets for their products.

Imperialism, characterised by Lenin as "the highest stage of capitalism," took, towards the end of the nineteenth century, the form of "the extension of capitalism into new territories, and the economic and political struggle among the older capitalist countries to gain these territories."[7] The "Scramble for Africa" culminated with the Berlin Conference of 1884-85, during which "the division of all territories of the globe among the great capitalist powers [was] completed."[8] Africa was now carved up into various European zones of influence, with the British and the French retaining for themselves the largest chunks of the continent.

Colonialism is essentially "a political phenomenon, whereby the sovereignty of a state and a people are totally alienated for the benefit of a foreign power:"[9] The colonial power puts itself in a position to decide which policies are best suited to the interests of the colonies and the indigenous people, and to firmly control the decision-making machinery, both national and local, designed to implement these policies.

Colonialism has been justified on a variety of grounds. These include: the elimination of the slave trade and of inter-ethnic disputes and wars (i.e. 'pacification'); the distribution to the indigenous people of the various social benefits of European civilization, notably education, religion, sanitation, and health; and the 'opening up' of underdeveloped areas to modern trade and industry by establishing foreign trading companies and transport infrastructures.

Of all these arguments the economic factor seems to be the most significant. According to Lord Lugard, architect of Britain's colonial policy of "indirect rule," "the partition of Africa was, as we all recognise, due primarily to the economic necessity of increasing the supplies of raw materials and food to meet the needs of the industrialised nations of Europe."[10]

Africa became the main supplier of raw materials and agricultural products to Europe, notably groundnuts, palm oil, coffee, cocoa, bananas, and timber. At the same time, Europe's manufactured goods found an ideal outlet in the new markets of the continent.

Under the protection of the colonial preferential trading areas, the prices of Africa's exports were set abnormally low, while imported goods were fixed artificially high.

Thus, the mechanisms and institutions of the *Économie de traite* (trade economy) of the early twentieth century were progressively established in accordance with the following "rules" applying to the colonies: they could only admit goods that originated from the *métropole*; they could only export to the *métropole* on a duty-free basis; they could not set up their own manufacturing industries; and they had to rely on the carriers of the *métropole* for the transportation of both their exports and imports.[11]

Under this international division of labor the colonies were restricted to the function of suppliers of raw materials and agricultural products, while the various European *métropoles* reserved for themselves the exclusivity of industrial production and the export of manufactured goods. Thus was established a system of "unequal exchange" whereby the exploitation of the colonies was manifested not only by underpricing African exports and overpricing imports from the *métropole*, but also by paying very low wages to the African labor force—despite long working hours and fairly high productivity—which resulted in the extraction of a substantial amount of surplus value to the benefit of the colonial administration.

This situation prevails to this day. Indeed, according to Arghiri Emmanuel's theory of unequal exchange, "a certain category of countries...whatever they undertake and whatever they produce, always exchange a larger amount of their national labor for a smaller amount of foreign labor."[12] One of the most serious and far-reaching consequences of the "trade economy" is to put the colonies in a situation of complete subservience to, and dependency on, the *métropole*. As one of the shrewdest analysts of French colonial policy has remarked, "The trade economy puts the colony in a state of total dependency vis-à-vis the *métropole*. The trading network is geared towards it: it buys only for export and sells only imported goods. The deeper the degree of penetration of the trade economy, the greater the dependency."[13]

Another major consequence of colonialism was to bring more and more farmers and laborers into the money economy by introducing the capitalist mode of production into the most remote parts of the continent, thereby helping to increase their dependence on the world economy. Africa was progressively drawn into an intricate network of economic relations with Europe from which it would find it difficult to extricate itself.

A further, far-reaching consequence of colonialism was the deliberate metropolitan policy of non-industrialization. One aim of the French in Africa was clearly to prevent the emergence of an industrial base that might undersell French manufacturers, both in the colonies and in France, and more significantly, provide the means for a progressive decrease in Africa's dependency on the *métropole*.

The first EurAfricanists appeared among metropolitan interest-groups with a stake in the colonial venture: politicians, military officers, businessmen, colonial administrators, educators, and missionaries. In Francophone Africa, the names of Joseph Caillaux, Anton Zischka, and Eugène Guernier, among others, are associated with the embryonic formulation of a EurAfrican ideology at the beginning of the twentieth century. These early ideologues attempted, with varying degree of success, to justify and rationalise the colonial venture on the basis of the natural complementarity and resultant "interdependence" of the two continents. As one of them succinctly put it:

> The African soil is too poor for Africa to be able to do without Europe. The African sub-soil is too rich for Europe to be able to do without Africa. Thus, it must be recognized that Africa is an indispensable complement to Europe.[14]

In short, the early EurAfricanists viewed Africa as a mere appendage of Europe, to be used to promote the latter's industrial development, to its exclusive economic benefit.

Consequently, from its inception, the ideology of EurAfrica appeared as a convenient—if somewhat unconvincing—justification of the colonial policies of the European powers (particularly of France) in Africa. More specifically, it was a rationalization of the inherently unequal and fundamentally exploitative economic policies implemented by the *métropoles* in their African territories, which contributed to further the latter's dependency on the "mother country." The genesis of the ideology of EurAfrica should be kept in mind when the post-colonial era of Africa is being analyzed.

THE IDEOLOGY OF EURAFRICA AS A JUSTIFICATION FOR NEO-COLONIALISM

Neo-colonialism is a strategy that has been devised by the European powers in order to allow them to carry on the economic exploitation of their former colonies, while relinquishing political power to a *comprador* national bourgeoisie, described by Frantz Fanon as nothing but "an intermediary...the transmission-belt between the nation and a capitalism...that is forced to put on the mask of neo-colonialism, thus becoming the mere business agents of the Western bourgeoisie."[15]

One of the main consequences of neo-colonialism has been to enable the former *métropoles* to continue to dominate the newly "independent" nations, militarily, economically, and culturally. Nkrumah's assessment of what has happened is quite appropriate:

> The essence of neo-colonialism is that the State which is subject to it, is in theory independent and has all the outward trappings of international sovereignty. In reality its economic system and thus its political policy is directed from outside.[16]

According to Johan Galtung, one of the main ploys of neo-colonialism is

...to make sure that the dominated countries do not

7

have too much direct, horizontal contact among themselves, particularly not economic interaction, trade. [Furthermore]...contact with the outside world should be vertical, towards the centre rather than horizontal, among the periphery countries.[17]

This age-old strategy of "divide and rule" manifests itself in "the principle of breaking up former large united colonial territories into a number of small non-viable States, which are incapable of independent development."[18] It is such a policy of "balkanization" that France has successfully carried out in Africa. Although the locally-elected nationalist leaders of most of the 12 territories of the *Fédération d'Afrique occidentale française* (AOF) and the *Fédération d'Afrique équatoriale française* (AEF) expressed their desire to obtain independence within these larger administrative frameworks, French officials, by engineering the *Loi Cadre* [framework law] of June 1956, manoeuvred in such a way that independence was finally granted to each territory separately.[19]

Neo-colonialism is a multi-faceted phenomenon including military, cultural, and technological dependency. However, the main focus of this chapter will be on the fundamental economic implications of dependence.

Association between Africa and Europe became formalized in 1958, when France obtained the necessary agreement of its five European partners that its colonies be granted preferential status under Part IV of the Treaty of Rome (which created the EEC) in terms of trade, aid, and investment. When these territories became independent in 1960, it became necessary to renegotiate the association status between the six EEC and the 18 African Associated States.[20]

While the first Yaoundé Convention (1964-1969) reproduced the Part IV provisions with hardly any modifications, the second (1971-1975) introduced minor innovations, still leaving the basic structure of the original agreement intact. Meanwhile, when Mauritius joined in 1972, the "Eighteen" became "Nineteen"—

including 12 former members of the French West and Central African Federations, as well as the three ex-Belgian colonies.[21]

From the outset, these formal EurAfrican ties provoked virulent criticisms from Ghana's first President, Kwame Nkrumah—a staunch Pan-Africanist– as well as from other African nationalist leaders. They suspiciously viewed this new association as the multilateralization of former bilateral dependency ties, whereby six powerful, developed countries were virtually annexing 18 of the poorest, most underdeveloped and powerless countries of Africa. It was, typically, an association of the rider and the horse, in which the former had everything to win and the latter everything to lose. This marked, in Nkrumah's words, "the last stage of imperialism":

> The Treaty of Rome, which brought into being the European Common Market, can be compared to the treaty that emanated from the Congress of Berlin in the 19th century; the latter treaty established the undisputed sway of colonialism in Africa; the former marks the advent of neo-colonialism in Africa.[22]

Europe's policy of association was viewed as a typical strategy of "divide and rule," as a deliberate attempt to preserve old colonial and linguistic cleavages, to prevent autonomous development, and to impede the formation of regional or continental political and economic groupings. Indeed, it was alleged that here was a new and convenient device to maintain the status of Africans as "hewers of wood and drawers of water"—that is as suppliers of raw materials and agricultural products.[23]

When the first Lomé Convention was signed in February 1975, policy-makers and academics exhibited a considerable degree of euphoria over what were considered to be far-reaching innovations as compared to the Yaoundé Conventions.

One of the main arguments of the advocates of Lomé I was that it would have a positive effect on African unity. Throughout the many months of preliminary meetings the African, Caribbean, and Pacific (ACP) states had negotiated as a group rather than separately, and, in the process, they had demonstrated a high degree of cohesion and bargaining skill. Furthermore, the fact that the African ACP countries included both French and English-speaking ex-colonies (following Britain's entry into the EEC in January 1973) was seen as another cohesive factor.[24]

On the other hand, since 1978 Europe has maintained separate co-operation agreements with four North African countries that are also members of the Organization of African Unity (OAU): Algeria, Morocco, Tunisia, and Egypt. Indeed, as argued by Timothy Shaw: "If the earlier Yaoundé, Arusha, and Nigeria agreements with the EEC served to divide Black Africa, then the EEC's Mediterranean policy tends to separate Black from Arab Africa, or Arab League from OAU."[25]

To what extent is the Lomé Convention less neo-colonial than its predecessors? Certainly the two concepts of "complementarity" and "interdependence," which are central to the ideology of EurAfrica, were frequently referred to by the European advocates of Lomé. For example, according to the former European Commissioner for Development Claude Cheysson:

> We are dependent on the Third World here and now as well as in the future. It, in turn, depends on us to a considerable degree. Our interests are linked. We should, therefore, try to express this dependence clearly and irrevocably.[26]

The new international division of labour is justified by this phraseology. On the one side, the countries of the Third World continue to specialize in the production and export of raw materials and agricultural products, and are allowed to conduct some limited, labor-intensive manufacturing activities, such as import-substitution, first-stage processing, and relatively "light" industries. On the other side, the industrialized countries reserve for themselves the most capital-intensive, technologically-advanced types of production, including electronics, computers, aeronautics, space industries, and nuclear energy.

In the transition from the colonial to the neo-colonial pact, the essence of unequal exchange remains unaffected. This situation results in a continued and increased dependency of the majority of African states on the metropoles. In the final analysis, Europe's main objective through the Lomé Conventions has been to obtain secure and stable access to Africa's strategic raw materials—notably, oil, uranium, bauxite, and non-ferrous metals—while gaining preferential access to additional markets, where the excess capacity of European industries can find a convenient outlet.

Politically, the Lomé Conventions, following typical Cold War alliances, linked the majority of African governments to the destinies of Western Europe. According to a European version of the Monroe Doctrine, the members of the EEC (and especially France) saw themselves as the watchdogs of the interests of this Western alliance in Africa. This policy was designed to counter the economic weight of the United States and Japan, as well as the political influence of the U.S.S.R.

Lomé I was indeed a neo-colonial pact, linking Europe and Africa in a contractual relationship of little value to the latter, but of great benefit to the former; the ideology of EurAfrica was used to justify this unequal relationship. As suggested by Michael Dolan, perhaps this Convention has been one of the European Community's greatest achievements, "but for Europe, not for the developing world."[27]

The ideology of EurAfrica is but an outgrowth of the neo-classical (or liberal) theory of international development. According to this theory, the goods that a nation should export and import ought to be decided according to its own specific factor endowment (i.e. availability of land, labor and capital).[28] On the basis of a cost-benefit analysis—and other things being equal—, all countries should be better off by opening up their economies to international transactions. Part of the domestic output will be exported, and part of the domestic demand will be satisfied by imports. As a result, the goods which the two partners are in a position to consume will be greater than would be the case in a closed economy. Hence the need for each country to specialize in the production of goods in which it has a relative cost advantage, resulting from a particular factor of production endowment.

The original formulation of this theory by David Ricardo has been frequently modernized and refined, notably by Heckscher, Ohlin, Samuelson, and Lerner. It is maintained that each country must specialize in the production and export of those goods which use most intensively the relatively more abundant factor. This means that, ultimately, the initial factor endowment plays a crucial role in the international specialization of each country in a particular type of production. According to the Heckscher-Ohlin-Samuelson formulation, trade will be most likely between unlike economies, and the gains will be maximized where conditions are most dissimilar. Therefore, trade will be greatest, and the gains largest, between North and South, where factor endowments and, consequently, costs of production differ most. It follows that the advanced economies will export capital-intensive goods to the underdeveloped world which, in return, will export labor-intensive goods to them.

A more elaborate international division of labor is envisaged by Raymond Vernon in his "product life-cycle" model, which asserts that there are successive stages for the development of each product.[29] New goods and processes are initially launched as a result of high income *per capita,* the relative availability of productive factors, and the considerable proportion of research and development activities. Thereafter, as production goes through the maturing and then the standardization stages, the location progressively shifts to take advantage of lower labor costs in different areas, initially in the United States itself, then in other, less-industrialized countries.[30]

According to the logic of this cyclical model, there is a tendency for production to move from the developed center towards the periphery. The more distant underdeveloped countries will eventually become the main producers of goods which have reached the standardization stage.

The key concepts of Eurafrica may now be reviewed in light of this brief summary of the neo-classical theory of international development . As regards "complementarity," each group of countries must continue to limit itself to the type of production that has been assigned by the international division of labor. The underdeveloped world must continue to produce and export agricultural products and mineral raw materials, as well as labor-intensive, standardized manufactured goods, while the developed economies will continue to produce the most sophisticated goods from their heavy, and technologically advanced industries. The meaning of "interdependence" in this situation hardly needs belaboring: Those countries that remain strictly specialized in a particular type of production must necessarily import goods which are not made locally.

More significantly, "interdependence" appears as an ideological justification for the perpetuation of dependency in a changing international environment. It seems to be a divisive manoeuver by Northern countries, alarmed at the disruptive potential of "commodity power" after the OPEC increases in the price of oil, designed to co-opt Southern countries into vertical-type (rather than South-South) relationships.

Rather than remaining within any dependency-inducing "interdependence" framework such as that formalized by Lomé, Väyrynen and others suggest that the countries of Africa should aim to achieve "relative" economic independence—"relative" because under the conditions prevailing in the contemporary international system, "total" independence is neither possible nor even desirable. Nevertheless, it should be possible for a number of African governments to create conditions which would allow them to maximize control over their national economies, and thereby to pursue the development strategy of their choice. This, in essence, is the meaning of "economic independence":

...namely, control over economic decision-making and the national economy, the establishment of a firm industrial structure, leading to a self-generating and self-sustaining growth, and a diversification of external economic contacts consistent with the nation's economic interests.[31]

ALTERNATIVES TO THE IDEOLOGY OF EURAFRICA

What, then, are the various African counter-strategies to neocolonialsm in the quest for economic independence? Three main alternatives will be briefly considered: cooperation with other developed countries; economic cooperation among developing countries; and African regional and continental integration.

Within the framework of a purely free-trade approach, a compelling argument could be made to de-link Africa's preferential economic relations with Europe in favor of a multiplicity of bilateral agreements with other developed countries. This certainly would strengthen the bargaining position of several African governments by enabling them to "play off" one capitalist state against the other.

In this connection, the United States, Japan, Australia, Canada, and Scandinavia would seem to have much to offer that many African economies might need—for example, market access, aid, and investment—possibly on much better terms than they are now getting from the European Community under Lomé. It could also be argued that it would be in the interest of Africa to increase economic relations with eastern European countries and Russia, presently at a very low level. There seems to be an extremely high-growth potential for such trade, as for increased flows of aid and investment from these countries as well as from China, since they have much to offer Africa in terms of industrialization models and appropriate technology.

In the pursuit of economic independence, however, it may be in the best interest of Africa to develop preferential economic links with the rest of the Third World rather than with developed countries.

Hence the strategy of collective self-reliance, which implies not only the creation of horizontal economic co-operation—namely, South/South, rather than North/South links—in trade, industrialization, and investment, but also the severance of various existing links between developed and developing countries.

The achievement of collective self-reliance depends on the capacity of the governments of the Third World to decide independently on matters affecting their economic and social development, to control both their human and physical resources, and to acquire on adequate terms the technology that is appropriate to their needs. In more concrete terms, this implies the promotion of economic cooperation among developing countries (ECDC). Such action was promoted, between 1973 and 1979, within the framework of the Non-Aligned Movement, the Group of 77, and the UNCTAD Secretariat. Recommendations put forward by the Third World fall under two broad headings, those designed to expand trade among developing countries, and those designed to increase production.[32]

The proposed trade measures include the establishment of a variety of collaborative ventures, such as: a global system of trade preferences among developing countries; cooperation among state-trading organizations; producers' cartels; and new multinational marketing enterprises. In the field of production, the developing countries could increase their own monetary and financial cooperation; create multinational production enterprises; work together in the transfer and development of technology; and jointly regulate direct foreign investment and technology transfer. Subregional and regional economic cooperation and integration among developing countries could also be strengthened and broadened.

In their search for economic independence and self-reliance, African governments have created a number of regional and inter-regional schemes of integration that have used different approaches and achieved various degrees of success.

The "concentric circles" aproach has been advocated by the functionalists who maintain that economic integration should be realized

15

progressively, in successive stages, starting from the existing regional economic organizations, evolving into an *African Common Market*, and ultimately leading to an *African Economic Community* by the year 2025.[33] By way of contrast, a number of pan-Africanists believe that the immediate and complete political and economic integration of the whole of Africa is the only road out of the present neo-colonial predicament,

Since the main advocate of the pan-Africanist strategy of integration, Kwame Nkrumah, disappeared from the African political scene in February 1966, the functionalist approach has been prevalent in African political, diplomatic, and academic circles.

Of the various attempts at regional integration in Africa, the promising East African Community failed dismally, was disbanded in 1977 and revived in December 2000. In Francophone Africa,, the *Union douanière et Économique de l'Afrique centrale* has somehow managed to maintain a fragile cohesive façade while not making much headway in terms of actual economic integration.[34] The *Communauté Économique de l'Afrique de l'ouest* (CEAO) has hardly been more successful in achieving its objectives. The CEAO was created in 1973 as a colonially-inspired regional integration scheme bringing together six former French West African states. Unfortunately, it has not managed yet to rid itself of this original blemish. A careful analysis of its structure, as well as of its trade pattern, reveals that it has remained a purely neo-colonial organization.[35] As such, it can hardly be presented as a successful example of regional integration in Africa.

The *Economic Community of West African States* (ECOWAS), which was set up in 1975, has achieved a measure of success in terms of trade liberalization and free movement of persons and capital. And to the extent that it is the first African regional integration scheme to transcend the traditional colonial and linguistic barriers by bringing together the 16 anglo-franco-luso-phone states of the West African sub-region, it seems to offer interesting prospects and potential in terms of African unity.

In the final analysis, the only path likely to lead to Africa's independent development is the economic and political integration of the continent. Thus, I totally agree with the view expressed in the late sixties by Reginald Green and Ann Seidman:

> African states should...take a firm collective decision to achieve continental planned development within the framework of African political unity if they are to achieve meaningful economic independence and higher living standards.[36]

Africa's economic future is tremendous in terms of its agricultural, forest, fishery, mineral, and energy resources.[37] But in order to realize this enormous potential, Africa must sever the umbilical cord that still ties it to Europe and start looking inwards. As Nkrumah put it, "Pan-Africa and not EurAfrica should be our watchword, and the guide to our policies."[38]

In this regard, the following plan for African continental integration presented by Nkrumah in 1963 still appears as a valid model that is worthy of being carefully studied and, ultimately, implemented. Political union being a prerequisite for economic integration, the first task must be to set up a Union Government of African States which should, *inter alia*, formulate a comprehensive policy based on the following continental mechanisms and institutions: an African Common Market, implying a common intra-African external trade policy; an integrated communications network; an integrated industrial structure; and a single integrated monetary zone, including a common currency and a central bank of issue.

In order to protect this economic structure, the Union Government of Africa should also adopt a unified defence strategy, based on an African Military High Command, and a unified foreign policy and diplomacy.[39]

Utopian as this blueprint may seem to some, it appears as the only solution to Africa's current problems. In this respect, I remain firmly convinced that the ideology of Pan-Africanism, as outlined by Nkrumah, offers the only way out of the neo-colonial predicament and towards the attainment of genuine and complete economic independence for the African continent.

ENDNOTES

1. Walter Rodney, *How Europe Underdeveloped Africa* (London & Dar es Salaam: Bogle-L'Ouverture, 1972), p. 29.
2. Quoted in Max Liniger-Goumaz, *L'Eurafrique: Utopie ou Réalité?* (Yaoundé: Editions CLÉ, 1972), p. 28.
3. A.G. Hopkins, *An Economic History of West Africa* (New York: Columbia University Press, 1973), p. 164.
4. Rodney, *op. cit.*, p. 103.
5. Hopkins, *op. cit.*, p. 129.
6. Rodney, *op. cit.*, p. 85.
7. Rosa Luxemburg, *L'Accumulation du capital*, vol 2. (Paris: Maspéro, 1976), p. 153.
8. V.I. Lenin, *Imperialism: The Highest Stage of Capitalism.* (New York: Progress Publishers, 1970), p. 89; on the Berlin Conference, see Thomas Pakenham, *The Scramble for Africa 1876-1912* (Johannesburg: Jonathan Ball, 1991), pp. 239-255.
9. Jack Woddis, *Introduction to Neo-Colonialism* (New York: International Publishers , 1967), p. 14.
10. Frederick D. Lugard, *The Dual Mandate in British Tropical Africa* (Edinburgh & London: William Blackwood & Sons, 1923), p. 613.
11. J.J. Poquin, *Les Relations économiques extérieures des pays d'Afrique noire de l'Union française, 1925-1955* (Paris: Armand Colin, 1957), p. 145 .
12. Arghiri Emmanuel, *Unequal Exchange* (New York: Monthly Review Press, 1972), p. xxxi.
13. Jean Suret-Canale, *Afrique noire occidentale et centrale;* vol. 2,

L'ère coloniale, 1900-1945 (Paris: Éditions Sociales, 1964), p. 250.

14. Quoted in Liniger-Goumaz, *op. cit.*, p. 27.
15. Frantz Fanon, *Les Damnés de la terre* (Paris: François Maspéro, 1979), p. 98.
16. Kwame Nkrumah, *Neo-Colonialism: The Last Stage of Imperialism* (London: Heinemann, 1965), p. ix.
17. Johan Galtung, *The European Community: a Superpower in the Making* (London: George Allen & Unwin, 1973), p. 42.
18. Nkrumah, *op. cit.*, p. xiii.
19. On this process, see: William J. Foltz, *From French West Africa to the Mali Federation* (New Haven: Yale University Press, 1965); Joseph-Roger de Benoist, *La Balkanisation de l'Afrique occidentale française* (Dakar: Nouvelles Éditions Africaines, 1979); and Guédel Ndiaye, *L'Échec de la Fédération du Mali* (Dakar: Nouvelles Éditions Africaines, 1980).
20. This section deliberately leaves out the political and economic analyses of the provisions, results, and impact of the Yaoundé I and II and Lomé I Conventions, which are examined in detail in Guy Martin, *The Political Economy of African-European Relations from Yaoundé I to Lomé II, 1963-1980: a Case Study in Neo-Colonialism and Dependency*, Ph.D. diss., Indiana University, 1982; see also John Ravenhill, *Collective Clientelism: The Lomé Conventions and North-South Relations* (New York: Columbia University Press, 1985).
21. The 19 A.A.M.S. were: (a) former French West African colonies: Benin, Côte d'Ivoire, Mali, Mauritania, Niger, Senegal, and Upper Volta; (b) former Central African colonies: Central African Republic, Chad, Congo, and Gabon; (c) the former French colony of Madagascar; (d) former U.N. trust territories under French mandate (Togo and Cameroon); (e) former Belgian colonies: Burundi, Rwanda, and Zaïre; and (f) others: Mauritius and Somalia.
22. Kwame Nkrumah, *Address to the Ghana National Assembly*, (30

May 1961), in Legum, Colin, *Pan Africanism: A Short Political Guide* (London: Pall <all Press, 1962), p. 119.

23. *Text of Joint Communiqué by President Nkrumah of Ghana and President Brezhnev of the Soviet Union* (24 July 1964), in Arnold Rivkin, *Africa and the European Common Market: A Perspective* (Denver: University of Denver, 1964), p. 35.

24. Jacqueline D. Matthews, *Association System of the European Community* (New York: Praeger Publishers, 1977), p. 41.

25. Timothy M. Shaw, "EEC-ACP Interactions and Images as Redefinitions of Eurafrica: exemplary, exclusive, and/or exploitative?," *Journal of Common Market Studies*, vol. 18, no. 2 (December 1979), p. 146.

26. Claude Cheysson, "Preface" to Michael Noelke, *Europe-Third World Interdependence* (Brussels: Commission of the EC, 1979), p. 7.

27. Michael B. Dolan, "The Lomé Convention and Europe's Relationship with the Third World: a critical analysis," *Journal of European Integration*, vol. 1, no. 3 (1978), p. 393.

28. For a standard presentation of the neo-classical theory of international development, see C.P. Kindleberger and P.H. Lindert, *International Economics* (Homewood, Ill.: Richard D. Irwin, 1978), pp. 13-103.

29. See Raymond Vernon, *Sovereignty at Bay* (New York: Basic Books, 1971), pp. 65-112; and "International Investment and International Trade in the Product Cycle", in John H. Dunning (ed), *International Investment*. (Harmondsworth: Penguin Books, 1972), pp. 305-325.

30. Raymond Vernon, "International Investment and International Trade in the Product Cycle," in J.H. Dunning (ed.), *op. cit.*, 318-19.

31. Justinian Rweyemamu, *Underdevelopment and Industrialisation in Tanzania* (Nairobi: Oxford University Press 1973), p. 38.

32. Cf. G. Seneviratne, *Economic Co-operation among Developing Countries* (New York: UN/UNCTAD, 1980).

33. For such views, see: Organization of African Unity, *What Kind*

of Africa by the Year 2000? (Addis Ababa, 1979); and United Nations, General Assembly, *Lagos Plan of Action for the implementation of the Monrovia Strategy for the Economic Development of Africa* (New York, 1980).

34. For a comprehensive survey and assessment, see: Lynn K. Mytelka, "Francophone African Regional Organizations," *Journal of Modern African Studies*, vol. 12, no. 2 (June 1974), pp. 297-320.

35. See, for instance: H. Kouvahé Amoko, *La Promotion des échanges commerciaux au sein de la CEAO*, Institut des Relations Internationales du Cameroun, Yaoundé (July 1981).

36. Reginald H. Green and Ann Seidman, *Unity or Poverty? The Economics of Pan-Africanism* (Harmondsworth: Penguin Books, 1968), p. 217.

37. On this point, see the fascinating book by: Cheikh Anta Diop, *Les Fondements Économiques et culturels d'un état fédéral d'Afrique noire* (Paris: Présence Africaine, 1974).

38. Kwame Nkrumah, *Africa Must Unite* (London: Panaf Books, 1963), p. 187.

39. *Ibid.*, pp. 150-72 and pp. 216-22.

Chapter 2

The European Union and Africa:
The Lomé Convention/Cotonou Agreement
into the 21st Century

The Lomé Convention—a comprehensive trade and aid agreement between the 15 member states of the European Union (EU) and 71 African, Carribean and Pacific (ACP) states—has constituted the framework of economic relations between Europe and Africa since 1975. For various reasons, the first three Lomé Conventions—Lomé I, 1975-80; Lomé II, 1980-85; and Lomé III, 1985-90—have not succeeded in altering the African countries' traditional trade and aid patterns and in launching them decisively on the path to self-sustained development. Despite some innovations and improvements, Lomé IV (1990-2000) was a disappointing trade and aid package given the African states' vast and growing economic and financial needs. The adoption of a successor agreement, the Cotonou Agreement, in June 2000 (2000-2020) constitutes an appropriate time to reflect on the 25 years of ACP-EU cooperation under the Lomé regime.

Since the conclusion of Lomé IV in 1990, major changes have occurred in the international political and economic environment: the end of the Cold War, globalization, the establishment of the World Trade Organization (WTO) as an overseer of a new multilateral trade regime, and growing environmental and developmental concerns. Furthermore, the end of the Cold War and German reunification have had a major impact on the process of European integration. The 1992 Treaty of Maastricht formed the EU's internal market—the Single European Market (SEM)—through implementation of the Single European Act (SEA). The European Monetary System (EMS) progressively evolved into an Economic and Monetary Union (EMU, 1999-2002), with a European Central Bank and a single currency (the euro) since January 1999 (effective January 2002). Austria, Finland and Sweden joined the Union in January 1995. By early 1998, the population of the EU reached 375 million, representing 51.4 per cent of Europe's total population (729 million). Negotiations on enlargement were initiated in March 1998. According to the current enlargement schedule, 12 Eastern and Southern European countries will become members of the EU between 2003 and 2012.[1] The 'Copenhagen' criteria for joining the Union include a secure democracy, a functioning market economy and a well-honed legal system that protects human rights.

This chapter explores the potential political and economic impact of the evolving European regionalism on the Lomé regime in general, and on the 47 Sub-Saharan African members of the ACP group in particular. Its central focus is the extent to which the Lomé regime might help mitigate the negative impact of Africa's increasing political and economic marginalization in the context of post-Cold War globalization. In particular, this chapter assesses the short and medium-term economic impact of the SEA and EMU, and the long-term political impact of European integration on the African ACP states.

24

EU-Africa Relations From the Treaty of Rome to Lomé IV

Association between Africa and Europe became formalized in 1958 when France convinced its five European Community (EC) partners to grant its African colonies preferential status regarding trade and capital flows under part IV of the Treaty of Rome. When these territories attained sovereignty in 1960, it became necessary to renegotiate the "Association Status" between the six-nation EC and the 18 African and Malagasy Associated States. While the first Yaoundé Convention (1964-69) reproduced the Part IV provisions with hardly any modifications, Yaoundé II (1971-75) introduced minor innovations, still leaving the basic structure of the original agreement intact. Britain's entry into the Community in 1973 required that its Commonwealth trading partners in Africa, the Caribbean and Pacific be part of a new, broader cooperation agreement between the EC-9 and the 46 ACP states. Thus, the first Lomé Convention (1975-80) was signed in February 1975 in a context of great optimism and with high expectations. The "Lomé Spirit" characterizing this new EurAfrican partnership was seen as an embodiment of the North-South dialogue and as an exemple of mutually beneficial North-South economic relations. The Lomé Convention may be defined as a legally binding contractual arrangement of limited duration (initially 5, then 10, now 20 years) based on partnership, reciprocity and equal benefits between the EC-15 and the 71 ACP states in the areas of trade, commodities, minerals, financial and technical assistance, and agricultural and industrial development. Lomé I was followed by the Lomé II (1980-85), Lomé III (1985-1990) Lomé IV (1990-2000) Conventions and by the Cotonou Agreement (2000-2020).

The Lomé Convention is a typically neo-colonial arrangement designed more to preserve and promote Europe's economic interests in the ACP countries than to assist in the economic transformation of these countries away from underdevelopment and dependency into self-sustainable development.[2] A cursory evaluation of the economic impact of fifteen years of Lomé regime (Lomé I to III, 1975-1990) points to a growing isolation of the ACP from the EC and the world economy as a whole.[3] The ACP share of imports from the EC fell from 6.8 per cent in 1975 to only 4.4 per cent in 1988. The ACP share of EC imports has declined even more when intra-EC trade is included in the EC figures, from 3.5 per cent in 1975 to only 1.9 per cent in 1988.[4] In 1990, the African ACP states accounted for only 0.9 per cent of the EC's world merchandise trade, and for only 1 per cent of the EC's world trade in manufactures. Conversely, the EC remains Africa's major trading partner. Thus, in 1990, the average share of the top three commodity exports from African ACP states to the EC (as a percentage of the share of merchandise exports to major markets) was 62 per cent.[5]

In the area of commodities, the EC's export earnings stabilization scheme (Stabex), which seeks to mitigate, through compensatory financial transfers, the damage resulting from a loss of earnings by ACP states on exports of certain agricultural products to the Community, has experienced serious dysfunctions. Nor has the scheme contributed to any transformation of the ACP's traditional economic role as suppliers of agricultural and mineral raw materials and tropical commodities to the processing industries of Europe. In addition, Stabex transfers tend to be concentrated on a few products and beneficiary countries.[6] Over the period 1975-1989 (Lomé I to III), 33.8 per cent of total Stabex transfers (569.5 million ecu[7]) were allocated to coffee, 17.5 per cent to groundnuts (168 million ecu), and 14 per cent to cocoa and cocoa products (203 million ecu). During the same period, 18.8 per cent of total Stabex transfers (437.7 million ecu) went to Côte d'Ivoire, 10.4 per cent (262.6 million ecu) to Senegal, and 9.2 per cent (232.4 million ecu) to Cameroon. In 1990, 69.5 per cent and 20.4 per cent of total Stabex transfers were allocated to coffee and cocoa respectively, the main beneficiary countries being Côte d'Ivoire (71.1 million ecu; 33 per cent of total transfers) and Cameroon (63.7 million ecu; 30 per cent of total transfers).[8]

EC aid to Africa is characterized·by inadequate amounts in relation to needs, slow disbursement procedures and significant concentration on a few beneficiary countries. This aid is administered by the European Development Fund (EDF) for grants and risk capital, and by the European Investment Bank (EIB) for loans. EC aid commitments under Lomé II (5th EDF) amounted to 4.6 billion ecu, while under Lomé III (6th EDF) they increased to 6.8 billion ecu. Out of the total Lomé III aid allocation, 464 million ecu (6.8%) have been allocated to Côte d'Ivoire; 391.2 million ecu (5.7 per cent) to Ethiopia; 277.9 million ecu (4 per cent) to Cameroon; 263.2 million ecu (3.9 per cent) to Senegal; 246.1 million ecu (3.6 per cent) to Nigeria; and 242.6 million ecu (3.5 per cent) to Sudan.[9]

Lomé IV, signed in December 1989 after 14 months of painstaking negotiations,[10] retains the long-term development aims of Lomé III—notably food security and rural development—while containing measures to help alleviate the ACP's economic crisis. The decision to extend the life of the Convention from five to ten years (with renewal of the Financial Protocol after five years) and the renewed emphasis on investment protection and on industrial cooperation are designed to increase the security and confidence of investors.

Lomé IV also retains the basic principles of duty and quota-free access to the EC market for almost all ACP exports, coupled with non-reciprocity. The EC also eased import restrictions on 40 major agricultural and food exports (such as rice, and fruits and vegetables) not covered by the free-access rule. In addition, the special arrangements for "sensitive" products such as beef and veal, sugar, rum, and bananas—governed by special protocols under Lomé IV—have been improved. The rules of origin—to determine whether a good is a genuine ACP product eligible for exemption from customs duties—were clarified, simplified, and further relaxed. An allocation of 70 million ecu was set aside for regional trade promotion, and more attention has been paid to the development of services, which are the subject of a separate chapter in the Convention.

The Stabex system—which now covers 49 agricultural products—was thoroughly overhauled and improved in several ways. The fund is substantially larger—1.5 billion ecu, 62 per cent more than the initial Lomé III allocation—and all transfers are in the form of grants. The reference period, dependency thresholds, and value base of Stabex calculations have been reduced and simplified in favor of the ACP beneficiary states. In addition to Stabex, Sysmin (a compensatory scheme for minerals) transfers are available to help restore the economic viability of troubled mining companies in ACP states, or in case of a substantial fall in an ACP state's mineral export earnings. An amount of 480 million ecu has been set aside from the 7th EDF for Sysmin operations (415 million ecu from the 6th EDF) in the form of grants to ACP states. Under Lomé IV, the list of products covered has been increased to nine (copper and cobalt, phosphates, manganese, bauxite and alumina, tin, iron ore and uranium).

Besides offering easier terms of financing (more grant aid, lower interest rates, partial acceptance by the Community of the exchange rate risk) and more economic aid (in the form of import programs and counterpart funds for structural adjustment measures), Lomé IV tries to make traditional project aid more effective and easier to administer. The volume of Community aid to ACP states has increased from 8.5 billion ecu in Lomé III to 12 billion ecu in Lomé IV. While this is a nominal increase of 40 per cent, it does not constitute an increase in real terms when demographic growth and inflation are taken into account.[11] The Lomé IV financial protocol (1990-95) includes 10.8 billion ecu of grants, emergency and refugee aid, and risk capital under the 7th EDF, as well as 1.2 billion ecu of EIB [European Investment Bank] loans. Because of the increasing indebtedness of the African ACP states (from US $ 56 billion in 1980 to 147 billion in 1989), and because debt repayments have become an obstacle to development, a section on debt has, for the first time, been included in an ACP-EC Convention. By late 1987, structural adjustment had become a major development issue. The Lomé IV Convention provides for a special structural adjustment fund of 1.15 billion ecu to ACP states undertaking International Monetary Fund (IMF) and World Bank-directed structural adjustment programs (SAPs).

Other significant innovations of EC-ACP cooperation include trade promotion and the development of trade in services; regional cooperation support; cultural and social cooperation; assistance in the area of population and demography; and protection of the environment (including an agreement to ban the shipment of hazardous and radioactive waste between the Community and ACP states).

The neo-colonial character of the Lomé regime has been mitigated in two ways. One is the increasing recognition that Lomé largely reflects the inequalities of the international economic system rather than being a significant cause of them. Thus, as Ravenhill suggests, it might be more appropriate "to conceive of Lomé as a form of clientelist relationship—an attempt by weak states to construct a particularistic arrangement that would preserve their position in the EC market and provide insurance against the insecurities of the marketplace."[12] The other has to do with the increasing economic and political marginalization of Africa in the world system resulting from the end of the Cold War and the demise of Socialism in eastern Europe and the former Soviet Union. These momentous changes have led the EU to shift the focus of its external relations away from the Third World and Africa to completion of the process of European integration and to the enlargement of this process to non-member countries in western, eastern and southern Europe.

The Impact of the Single European Market and of the European Monetary Union on the African ACP States and on the Lomé Regime[13]

The founding treaties stated as the European Community's primary goals "a harmonious development of economic activities, an accelerated raising of the standard of living and closer relations between the States belonging to it."[14] These goals are to be achieved through the progressive harmonization of economic policies and the establishment of a common market. The first step taken by the EC towards the creation of a common market was to establish a customs union. This entailed removing duties on trade between EC member states and fixing a common external tariff—a process that was completed by July 1968. Despite these achievements, some old barriers remained and new ones were erected during the 1970s. By the mid-1980s, the Community was compelled to admit that its primary aim—the creation of a true common market—had not been accomplished. The Community commissioned a White Paper (1985), which mapped out the road for completion of the internal market by the end of 1992.

"Europe 1992" was a plan for deregulation and liberalization. By the end of 1992, the EC became a true common market—a unified economic area without internal frontiers within which people, goods, capital and service could circulate freely. The Single European Act (SEA) went into force in July 1992. The SEA contains the amendments to the EC treaties necessary to ensure the timely achievement of the 1992 program, as well as providing for significant developments in economic and monetary policy, social policy, research and technology, and the environment.

The 1992 single market opened up new prospects for the Community, including that of Economic and Monetary Union (EMU).[15] Without EMU, the internal market would have remained fragmented in 15 different currencies, involving exchange rate risks and unnecessary transaction costs for European citizens and businesses.

The EMU was achieved in three stages. Stage one (initiated in July 1990) improved economic and monetary policy convergence among member states and removed exchange controls in most member states. The 1992 Maastricht Treaty provided the legal foundation for stage two (initiated in January 1994) involving the setting up of an interim European Monetary Institute. In May 1998, a single European currency, the euro, was launched in 11 of the 15 member states (stage three).[16] In January 1999, the euro—managed by the European Central Bank/ECB—became the single European unit of account for all intra and extra-EU monetary and financial transactions. At the end of the transitional stage (January 2002), euro notes and coins replaced all national notes and coins.

The impact of the SEA on African ACP states must be considered from three related perspectives. First, what does this process mean for market access? Will it, on balance, be trade-creating or trade-diverting? Second, what impact will it have on patterns of capital flows— aid and investment—to Africa? Third, will the African ACP states be able to exploit the opportunities of the wider, more integrated market and be able to meet the challenges of more intense competition or tougher technical standards?[17]

As far as market access is concerned, a distinction must be made between the short-term and long-term impact. In the short run, elimination of internal non-tariff barriers (NTBs) to trade in goods and services within the EU may not have any significant impact on Africa. Most of the African exports to the EU are primary products not directly affected by the proposed changes in NTBs. In fact, African exports have been more directly affected by the Uruguay Round of GATT tariff negotiations, which reduced the margin of preference enjoyed by the African countries on the EU market under the Lomé Convention. Because of the limited overlap between African and EU exports, the trade diversion potential deriving from stiffer competition from European producers is limited to a few key export sectors in many African countries. The trade diversion potential may be amplified by the related investment diversion, for example in favor of new and more profitable ventures in Eastern Europe. In fact, ACP effective trade preferences under the Lomé regime have been substantially eroded as a result of gradual intra-EU tariff reductions. As a result, over 60 per cent of ACP exports to the EU no longer enjoy any preference over Asian or Latin-American exports to Europe, and only 7 per cent—including bananas, rum, sugar and beef—still benefit from a substantial preferential margin.[18]

Short-term effects that concern exclusively African exports of goods include: the elimination of quantitative restrictions and other border controls and barriers; the harmonization of fiscal measures; the elimination of technical barriers; services; and visas and other entry requirements. To what extent are the new EU-wide arrangements replacing previous bilateral arrangements governing imports of "sensitive products" of export interest to African countries—such as beef and veal, sugar, rum, bananas, textiles and footwear—more or less restrictive than those previously faced by African exporters? Second, how will harmonization of taxes within the EU affect the price and demand for imports from Africa?

The Lomé protocol on beef and veal provides for the abolition of the *ad valorem* element of customs duties granted to all ACP countries, as well as for a reduction of 92 per cent in the specific right for a total quantity of 52,100 tons shared out among traditional ACP suppliers (seven African ACP states).[19] While resulting in a substantial increase in export earnings for the beneficiary ACP countries (over 30 million ecu in 1996), the protocol on beef and veal has never been fully exploited by these countries. Thus, the utilization rate has fallen from almost 80 per cent in 1995 to under 50 per cent in 1997.

The EU had always sought to protect traditional European banana markets for suppliers from Africa and the Caribbean. Lomé IV provided for the renewal of the banana protocol as it existed under Lomé III, maintaining protection for bananas from the ACP states in the French, Italian, and British markets. The provisions of the banana protocol are implemented within the framework of the common market organization for bananas. The 12 beneficiary ACP countries (including Cameroon, Cape Verde, Côte d'Ivoire, Madagascar, and Somalia) have a quota of 857,000 tons (380,700 tons for the five African ACP countries) free of customs duty, distributed among traditional exporters. In 1997, the banana protocol generated exports worth 400 million ecu for the 12 beneficiary ACP countries (205.2 million ecu for the five African ACP countries), although the total quota was not filled.

Under the sugar protocol of the Lomé Convention, the EU undertakes to import, for an indefinite period, specific quantities agreed with ACP countries at guaranteed prices. ACP sugar is needed to enable EU refiners to stay in business since they work with raw cane sugar. The provisions of this protocol remain in force after the expiration of the Lomé IV Convention, even if the Convention ceases to be operative. The EU commitments to the ACP countries regarding sugar take the form of an annual duty-free quota of 1,304,700 tons for all ACP states (701,243 tons for the 9 African ACP states).[20] Only 245,000 (170,997 for the 9 African ACP states) were actually used in 1997.

In 1997, ACP countries exported 7.4 billion ecu worth of manufactured goods to the Community. For these products, the margin of preference in 2000 is about 1.6 per cent. The sectors where the preferential margin will remain substantial are chemicals, footwear and textiles (together generating 2 billion ecu of exports in 1997). The ACP countries were unable to develop their potential for exporting manufactured goods, the overall volume growth rate being only 1.5 per cent (3.6 per cent for all exports) between 1988 and 1997; only textile exports (including those from Mauritius and Madagascar) saw a relatively large increase (66.5 per cent) over that period. However, the current dismantling of the Multi-Fibre Arrangement will generate greater competition and further erosion of preferences in coming years. Other African ACP countries which were able to increase their export of manufactured goods between 1988 and 1997 are Kenya and Zimbabwe (cut flower, fruit and vegetable). If the use of preferences is analyzed in terms of development of production capacity in existing or new sectors, only four countries registered positive results, namely Mauritius, Madagascar, Kenya and Zimbabwe.[21]

The elimination of the EU excise tax on tropical beverages (coffee, tea and cocoa) did benefit ACP exporters of these goods. In the case of coffee, where taxes were highest and the value of trade greatest, the gains were significant. In particular, African coffee producers such as Kenya and Uganda benefitted from the elimination of Germany's excise tax on coffee. German consumption increased by about 8 per cent, representing an increase of 3 per cent in EU consumption and translating into US $ 200 million additional African coffee exports to the Community. In addition, some African exporters of jewelry, gold, silver and precious and semi-precious stones—such as Angola, the Central African Republic, Congo, Guinea, Liberia, Sierra Leone, Zaire and Zambia—benefitted from the reduction from previous levels (ranging from 25 per cent to 36 per cent) to 20 per cent of the Value Added Tax (VAT) rate applied by France, Belgium, Italy, Spain, Greece and Portugal.[22] The harmonization of taxes on tobacco products led to an increase in average excise tax levels. However, Zimbabwe and other African tobacco-exporting countries (such as Malawi) managed to slow down the potential loss of exports by adjusting their production to the evolving demand for lighter cigarettes and the continued growth in world consumption of tobacco.

The harmonization or mutual recognition of norms, technical standards, and certification procedures affected African countries new EU regimes for six categories of products exported to the EU: phosphates, tobacco, cocoa, palm oil, meat and fish. The EU has adopted new norms to reduce the use of cadmium-rich phosphates such as those exported by Senegal and Togo. While strict norms were being enforced, the EU provided a transition period allowed these two African countries to adjust to them. The EU also harmonized member states' rules concerning maximum cigarette tar content by the end of 1995. This gave African tobacco producers (Malawi and Zimbabwe) sufficient time to adjust to the new, stricter norms. The harmonization of the definition of chocolate, raising the level of vegetable oil allowed by French and Belgian producers, allowing them to reduce the cocoa content of their chocolates. These trends adversely affected cocoa beans or cocoa butter exports from Cameroon, Côte d'Ivoire, Ghana, Nigeria and Togo. But African exporters of palm oil such as Cameroon, Côte d'Ivoire and Nigeria benefitted as demand for their palm oil rose. New standards on food hygiene and meat products (notably the strengthening of the EU inspectorate system of slaughterhouses) negatively impacted African meat exporters such as Botswana, Kenya, Madagascar, Namibia , Swaziland and Zimbabwe. These countries have been hampered by the lack of information about the technical details required to meet the new norms and have accused the Community of deliberate protectionism under the guise of stringent monitoring of health and hygiene rules. The same applies to new health norms on fresh or preserved fish products, exported mainly by Côte d'Ivoire, Madagascar, Mauritania, Mauritius, Senegal and Seychelles. Whenever there are unified quality norms, the tendency is to raise the quality and environmental standards. In any event, quality and health norms were unified in 1993 following norms applied by the strictest EU country.

With regard to services, the impact of the Single European Market (SEM) was trade-creating within the Community, and trade-diverting as regards ACP countries. Many services opened up in which intra-EU trade was virtually impossible because of controls and regulatory structures. Many of the trade barriers reduced by the SEM are related to previously non-freely traded services, notably in transport, banking and insurance. There was, however, no commitment to reduce barriers to non-EU suppliers. Among the issues related to African countries' export of services to the EU, the most important is air transport deregulation, which led to a 10 to 20 per cent reduction in most intra-EU air fares. Consequently, European-African routes were progressively deregulated, and African countries with air routes to the EU had to adopt "open skies" policies. As a result, most African countries offering tourism products in the EU—such as Côte d'Ivoire, Kenya, Mauritius and Seychelles—benefitted from the SEM as they became more attractive to European tourists.[23]

Some African visitors and migrants to the EU faced more restrictive entry requirements into the Community as a result of the elimination of internal controls at EU borders. African residents must now obtain visitors visas to travel to the 15 EU countries, which was not previously the case for 19 African countries.

While EU officials insist that there is no evidence of any aid or investment diversion away from the ACP states, and that allocation of aid for eastern European countries is definitely not at ACP expense, aid budgets are finite. If we view the total aid budget as a cake, the size of the portion allocated to the ACP is likely to affect the slice available to the eastern Europan countries, and vice versa. In this regard, it is interesting to note that the European Bank for Reconstruction and Development, created in April 1991 by the EU to promote economic development in central and eastern Europe, was endowed with a starting capital of 12 billion ecu, an amount equivalent to the Lomé IV first financial protocol allocated to the (then) 69 ACP states for five years (1990-95), which amounted to 35 million ecu per state per year. Put differently, "the annual payment per cow under the EU's livestock subsidy is greater than the EDF's annual allocation per person to the ACP."[24] After protracted negotiations, the EU heads of government finally agreed, in June 1995, on the amount of EDF funding under the second financial protocol of Lomé IV (1995-2000). The financial package agreed upon is 14.6 billion ecu, somewhat less than the 15.8 billion ecu originally sought by the ACP group, but equal to the amount proposed by the French.[25] France is now the largest EDF contributor, followed by Germany, while Britain's contribution fell by 8 per cent.Of the total APC aid package of 14.6 billion ecu, 12.97 billion have been earmarked for the EDF, and 1.66 billion for the EIB [European Investment Bank]; 11 billion are in the form of subsidies, and 1 billion is risk capital. Special allocations for Stabex, Sysmin, structural adjustment and regional cooperation amount to 1.8 billion, 1.4 billion and 1.3 billion ecu, respectively.[26] In 1990, 46 per cent of French and 87 per cent of Italian concessionary aid to Africa (that is, 60 per cent of the EU's bilateral aid) was tied to procurement in these countries. Given the impossibility of maintaining tied bilateral aid, the larger donor countries (Britain, France, Germany and Italy) are progressively replacing bilateral concessionary aid with multilateral aid channeled through the Community's EDF and European Investment Bank.

Lomé IV for the first time included a human rights clause in its main text, explicitly linking human rights to development (Article 5). Following the mid-term review process, the revised version of Article

5 of Lomé IV now expressly links development policy and cooperation not only to respect for human rights but also to the recognition
and application of democratic principles, the consolidation of the rule
of law and good governance. Indeed, the EU has increasingly resort-
ed to the unilateral suspension of Lomé benefits because of (alleged)
violations of human rights or democratic principles in a particular
ACP country.[27] However, a recent study focusing on European aid
policies towards Africa (Algeria, Niger, Kenya and South Africa) in
the 1990s shows that these policies have been primarily influenced by
the security concerns and narrow national interests of individual
donor countries (particularly France). Despite the Convention's provisions and EU's policy statements to the contrary, the lofty aim of
promoting democracy and respect for human rights in post-Cold War
Africa has clearly been secondary to other objectives of Europe's policies towards the continent: "only in very few exceptional instances is
it in the national interest of European donor states to promote moral
issues such as democracy and respect for human rights." Thus, as was
the case during the Cold War, *realpolitik* tends to prevail over moral
considerations.[28]

The SEM's impact on investment in African ACP states is mostly
negative. Removing barriers to capital flows and improving information to permit companies to treat the Community as a single market
are central to the program. There was an increase in investment in the
EU by those engaged in intra-EU trade, and a decrease by those
exporting to it. Additionally, there was a relative rise in the level and
growth rate of demand and an opening up of the market for financial
and other investment-related services. Finally, the removal of
exchange controls by France diverted investment away from the franc
zone African countries. All these effects are reinforced by increased
awareness of opportunities in Europe.[29]

The European Monetary Union (EMU) and the Franc Zone

The franc zone is a monetary cooperation arrangement set up between France and its former colonies in west and central Africa in the early 1960s. The franc zone operates according to four basic principles: fixed parity between the french franc and the CFA franc;[30] free and unlimited transfers between countries and currencies; harmonization of exchange regulations; and common management of foreign exchange reserves through the French Treasury. The franc zone constitutes a de facto preferential trading area between France and the francophone African states.[31] The Comoros, Equatorial Guinea, and Guinea-Bisssau joined the franc zone in 1979, 1985 and 1997, respectively. Two treaties, the *Union monétaire de l'Ouest africain* (UMOA, June 1994) and the *Communauté Économique et monétaire de l'Afrique centrale* (CEMAC, March 1994), created west and central African monetary unions evolving towards economic unions. On January 12, 1994, the CFA franc was devalued by 50 per cent vis-à-vis the French franc.

An EU Council decision of 23 November 1998 (effective 1 January 1999) formally linked the CFA franc to the euro (1 euro = 655,957 CFA francs). To the extent that the monetary agreements between France, UEMOA and CEMAC remain in force and that the French Treasury continues to guarantee the free convertibility of the CFA franc, the basic structure of the franc zone remains intact. However, its functioning is modified in the sense that the linkage of the CFA franc to the euro signals a shift from a bilateral to a multilateral exchange rate system; the exchange rate has been modified, and the euro's exchange rate fluctuates vis-à-vis the U.S. dollar; and strict public deficit rules linked to specific convergence criteria will have a definite impact on relations between the French Treasury and the African countries that are members of the franc zone.[32] To the extent that it preserves the basic structure of the franc zone and links the CFA franc to a strong and stable currency, the CFA franc-euro linkage has been presented as a factor of stability for the franc zone.

It is also argued that by broadening their trade and financial opportunities, and by allowing them to reschedule their debts among different currencies and to take advantage of the euro's current low long-term interest rates, the CFA franc-euro linkage offers real developmental opportunities to African members of the franc zone.[33] As correctly observed by Philippe Hugon, the maintenance of monetary stability must not be at the cost of creating rent and monopoly situations, and clientelist networks. More significantly, the CFA franc-euro linkage evokes strategic choices regarding the survival of a Euro-African solidarity zone beyond Lomé IV.[34] Ultimately, the African members of the franc zone will have to devise new strategies of endogenous development and take charge of the processes and institutions of the west and central African monetary unions.

The Post-Lomé Convention in the Context of the EU-South Africa Agreement and the New World Trade Regime

After almost four years of complex and protracted negotiations, a Trade, Development and Co-operation Agreement (TDCA) between the EU and South Africa was approved by the EU heads of state on March 24, 1999 and formally signed in Pretoria on October 11, 1999. This agreement, which establishes a free trade area between the contracting parties over the next 12 years, liberalizing about 95 per cent of trade, will give South Africa preferential access to the world's largest market. In particular, the TDCA will open up important opportunities for South African companies in sectors such as textiles and clothing, chemicals, food and vegetables. According to the agreement, South Africa will grant duty-free status to 86 per cent of its EU imports, whereas the EU will give duty free status to 95 per cent of South African exports. In addition, the EU will implement its tariff reductions faster, with most EU liberalization being completed by 2002. South Africa's tariff cuts will, on the other hand, concentrate on the second half of the 12 year transition period, between

2006 and 2012. The treaty also provides for EU financial assistance to South Africa to the tune of about 125 million euro per year. This funding will be channeled through the European Programme for Reconstruction and Development, which will continue to work with the South African government to help redress the inequalities of the past and assist in the process of transformation. Parallel agreements in other areas include a science and technology pact (1997), an agreement on wines and spirits, and a fisheries deal.[35]

To prevent concessions granted under the TDCA from harming its traditional Lomé partners, the EU excluded certain product groups, like sugar and red meat, from the treaty and provided aid from the general EU budget (rather than from Lomé funds). Concerns have been expressed by some member states of the Southern African Development Community (SADC), of which South Africa is also a member, about the degree of preference enjoyed by some sensitive products of particular export interest to them (such as beef and sugar) on the EU market vis-à-vis similar South African exports and, as a result, are promoting the concept of "SADC first". A trade dispute between the South African Milk Buyers Organization (SAMBO) and the EU has arisen over the administration of the 5,000-ton cheese quota awarded to South Africa. As a result of the unilateral implementation of administrative measures by some EU member states in contravention of a verbal agreement to the contrary, South African cheese manufacturers expect to lose as much as US $1.50 per kilogram. "For us it is clear proof of the fact that the EU is not honest in its efforts to provide free entry to European markets to South African farmers," said Martiens Hermann, chairman of SAMBO.[36]

At the opening of negotiations for a successor Convention to Lomé IV (which expired in February 2000), the EU proposed an overall package with three components: political dialogue, support for development and economic and trade cooperation. The Commissioner responsible for relations with the ACP countries, João de Deus Pinheiro, stressed that the responsibility for development, reducing poverty, and the preservation of a political environment conducive to peace, security, and respect for human rights lay with each ACP country. The eradication of poverty is the main objective of this agreement, which requires reforms in the ACP countries to achieve sustainable development, greater competitiveness, development of the private sector, creation of productive jobs, improved access to social services, and extension of the EU-ACP partnership to civil society. The partnership will adjust and adapt these priorities and approaches according to the level of development and vulnerability of each country, so as to take account of national and regional conditions. Economic and trade cooperation should enable the ACP countries to participate fully in a liberalized international trade system. At the Brussels ACP-EU ministerial conference in December 1999, agreement was reached on the future trade arrangement. Negotiations between the EU and the ACP Group for a World Trade Organization/WTO-compliant trade regime will be initiated in 2002, and will enter into force no later than 2008. In 2004 the EU will assess the situation of the non-Less Developed Countries/LDCs which will not be in a position to negotiate free-trade regional agreements. The EU will try to provide these countries with a new WTO-compliant trade framework equivalent to their present situation. In 2006, the parties will undertake a comprehensive review of these agreements. Furthermore, in 2000, the EU embarked on a process that will give free access to a range of products from all LDCs by 2005 at the latest. The ACP States and the Community will ask the WTO for a waiver that will allow them to keep the present preferential arrangements during the preparatory period.[37]

The EU financial offer for a 9th EDF (2000-2005) amounts to 13.5 billion euros (including 10 billion for development, 1.3 billion for regional cooperation, and 2.2 billion for the investment facility). If one adds the 1.7 billion earmarked for EIB loans, the total aid package amounts to 15.2 billion euros.[38]

In adopting the report by Michel Rocard in April 1998, the European Parliament endorsed the following principles: a convention between the EU and the ACP should be maintained;

the geographical scope of the convention should remain as it is (Africa, Caribbean, Pacific); a political dimension (support for democracy, security arrangements, good governance) should be included alongside the economic dimension; security arrangements should include a regional conflict early warning system, a conflict-prevention mechanism, and an inter-African peace-keeping force; the EU-ACP partnership should be improved: cooperation should be decentralized and the partnership should be extended to include local authorities and members of civil society; regional structures should be set up, and economic cooperation encouraged; ACP debts should be reduced, and obstacles to development eliminated.[39]

In her statement at the opening of the negotiations for a successor agreement to Lomé IV (September 30, 1998), the president of the ACP council of ministers, Billie Miller, echoed an earlier statement by prime minister Owen Arthur of Barbados, saying: "In a global context, the Lomé body of relationships represents still the most effective, the most meaningful model of North-South arrangements ever conceived by man...In a changing world, in a world of liberalization and globalization, Lomé too will and must change. But the soul of Lomé must not be lost..."[40] Indeed, one could argue that for the ACP states, the Lomé Convention remains the most effective body of North-South arrangements in the post-Cold War era. In spite of disappointments in realizing the goals of the Convention, there is no question of "losing Lomé"; the point is rather to revitalize this partnership for development. Given the fact that half of the ACP states are among the world's poorest countries (39 out of 48), and that they are dealing with the world largest trade partner (and, with 375 million citizens, also the biggest single market in the world), the ACP asks the EU to understand this fundamental reality of inequality, and demands fairness in these negotiations. In other words, post-Lomé arrangements should start from the most basic reality of differentiation between rich and poor countries. Beyond the traditional arguments for "free trade" and "open markets," the ACP's basic position of principle is that between unequal partners, what equity requires is not reciprocity but proportionality. Given the great disparities in economic power, poor countries and people are not empowered but endangered by unqualified reciprocity, and "free trade" is, by no means, "fair trade." The ACP countries thus have a fundamental interest in the renewal of the basic non-reciprocal character of the Lomé regime, a principle which they would also like to see enshrined in the new world trade regime.[41]

Both the Libreville Declaration and the Santo Domingo Declaration reaffirm the attachment of the ACP states to the general framework of ACP-EU cooperation based on the principles of solidarity, sovereignty and equality between partners, and characterized by predictability, dialogue, partnership, and its contractual nature. The ACP also subscribe to the principle of positive differentiation and adaptation of cooperation policies and actions to the needs and specificities of individual countries and regions and to the principle of regionalization (that is, promoting regional cooperation and integration). According to the ACP, the new development cooperation agreement should be a true "strategic" partnership for development. A such, it should place greater emphasis on the development of human resources, particularly in the agricultural and service sectors; on improved access to science and technology, on promotion of industrialization and preservation of the environment . The ACP states believe that a broader and deeper political dialogue with the EU would improve this partnership and cooperation and would also contribute to strengthening regional mechanisms for conflict prevention, management, and resolution. In the area of trade and investment, the ACP calls on the EU to: maintain the preferential commodity protocols and arrangements; consult with the ACP Group prior to the adoption of restrictive trade measures likely to adversely affect ACP states; liberalize and improve the existing rules of origins so as to facilitate ACP exports; maintain and improve the Stabex and Sysmin schemes; encourage the development of the service sector, including tourism; promote industrial development activities in the ACP private sector, notably by strengthening the role of the Centre for the Development of Industry.

With regard to financial and technical assistance, the ACP believe that a post-Lomé agreement should: provide adequate financial resources for the development of the ACP countries; be based on mutual and reciprocal rights and obligations; be tailored to specific circumstances of individual ACP states and sensitive to the different needs and conditions in the ACP regions; establish a post-conflict financial facility (as well as flora and fauna rehabilitation programs) for countries victims of wars and host to refugees; ensure transparency, efficiency and accountability in the use of resources, and rationalize aid mechanisms and instruments; and establish an investment guarantee agency to facilitate investment flows from the EU to the ACP regions.[42]

According to the fundamental principle of ACP solidarity, the ACP will not allow regionalization to be used as an excuse for splitting up the ACP: "The ACP did not forge its unity only to negotiate its division into three or perhaps even six parts. A Europe that has succeeded so well in the strengthening of its own integration should be the last to seek to take the ACP down the road of disintegration."[43] With respect to the EU's proposal for a new trading framework equivalent to the Lomé regime and in conformity with WTO rules, the ACP are of the view that a roll-over of the existing Convention is necessary and that realistically, the time-frame must allow ACP countries to prepare adequately for alternative arrangements (ideally eight years). This proposal is considered acceptable by Europe. Beyond that, the ACP call for the application of WTO rules on a basis of flexibility that would make them compatible with the basic objectives of development.

Both the ACP and the EU agree on the need to foster the participation of agents of the civil society in the management of ACP societies, though the issues of representativeness and governance are still subject to debate. Democracy, the rule of law, and respect for human rights have, by and large, become part of the ACP's national civic ethics. Although the existing Convention has given attention to services, it needs to be broadened to include new service sectors of importance to the ACP such as tourism, entertainment, and sports. The ACP want to make a strong case for maintaining what is best in Lomé: Stabex and the various commodity protocols (beef and veal, bananas, sugar and rum). The ACP are committed to the fight against poverty, and they want to make poverty alleviation the centerpiece of the new Lomé Convention. The ACP are concerned about the debilitating external debt burden of many ACP countries and the decline of both official development assistance in real terms, and foreign direct investment flows to ACP countries. In particular, it believes that the new agreement should include provision for additional debt relief, including the write-off of all the debt incurred by the ACP states under the previous Lomé Convention. The ACP accepts the value of a political dialogue between the EU and the ACP as between partners for development cooperation, but it believes that this partnership must not be tarnished by intimations of political dictation or tainted with notions of conditionality. Among the new areas of dialogue that are of shared concern and mutual importance are intra-ACP conflict prevention and resolution; gender issues (particularly the role of women in development); a simpler, clearer, and more logical convention; improved administrative and budgetary procedures; and decentralized decision-making in the management of the convention.

Conclusion

A quarter-century of the Lomé regime (1975-2000) has not succeeded in significantly altering the African ACP states' traditional trade and aid patterns and in launching them decisively on the path to self-sustained development. In a changing international economic environment characterized by the end of the Cold War, globalization, the establishment of a new international trade regime managed by the WTO, and the gradual erosion of trade preferences, the African countries are becoming increasingly marginalized. As the Malagasy president, Didier Ratsiraka, declared at the Santo Domingo summit meeting of the ACP Group in November 1999, "We perceive globalization as being a totalitarian doctrine framed within a unifying thought process imposed by the only remaining world power." And Ratsiraka went on to denounce the WTO as "the main agent of globalization which is going to regulate all types of human activities henceforth subject to trade."[44]

Because of their structural weaknesses and persistent underdevelopment and dependency, the African ACP states have been unable to take advantage of the positive elements of the SEM and EMU, and to limit the damage from the negative elements. The present asymmetrical relationship between the EU and the ACP is likely to be further aggravated when the current enlargement process—probably resulting in an EU of 27 member states by 2012—is completed. It is interesting to note in this regard that the 'Copenhagen' criteria for joining the Union—democracy, a functioning market economy, and a well-honed legal system that protects human rights—are the same political conditionalities imposed on the ACP before any financial aid is disbursed. The "Abidjan Doctrine" of 1994 according to which French bilateral aid was made conditional upon the conclusion of agreements between the African states and the international financial institutions, is symptomatic of a gradual process of multilateralization of French aid through the World Bank, the International Monetary Fund and the EU's EDF.

In view of this evolving international environment and chronic structural asymmetries and constraints, does the Lomé regime really have a future? As Robert Kappel observes, the self-proclaimed goals of Lomé—elimination of poverty, promotion of self-sustainable development and of democratic governance—have not been achieved to any significant degree. This, he argues, is because geo-strategic and economic interests—as well as clientelist relations between the European and ACP/African elites—have largely prevailed over developmental concerns: "The Lomé economic instruments...reinforce asymmetries, impede the development of endogenous potentials in agriculture and industry. They have not helped to develop adequate potentials. They forcibly bind Africa to a division of labor non-conducive to sustainable development."[45] Ultimately, the post-Cold War situation characterized by the liberalization of world trade, the emergence of a tri-polar world (U.S., Europe, and Japan), the implementation of the Maastricht Treaty and the broadening of the EU call for an end of the preferential, non-reciprocal Lomé relationship and the eventual discontinuation of the Lomé regime.

Faced with such momentous changes, the ACP's attitude has generally been reactive (one of "wait and see") rather than pro-active. As Kappel suggests, the ACP elites should extricate themselves from the clientelistic relations they entertain with their EU counterparts and should "stop playing the 'petitioner' and seek to create conditions for reciprocal cooperation."[46] Indeed, the only way the ACP could radically transform their cooperation with Europe would be to initiate truly endogenous processes of democratization, development, and regional cooperation and integration as a prerequisite for a successful strategy of de-linking. In this regard, one positive consequence of the EU's push for subregional free trade areas might be an acceleration of the pace of economic integration in the various African subregions. The consolidation of existing subregional economic groupings would ideally lead to the gradual establishment of an African Common Market by the year 2020 and an African Economic Community by the year 2025. Should this optimistic scenario materialize, the African ACP states would have rendered the Lomé regime irrelevant and obsolete by virtue of following the European model of economic and political integration to its logical, ultimate conclusion.

Endnotes

1. Hungary, Poland, Cyprus, Estonia, Czech Republic and Slovenia initiated accession negotiations with the EU in March 1998,

while Latvia, Lithuania, Slovakia, Bulgaria, Romania and Malta shall initiate theirs in February 2000; Turkey was officially recognized as the EU's 13th candidate—and Ukraine as a serious contender—at the Helsinki European summit meeting [10-11 December 1999] (see "Enlarging the European Union: A new pace?" *The Economist* [2-8 October 1999], pp. 54-5; Philippe Lemaître & Laurent Zecchini, "Helsinki: élargissement, défense commune... et Tchétchénie," *Le Monde* [10 décembre 1999]; "Union européenne: un sommet 'historique' qui a ouvert la porte à la Turquie, *Le Parisien* [11 décembre 1999]; Nathalie Dubois & Jean Quatremer, "Vers une Europe sans frontières," *Libération* [13 décembre 1999]).

2. See Guy Martin, *The Political Economy of African-European Relations from Yaoundé I to Lomé II, 1963-1980: A Case Study in Neo-Colonialism and Dependency*, Ph.D. dissertation, Indiana University, 1982; and chapter 1: "Africa and the Ideology of Eurafrica: Neo-Colonialism or Pan-Africanism?" in this volume.

3. Pierre Audinet, *Lomé IV: Une nouvelle stratégie de développement? Éléments critiques sur la coopération CEE-ACP* (Paris: Centre d'Observation des Économies Africaines/COBEA, 1990).

4. Vincent A. Mahler, *The Lomé Convention and North-South Commodity Trade*. Paper presented at the annual meeting of the International Studies Association, Atlanta, GA (1-4 April 1992).

5. *Global Economic Prospects and the Developing Countries* (Washington, DC: The World Bank, 1992), tables E8, E10 & E12, pp. 64-7.

6. Guy Martin, "African-European Economic Relations under the Lomé Convention: Commodities and Stabex," *African Studies Review* vol. 27, no. 3 (September 1984), pp. 41-66; John Ravenhill, "What is to be done for Third World commodity exporters? An evaluation of the EEC's Stabex scheme, *International Organization* vol. 38, no. 3 (1984), pp. 537-574

7. The European currency unit (ecu) was initially created as a mere

unit of account and later became a full-fledged currency, the euro.

8. *The Export Earnings Stabilization System (Stabex)* (Brussels: Commission of the EC, January 1990) [Europe Information/Development no. DE 63].

9. *From Lomé III to Lomé IV: Review of Aid from the Lomé Conventions at the End of 1990* (Brussels: Commission of the EC, April 1992) [Europe Information/Development no. DE 74].

10. P. Audinet, *op. cit.*; John Ravenhill, "When Weakness is Strength: The Lomé IV Negotiations," in I. William Zartman (ed.), *Europe and Africa: The New Phase* (Boulder: Lynne Rienner Publishers, 1993), pp. 41-61.

11. Carol Cosgrove & Pierre-Henri Laurent, "EC Relations with the ACP States,"in John Redmond (ed.), *The External Relations of the European Community: The International Response to 1992* (New York: St. Martin's Press, 1991).

12. John Ravenhill, *Collective Clientelism: The Lomé Conventions and North-South Relations* (New York: Columbia University Press, 1985), p. 3.

13. *The European Community in the Nineties* (Washington, DC: EC Delegation to the U.S., 1992), pp. 10-11.

14. *EEC Treaty*, Article 1.

15. *The European Community in the Ninenties*, pp. 12-13; Michel Foucher & Catherine Baulamon, "Europe occidentale et médiane," in *L'État du monde 1999: Annuaire Économique & géopolitique mondial* (Paris: La Découverte, 1998), pp.440-445.

16. The four EMU non-member countries are Britain, Denmark, Greece and Sweden. The last three are now poised to join the Union and the euro by early 2001, while in Britain the issue shall be decided in a referendum in late 2001-early 2002 (see "The euro's in-and-out club," *The Economist* (16-22 October 1999), pp. 51-2; and "Single currency, many voices," in *op. cit.*, pp. 57-8.

17. See in particular: Carol Cosgrove, "The Impact of 1992 on EC-ACP Trade and Investment," in I. William Zartman (ed.), *Europe*

and Africa, pp. 63-73; Michael Davenport (with Sheila Page), *Europe: 1992 and the Developing World* (London: Overseas Development Institute, 1991); John Redmond (ed.), *The External Relations of the EC*; and Alfred Tovias, *The European Communities' Single Market. The Challenge of 1992 for Sub-Saharan Africa.* (Washington DC: The World Bank, 1990).

18. Anne-Marie Mouradian, "Menaces sur la Convention de Lomé," *Le Monde diplomatique* (juin 1998), p. 7.

19. According to Article 2 of *Protocol 7 on beef and veal* of the *Lomé IV Convention*, the African ACP beneficiary states are Botswana, Kenya, Madagascar, Swaziland, Zimbabwe and Namibia.

20. The nine African ACP states beneficiary of the sugar protocol are Congo, Côte d'Ivoire, Madagascar, Malawi, Mauritius, Swaziland, Tanzania, Zambia and Zimbabwe.

21. See *Analysis of trends in the Lomé Trade Regime*, pp. 8-11.

22. It should be noted that the production and export of coffee in Burundi, Rwanda and the DRC/Zaire, and the production of precious and semi-precious stones in Angola, the CAR, Congo, Liberia, Sierra Leone, and the DRC/Zaire has been adversely affected by the endemic warfare and civil strife that these countries have experienced, on and off, over the last ten years (see chapter 6 in this volume).

23. Plagued by endemic political and ethnic violence—in which a number of foreign tourists have been killed—over the last five years, Kenya' s tourism sector has been in serious crisis.

24. ACP Group, *Statement by the Hon. Ms Billie A. Miller, President of the ACP Council of Ministers at the Opening of the Negotiations for a successor Agreement to Lomé IV* (Brussels, 30 September 1998), p. 3.

25. Note that the financial aid package offered to South Africa as part of the *EU-SA Agreement* on *Trade, Development & Cooperation* (11 October 1999) provides for an average annual allocation of 125 million euro over 12 years (2000-2012), amounting to a total of 1.5 billion euro (representing 10.2% of the 1995-2000

ACP aid package). However, EU aid to SA is taken from the general EU budget, not from Lomé funds.

26. Karin Arts & Jessica Byron, "The mid-term review of the Lomé IV Convention: heralding the future?" *Third World Quarterly* vol. 18, no. 1 (1997), pp. 82-3; European Commission/EC, *Grants and loans from the European Union; III: Practicalities (Lomé Convention instruments)* (Brussels: EC, 27 November 1999), p. 2.

27. K. Arts & J. Byron, *art. cit.*, pp. 83-4.

28. This argument is eloquently and convincingly made by Gorm Rye Olsen, "Europe and the Promotion of Democracy in Post Cold War Africa: How Serious is Europe and for what Reasons?" *African Affairs* no. 97 (1998), pp. 343-367 (the quote is from p. 343).

29. See P. Economou, M. Gittelman & M. Wubneh, "Europe 1992 and Foreign Direct Investment in Africa," in I.W. Zartman (ed.), *Europe and Africa*, pp. 95-119.

30. CFA stands for *Communauté financière africaine* (African financial community).

31. On the franc zone, see in particular Patrick Guillaumont, *Franc Zone in Africa: Problems and Prospects* (Clermont-Ferrand: CERDI, 1991); Guy Martin, "The franc zone, underdevelopment and dependency in francophone Africa,' *Third World Quarterly* vol. 8, no. 1 (January 1986), pp. 205-235; G. Martin, "Zone franc, sous-développement et dépendance en Afrique noire francophone," *Africa development* vol. 12, no. 1 (1987), pp. 55-100; Olivier Vallée, *Le prix de l'argent CFA* (Paris: Karthala, 1989).

32. The most comprehensive, up-to-date and perceptive study of these issues is Philippe Hugon, *La zone franc à l'heure de l'euro* (Paris: Karthala, 1999).

33. Yves-Thibault de Silguy [membre de la Commission du Parlement européen responsable des affaires économiques, monétaires et financières], *L'Euro et le franc CFA* (speech delivered in Dakar, Senegal, 18 June 1999).

34. Ph. Hugon, *op. cit.*, pp. 272-4.

35. *EU and South Africa sign a historic Trade and Development Cooperation Agreement* [DN: IP/99/735] (Brussels, 11 October 1999).

36. "Dairy Industry Threatens to Sue EU and SA," *Panafrican News Agency* (13 December 1999).

37. EC Commission/Development, "EU-ACP Negotiations: Conclusions of the Brussels Ministerial Conference (7-8 December 1999), *Information Memo* no. 9, p. 2.

38. *Ibidem*, p. 3.

39. ACP-Info, *EU-ACP relations on the eve of the 21st century: Challenges and options for a new partnership* (Brussels: ACP Secretariat, September 1998).

40. ACP Group, *Statement by the Hon. Ms Billie A. Miller, President of the ACP Council of Ministers at the Opening of the Negotiations for a successor Agreement to Lomé IV* (Brussels: ACP Group, 30 September 1998), p. 1.

41. By the *Santo-Domingo Declaration* of 26 November 1999, the ACP Group requests that the WTO ministerial meeting of Seattle "reaffirms clearly and unequivocally the principle of preferential treatment of developing countries as a fundamental element of the multilateral trade regime" (Jean-Michel Caroît, "Les pays du groupe ACP expriment leur défiance face à la globalisation," *Le Monde* (27 novembre 1999).

42. *The Libreville Declaration Adopted by the First Summit of ACP Heads of State and Government* [ACP/28/051/97/Final], Libreville, Gabon (7 November 1997), pp. 6-9.

43. ACP Group, *Statement by the Hon. Billie A. Miller*, p. 5.

44. Quoted in J.M. Caroît, *art. cit.*; see also *The Santo Domingo Declaration Adopted by the Second Summit of ACP Heads of State and Government* [ACP/28/015/99/Final], Santo Domingo (26 November 1999).

45. Robert Kappel, *European Development Cooperation with Africa: The future of Lomé* [University of Leipzig Papers on Africa no. 3]

(Leipzig: University of Leipzig, 1996), pp. 30-35 (the quote is from p. 34); see also R. Kappel, *The Future of Lomé: German Options for a Reform in Development Co-operation between the EU and the ACP Group of States* [Working paper on EU Development policy no. 6-E] (Bonn: Friedrich-Ebert-Stiftung, 1998).

46. R. Kappel, *European Development Cooperation with Africa: The future of Lomé*, p. 33.

Chapter 3

Continuity and Change in Franco-African Relations

While noticeable signs of change in relations between France and its former colonies in Africa began to appear in the post-Cold War era, elements of continuity include their enduring historical and cultural ties; their informal, intimate, and secretive politico-diplomatic relations, typified by the bi-annual Franco-African summit meetings; and the fact that the continent remains of great economic importance to France. The gradual process of democratization which has swept throughout Francophone Africa in recent years has been selectively supported by France for reasons pertaining more to its core foreign-policy interests in Africa than to ideological, legalistic, or humanitarian considerations. Arguably the most profound changes have occurred in the economic domain. The first was the redirection of French trade and capital investment away from Francophone states to others in the continent, followed by the 50 per cent devaluation of the CFA franc in January 1994, which signalled the demise of the Franco-African preferential monetary and trading area known as *la zone franc*. This, more than any other single event since independence, might truly mark the dawn of a new era in Franco-African relations.

The Salience of History and Culture in Franco-African Relations

France prides itself on being the home of a particularly rich culture, and on having a vocation to spread it overseas. Stimulated by the universalist ideals of the Revolution of 1789—notably, *Liberté, Égalité, Fraternité*—in the nineteenth century this vocation became a *mission civilisatrice*, intimately linked with French imperialist expansion and rule in Africa. Even after decolonization, France retained its claim to be the centre of a transnational culture and pursued a policy of cultural *rayonnement*. Underlying this quest is a belief in the innate value of the French language. According to French historian Fernand Braudel, "*La France, c'est la langue française.*"[1] But cultural pride has also been mixed with a need to associate or assimilate Africans into the ideals of French civilization by imparting to them the essentials of that language and culture.

Cultural diffusion thus entails elements of an ideology and policy that have been used to reinforce France's presence overseas. The vision of *France-Afrique* as a single geo-political whole was offered as the goal of continued French presence in Africa. Sometimes the ideal of *EurAfrique* was propounded by those who believed that France should be the leading European power in Africa. Both concepts symbolized the intensity with which many French people came to believe that links with Africa were indissoluble.[2]

The first EurAfricanists appeared among interest groups with a stake in continued French rule, the *parti colonial*: politicians, military officers, and businessmen. They attempted to justify and to rationalize the colonial venture on the grounds of the natural complementarity and related "interdependence" of the two continents: Africa as provider of raw materials, and Europe as supplier of finished goods. Prominent members of this French lobby argued that in order to preserve and manage such intercontinental complementarity it was necessary to unite Africa and Europe, and to link their future together, thereby ensuring the economic prosperity of both.[3] Thus, from its inception, the concept of *Eurafrique* appeared as a convenient justification of the historic role of Britain, Portugal, and particularly France in Africa, and as a rationalization of the inherently unequal and fundamentally exploitative economic policies implemented by the metropoles in their colonies.

The central tenets of complementarity, solidarity, and interdependence continued to be invoked by post-colonial EurAfricanists such as Léopold Sédar Senghor. According to this updated ideal, the creation of *Eurafrique* appears as a strategic and economic necessity for those countries and regions (such as Europe, France and Africa) trying to combat the influence of the superpowers (the United States and the Soviet Union) on the continent. However, the tensions created by the question of which should be given preeminence, bilateral relations between France and its former colonies or multilateral relations between Europe and Africa, would always remain. While France retains a special rapport with its ex-colonies, Europe presents a coherent and largely favourable image of itself in the developing world through the Lomé Convention. This comprehensive trade and aid agreement—between the 15 members of the European Union (EU) and 71 African, Caribbean, and Pacific (ACP) states—has constituted the framework of economic relations between Europe and Africa since 1975.[4]

In the aftermath of World War II, French policy-makers initiated a process of decolonization from above in Africa as they came to realize that the ending of formal control need not be accompanied by a loss of real power and influence on the continent. Shortly after assuming power in June 1958 as the first President of France's Fifth Republic, General Charles de Gaulle, who was trying to revive French *grandeur*, nurtured a special relationship with those Francophone African nationalist leaders who thought that if they could share in the creation of a new France they would also have a part in its success. De

Gaulle's personal conception of *France-Afrique* was translated into his project of a *Communauté franco-africaine* granting autonomy and internal self-government to the African colonies, while France would retain control over such essential matters as defence and foreign affairs, as well as economic, monetary, and strategic-minerals policy.

This Gaullist proposal was presented to the African peoples in the September 1958 Referendum which, although formally offering the option of immediate independence, in effect strongly discouraged it. All the French African territories voted overwhelmingly in favour of the *Communauté franco-africaine* except Guinea, where Sékou Touré had intimated to de Gaulle that the inhabitants preferred "poverty in liberty to wealth in slavery"—which, with hindsight, proved to be a sadly prophetic statement.[5] However, following the independence of Ghana in March 1957 and Guinea in October 1958, the movement toward independence proved irresistible. By August 1960, virtually all the ex-French African colonies had become independent.

The ideologies of *Eurafrique* and *France-Afrique,* which had been used to justify French colonialism, as well as the still-born *Communauté franco-africaine*, became applicable to post-independence relationships, albeit conveniently renamed *coopération*. Before the formal granting of independence, comprehensive bilateral agreements were negotiated covering defence and security; foreign policy and diplomatic consultation; economic, financial, commercial, and monetary matters; and technical assistance. Through the linkage established between the accession to international sovereignty, the signing of model *Accords de coopération*, and the wholesale adoption of the constitutional model of the Fifth Republic, France managed to institutionalize its political, economic, monetary, and cultural pre-eminence over its former African colonies, which thereby remained excessively dependent on it.

Though the first generation of cooperation agreements were subsequently revised in the mid-1970s as a result of African requests, they still gave exorbitant privileges to France.[6] The small Francophone political elites which had been carefully nurtured through many years of what might be described as "on-the-job train-ing" as members of various French legislatures, advisory councils, and even governments, and which had earlier so enthusiastically adhered to de Gaulle's *Communauté franco-africaine*, now unreservedly acquiesced to the new .cooperation agreements in so far as these helped to sustain their own power base, while giving them a degree of influence over the French political agenda. With a stake in the fran-co-African system, these elites generally opted for a gradual process of decolonization rather than a radical break with the past.

The concept used to organize the world's French-speakers and the countries sharing, at least partly, French civilisation is known as *la francophonie*.[7] For some, this means only the use of the French language; for others it refers to countries where it has an official sta-tus. Most users of French see *francophonie* as an element of shared identity by which citizens of states with no indigenous national lan-guage (such as most in Francophone Africa) can communicate with each other and in their regions. Promoters of *francophonie* in Africa also see it as demarcating a distinctive 'Latin' world—inclusive of the Portuguese and Spanish-speaking African elites—separate from that of the English-speaking one, and a way of guarding against encroach-ment from "Anglo-Saxon" civilization.

In its nationalist extreme, *francophonie* becomes *francité*, the dis-tinguishing mark of French civilisation. Ultimately, this appears as a post-colonial modernization of the French policies of "assimilation" (the total political, economic, and cultural absorption of colonies and their peoples into France) and *"association"* (which recognized the autonomous identity of African colonies and cultures). To the extent that it implies the inclusion of people outside France in the culture of France itself, *francophonie* is a truly neocolonial concept.

Permanence of Diplomatic Relations

France's African policy is characterized by exclusivity, stability, and continuity. During the heyday of imperial expansion, the nation's economic dynamism and level of industrial development never quite matched those of its major European competitors, Britain and Germany. This explains why protectionism and autarky were systematically applied to France's African empire and continued to shape its colonial and postcolonial policies. France's heavy reliance on explicit legal instruments is codified in the form of a highly normalized set of binding documents (the cooperation agreements) supported by a number of multilateral arrangements ranging from *la zone franc* to the Franco-African summits.

To this day, Francophone Africa is perceived as belonging to France's traditional sphere of influence by virtue of historical links and geographical proximity. According to this French version of the Monroe Doctrine, it is seen as constituting a natural French preserve—*domaine réservé* or *pré-carré*—off-limits to other foreign powers, whether perceived as friends or foes. Indeed, France has, on several occasions, shown a deep suspicion of the motives and actions of other powers in Africa.[8] Although camouflaged under the mantle of *coopération*, France's African policy is primarily motivated by a narrow conception of its national interests, and blatantly disregards African concerns and interests. As former President Valéry Giscard d'Estaing once bluntly declared, "I am dealing with African affairs, namely with France's interests in Africa."[9]

Because they are said to be based on historical links, geographical proximity, and linguistic and cultural affinity, relations between France and Francophone Africa are invested with a close and intimate—indeed quasi-familial—quality. According to Jean-Pierre Cot, a former *Ministre de la Coopération*, "The relationship between France and its Francophone African partners is based on traditional complicity, on a background of common friendship and references which facilitate contact and dialogue."[10] Thus, while family feuds may occasionally erupt, differences are never such that they cannot be quickly reconciled within the informal, warm, and friendly atmosphere of Franco-African institutions.

One of the most striking features of France's African policy has been its continuity throughout the Fifth French Republic, from 1958 to 1995, transcending traditional political cleavages as well as various governments and individual leaders. The successive governments of Charles de Gaulle, Georges Pòmpidou, and Valéry Giscard d'Estaing have initiated and nurtured this policy. Although François Mitterrand had proclaimed his intention to decolonize the policy, his socialist régime (inaugurated in May 1981) found its room for manoeuver strictly limited by historical constraints, and by the sheer weight of economic, political, and strategic interests. Mitterrand was thus left to manage, rather than to radically transform, this inheritance.[11] The two periods of *cohabitation* during which Mitterand was forced to share power with a rightist parliamentary majority and Prime Minister (Jacques Chirac, 1986-88; Édouard Balladur, 1993-95) revealed the broad agreement that exists across party lines on the substance of France's African policy.

At a more general level, one of the constant preoccupations of French policy-makers in Africa has been to inspire and sustain formal or informal institutions by bringing together all the Francophone African states under the aegis of France. Such concerns led to the creation of a series of Francophone African organizations, including the five-member *Conseil de l'Entente* in May 1959, followed by the *Union africaine et malgache* (UAM) in September 1961, transformed briefly into the *Union africaine et malgache de coopération Économique* (UAMCE) in February 1965, and then into the 13-member *Organisation commune africaine et malgache* (OCAM) in June 1966.[12]

It was partly to make up for the deficiencies of the rather ineffectual and dormant OCAM that President Pompidou initiated the Franco-African summits in November 1973. Since then, 20 have been held, alternatively in France and in Africa.[13] In spite of their progressive inclusion of an ever greater number of non-Francophone African participants—prompting some observers to suggest that they act as a kind of surrogate Organization of African Unity (OAU)—these meetings essentially retain their familial character and constitute the cornerstone of the Franco-African institutional edifice. In addition, a kind of permanent *tête-à-tête* exists between the French president and each of the Francophone heads of state, either directly or via the presidential advisory unit on African affairs, headed from October 1986 to March 1992 by none other than Mitterrand's own son, Jean-Christophe.[14] Such intimate contacts are also preserved through the frequent (official, working, or private) visits of the Francophone African leaders to France, as well as the numerous African tours undertaken by the French president.

At a lower level, a number of *ad hoc* conferences periodically bring together the French and African ministers who deal with similar areas of competence in their respective countries—foreign affairs, economy and finance, telecommunications, justice, education and culture, health, sports, etc. Finally, a wide network of inter-governmental organizations and conferences—whose hub is the *Agence de la francophonie,* formerly the *Agence de coopération culturelle et technique* (ACCT)—tries, under the label of *la francophonie,* to institutionalize the linguistic, cultural, educational, and communication links existing between France and its African partners. President's Mitterrand's decision to revive this concept led to the organization of the broader summit conferences of all Francophone heads of state and government inaugurated in Paris in February 1986, and the creation of a full-fledged *Ministère de la francophonie* in June 1988.[15]

During the Cold War, France was perceived by most African states as a respectable middle power, free from superpower hegemony, non-aligned, and thus a natural ally of the Third World. Francophone Africa constituted a base from which France was able to develop political and economic relations with countries located outside its traditional sphere of influence, notably Nigeria, Angola, Mozambique, Kenya, Zimbabwe, and South Africa. The recent broadening of participation in Franco-African summits to include non-Francophone régimes—25 of which were represented at the 20th summit in Paris in November 1998, including 16 at head of state and government level—derives from the same policy.[16] And while all the French-speaking African states nominally belonged to the Non-Aligned Movement, they effectively retained close political, military, and economic ties with France throughout the Cold War. In reality, France was acting in Africa not only in defence of its own national interests, but also as a proxy gendarme of the West. Today, Africa remains the only area of the world where France retains enough power and influence to support its claim to medium-power status in the international system.[17]

The Economics of Franco-African Relations

It has become fashionable to argue among revisionist historians that France never derived any substantial economic benefits from its African colonies, which were perceived as costing, rather than earning, money, and which—so the argument goes—contributed to slowing down the modernization of France's productive capacity and retarded the development of French capitalism.[18] As one former French foreign minister succinctly put it, "Black Africa is not an indispensable source of raw materials for France. Our investments there are minimal and our trading relations remain fairly limited."[19] In reality, Africa has always been (and remains) an important economic partner for France as a source of strategic raw materials, as a market for its manufactured goods, as an outlet for its capital investment, and as a prop to its currency.

Trade and Strategic Raw Materials

The perennial question of assured access to strategic raw materials places Africa squarely at the center of French geopolitical designs.

Europe in general, and France in particular, are highly dependent on the import of certain minerals that are vital to the functioning of their high-technology industries. Thus, in the early 1980s, France's rate of dependency on mineral imports from Africa ranged from 100 per cent for uranium (Gabon, Niger) to 90 per cent for bauxite (Guinea); 76 per cent for manganese (Gabon, South Africa); 59 per cent for cobalt (Congo/Zaïre, Zambia); 57 per cent for copper (Congo/Zaïre, Zambia); 56 per cent for chromium (Madagascar, South Africa); 55 per cent for phosphate (Morocco, Togo); and 31 per cent for iron ore (Liberia, Mauritania).[20] More generally, France's energy dependency on Africa has increased from 30 per cent in 1950 to 80 per cent in 1988-9. Indeed, almost 70 per cent of the oil extracted world wide by the French state-owned Elf-Aquitaine came from its African deposits (Angola, Cameroon, Congo, and Gabon). Furthermore, the post-independence cooperation and defence agreements concluded between France and the Francophone African states contain special provisions concerning exclusive French access to such strategic raw materials as oil, natural gas, uranium, thorium, lithium, beryllium, and helium. These must be sold to France on a priority basis, as required by "the interests of common defence."[21]

The European Union's share in Francophone Africa's total trade remains as high as 45 per cent, while France's share has now levelled off at around 32 per cent (21.4 per cent of Africa's total trade).[22] Most trade, marketing, and shipping activities in those states are still monopolized by the old colonial trading companies—notably the *Compagnie française de l'Afrique occidentale* (CFAO) and the *Société commerciale de l'ouest africain* (SCOA)—which have recently diversified into import-export activities, and which operate within the vast protected market circumscribed by *la zone franc.* Almost four decades after independence, the foreign trade of Francophone African countries is still largely functioning according to the rules of the *économie de traite*, which means that Africa is restricted to the function of commodity producer, while the European countries retain exclusive control over the export of manufactured goods. As late as 1991, 20 per cent of France's imports from Africa were made up of agricultural and food products, and 45 per cent were energy and fuel products.[23]

France's main trading partners remain the "chosen few" who still constitute the core of the Franco-African "family," namely Cameroon, Congo, Côte d'Ivoire, Gabon, Niger, and Senegal. In 1992, these six countries together accounted for 22 per cent of France's imports from Africa, and for 26 per cent of her exports to the continent. France's balance of trade, which is in chronic deficit with the rest of the world, has always been positive with Africa (+20.3 billion FF in 1986; +24.6 billion in 1991; +27.7 billion in 1992; and +29 billion in 1993). Thus, despite a gradual decline in Franco-African trade since 1986, French exports to Africa have stabilized or even increased, amounting to 82 billion FF in 1993 (with Africa ranking as France's third main export market behind Europe and North America).[24]

French Aid to Africa

French official development assistance (ODA) to sub-Saharan Africa increased from FF12.1 billion (representing 70 per cent of total ODA to the region) in 1985 to 18.1 billion (85 per cent) in 1990, and 18.3 billion (81 per cent) in 1991, to finally stabilize at FF7.7 billion in 1994 and 1995. While the total amount of French aid has increased, the quality has substantially deteriorated. Thus, over the last 15 years, the degree of concessionality has steadily decreased: grants, which represented 80 per cent of French ODA to sub-Saharan Africa in 1975, only accounted for 65 per cent in 1985. In 1992, 59.4 per cent was allocated to economic, social, educational, and administrative infrastructure, 10 per cent to industrial production, 7 per cent to agriculture, and 2.6 per cent to food aid. In keeping with France's policy of *rayonnement culturel* and promotion of *francophonie*, its bilateral aid to Africa remains heavily biased in favor of cultural and technical cooperation. Indeed, in 1991, France still maintained over 7,000 French technical assistance personnel in Francophone Africa.[25]

Since the mid-1980s, a gradual process of multilateralization of aid has been under way, whereby increasing amounts of French ODA are channelled through either the EU-ACP Lomé Convention's European Development Fund or the International Monetary Fund and the World Bank. While purporting to be the advocate of the Francophone African states in North-South fora and in the Washington-based financial institutions, France increasingly defers to their dominant (neo-liberal) development ideology as reflected in the structural adjustment programmes (SAPs) imposed on African countries.[26]

Monetary Dependency

France continues to play a dominant rôle in formulating and implementing monetary policies in Francophone Africa. Through the arrangements made with 13 of its former colonies in sub-Saharan Africa (plus Equatorial Guinea) following their independence in the early 1960s, France controls their money supply (that is, the issue and circulation of their currencies), their monetary and financial regulations, their banking activities, their credit allocation and, ultimately, their budgetary and economic policies.[27] Through their acceptance of the draconian membership rules of *la zone franc*—such as the joint management of all foreign exchange reserves by the French Treasury, and the quasi-veto right retained by French administrators in the decision-making process of the African central banks—the member states have entrusted all their monetary and financial responsibilities to France in what amounts to a voluntary surrender of sovereignty. Indeed, any modification in the value of the French franc against other currencies automatically and fully affects the CFA franc without African governments being consulted prior to any devaluation decision. The CFA franc is a mere appendage of the French franc, with no real autonomy of its own.[28]

French Military Presence and Intervention in Africa

Since independence, France has maintained eight defence and 24 military technical assistance agreements with its former African colonies (including those in North Africa) and with African countries situated outside its traditional sphere of influence (such as Burundi, Rwanda, Congo/Zaïre, and Zimbabwe). With an estimated 8,450 troops. France maintains a significant permanent military presence in Africa, including Central African Republic (1,200), Chad (750), Côte d'Ivoire (500), Djibouti (4,000), Gabon (800), and Senegal (1,200).[29] 792 French military advisers are assigned to 20 African countries. Although its military bases on the continent have been gradually phased out since independence, in 1993 France set up *La Force d'action rapide* (FAR) composed of five units totalling 44,500 men that are capable of intervening at short notice almost anywhere in Africa from bases in France. This elaborate network of agreements and logistical support structures has enabled the French army to intervene at least 30 times in Africa since 1963. According to the official French doctrine, such military interventions are *ad hoc*, always conducted at the concerned government's specific request, within the framework of an existing defence agreement, and designed to counter actual or potential external aggression.[30]

French leaders tend to link the concepts of security and development by arguing that their military assistance has contributed to the stability, and hence to the economic benefit, of all concerned. In fact, their objective in creating African national armies at the time of independence was to ensure that these would work closely with French units and effectively serve as branches of the French army overseas. The Ministry of Cooperation continues to subordinate particular African requests to France's general strategy for Africa. Here, as elsewhere, continuity has prevailed over change. Although the Socialist's pre-election policy paper on Africa stated that the whole question of the French military presence would have to be reviewed, the Mitterrand Government decided to intervene in Africa on nine separate occasions between 1981 and 1994.[31] France's policy of military co-operation (which had reportedly produced some 40,000 African officers by 1992),[32] enables it to control the size and capabilities of most Francophone armies—and hence the defence systems of their states and further exacerbates their already acute dependency on Paris.

In the final analysis, France's military presence in Africa is determined by three main factors: the size and degree of its economic interests and involvement; the number of French residents; and the nature of the links existing between France and the national ruling elites. The countries linked by defense agreements are those central to France's economic interests: Cameroon, Central African Republic, Côte d'Ivoire, Gabon, Senegal, and Togo. Ultimately, one suspects that the main objective is to help pro-French régimes stay in power, as the remarkable political stability and exceptional élite longevity of these states seem to indicate.

Changes in Franco-African Relations

After three decades of authoritarian one-party rule characterized by political repression, human rights abuses, economic mismanagement, nepotism, and corruption, the winds of change have swept throughout Africa, signalling the dawn of a new era variously referred to as the "second independence," the "second liberation," or the '"Springtime of Africa."[33]

Democratisation in Francophone Africa

France observed with some trepidation a process of democratization that it had not expected, and over which it had no control, unfolding in its former African colonies. However, France soon realized the inevitability of that process and promptly initiated a policy of "political conditionality" that established an explicit linkage between the provision of economic and financial assistance and the adoption of political reforms leading to liberal, multi-party democracy. Thus, at the June 1990 La Baule Franco-African summit meeting , president Mitterrand stressed the link between democracy and development, and declared that "French aid will be lukewarm towards authoritarian régimes and more enthusiastic for those initiating a democratic transition."[34] However, France has not actually matched its words with its deeds and, as is often the case, official pronouncements have not been followed by concrete and appropriate policy measures.

Total French ODA to Francophone Africa in 1991 amounted to FF8 billion. A country-by-country breakdown reveals that the French share of aid to those in transition to democracy (such as Benin, Mali, and Niger) has actually been reduced (as in Benin, from FF588 million in 1989 to 300 million in 1990), while authoritarian régimes or reluctant democrats saw their share increase during the same period (from FF628 to 963 million in Cameroon, from FF305 to 519 million in Togo, and from FF669 to 1 billion in Zaïre).[35] Similarly, the only concrete decision of the Libreville Franco-African summit in October 1992 was for France to create a "Debt Conversion Fund for Development" endowed with FF4 billion to provide debt relief to Cameroon, Côte d'Ivoire, Congo, and Gabon where democratisation processes have been either blocked or derailed. While France officially discontinued its ODA to Congo/Zaïre following the 1991 riots, "humanitarian assistance" continued. And barely two months after having been reelected in seriously flawed elections in October 1992, president Paul Biya of Cameroon was allocated FF650 million in French economic aid.[36]

The "oil war" between Congo and the French state-owned Elf-Aquitaine in the early 1990s illustrates the ambiguity of France's African policy and is worth recounting in some detail. The August 1992 presidential elections in Congo brought to power Pascal Lissouba and his radical *Union panafricaine pour la démocratie sociale*. The new president inherited from his predecessor Denis Sassou-Nguesso a disastrous economic and financial situation: the state's coffers were empty, the oil revenues were mortgaged until 1999 for FF1.8 billion, and the country's foreign debt amounted to a staggering US$5 billion. Since Lissouba urgently needed to renew the payment of civil service salaries and pensions as soon as possible (and definitely before the legislative elections scheduled for May 1993), he naturally turned for help to *Elf-Aquitaine* (which controls 80 per cent of the country's oil production) and its French manager, Loïk le Floch-Prigent; first in February when he sought a $300 million loan, and again in March, when he requested a $300 million mortgage on the future production of three promising new off-shore oil deposits.

Having met with a categorical refusal from Elf-Aquitaine and le Floch-Prigent, Lissouba then initiated (with the assistance of former U.S. President Jimmy Carter) secret negotiations with Occidental Petroleum Corporation (Oxy), one of the most enterprising US "minors," represented by David Marten. On April 27, 1993 the government committed itself to deliver to Oxy 75 million barrels of Elf-Congo's projected share of the three new off-shore oil deposits in exchange for a cash payment of $150 million. The money reached Brazzaville on May 1st, just in time to pay the salaries of the 80,000 Congolese civil servants before the first round of parliamentary elections the following day, when Lissouba's 'presidential majority' obtained 62 of the 125 seats in the National Assembly.

Three lessons can be drawn from this revealing story. First, Elf-Aquitaine and its senior staff exhibited a total lack of empathy for, and sensitivity to, the priorities and needs of the Congolese, and generally acted in a most paternalistic and neo-colonial fashion. Second, paranoid senior French officials viewed the Congo-Oxy agreement as yet another inadmissible intrusion of American capitalism into a region considered to be an exclusive French preserve. Third, by denying Lissouba's régime financial resources vital to its survival, Elf-Aquitaine (and by extension the French state) could rightly be perceived as favouring opposition leaders close to them (such as Sassou-Nguesso and Jean-Pierre Thystère Tchicaya) against the democratically elected (but non-compliant) Lissouba. This oil war shows that true to its economic and strategic interests, France deliberately chose to back the forces of authoritarian reaction against those in favor of change.[37]

Not only does France financially support non democratic régimes, but it also comes to their rescue whenever their internal security and stability is threatened. France embarked on ten military interventions in support of those in power between 1986 and 1993 in Chad, the Comoros, Côte d'Ivoire, Gabon, Rwanda, Togo, and Congo/Zaïre. The cost between October 1990 and October 1991 has been conservatively estimated at FF6 billion, an amount almost equivalent to total French ODA to Francophone Africa during that year. Indeed, French military aid appears to be increasingly redirected to satisfy the urgent internal security needs of embattled African régimes attempting to resist popular pressures for democracy. Hence the deployment of 700 officers of the French *Gendarmerie* to eight countries—Benin, Central African Republic, Chad, Comoros, Congo, Madagascar, Niger, and Togo—as well as technical help and material/logistical support for their police forces, riot control units, presidential guards, secret services, and intelligence agencies. In 1993, FF200 million were earmarked for this on-going program designed to benefit the 24 African states linked to France by defence and/or military technical assistance agreements.[38]

Implicitly recognizing the ambiguity of France's African policy, in the mid-1990s the government down-played the linkage between the provision of French aid and the initiation of democratic reforms in favor of the prevailing norm, namely economic conditionality. Thus, then prime minister Balladur insisted that African states should work toward the establishment of definite and stable political and social norms and rules (*L'État de droit*), and that the processes of democratization should not be externally induced according to a presumed ideal model, but allowed to follow their own individual course.[39] According to former *Ministre de la coopération* Bernard Debré, "Democratization in Africa leads to instability and institutional weakness. We must therefore encourage, assist, and help stabilise those régimes and leaders who are progressing on the path to democratization at their own pace."[40] While officially proclaiming support for democratization and human rights, France continues to back the régimes and leaders of the core countries in terms of its economic and politico-strategic interests in Africa. France thus maintains a deliberate (though recently toned-down) "creative ambiguity" in its African policy pronouncements and actions. Continuity and stability tend to prevail over justice and equity

The Devaluation of the CFA Franc

Following an extraordinary Franco-African summit meeting in Dakar in January 1994, the CFA franc—whose exchange rate had remained unchanged since 1948—was officially devalued by 50 per cent. The French decision—apparently arrived at in July 1992 but delayed for political reasons—was motivated by several factors. First the CFA franc was grossly overvalued, thereby making goods in *la zone franc* uncompetitive on African markets and encouraging cross-border smuggling with non-CFA countries. Capital transfer between Francophone states and European banks had sharply increased over the last year-and-a-half, prompting monetary authorities to suspend the free convertibility of the CFA franc starting in August 1993. In addition, the French Treasury had been repeatedly called upon to bail out Francophone African states on the verge of financial bankruptcy (notably Cameroon, Congo, Côte d'Ivoire, Gabon, and Senegal) either by providing direct budgetary support or by paying their arrears to the IMF and the World Bank. Such short-term aid relief had amounted to more than FF1.5 billion over the six-month period from December 1992 to May 1993.

Ultimately, the deepening economic and financial crisis in Francophone Africa, coupled with a severe recession in France, led to the sobering realization that the latter could no longer afford to foot the bill. As Balladur candidly admitted, "France alone cannot solve all the economic and financial problems of all the African countries. The international [financial] institutions must become much more involved in Africa than they are at present."[41] This explains the decision to make any new French aid commitment to régimes in *la zone franc* conditional upon a prior agreement with the IMF and the World Bank as of January 1994.

From the French government's perspective, the devaluation of the CFA franc was a rational economic decision that transferred the burden of the huge foreign debts of, for example, Cameroon, and Côte d'Ivoire, from the French Treasury to the Washington-based financial institutions.[42] On balance, the devaluation had negative economic and social consequences for the African countries and peoples, sharply reducing foreign-exchange earnings, household incomes, and standards of living. Recent proposals for reform of *la zone franc* center on the strengthening of intra-regional monetary, financial, and economic unions in Africa, and on the creation, within the framework of the ACP-EU Lomé Convention, of a new Euro-African monetary zone in which the new European currency (euro) will replace the French franc as the monetary unit of reference. While a degree of Franco-African monetary cooperation might subsist, this severing of the link between the CFA franc and the French franc—a logical outcome of the circulation of the euro in January 2002—in effect signals the beginning of the end for *la zone franc*.[43]

Conclusion

In the post-Cold War era, Africa remains the only continent where France retains enough power and influence to support its claim to medium-power status in the international system. In a context of increasing globalization of the world economy and European integration, France no longer has the wherewithal and the political will to maintain an autonomous African policy distinct from that of its Western partners. Thus, the devaluation of the CFA franc is likely to result in France's gradual (but substantial) loss of political, diplomatic, and economic power and influence in the Francophone African states. The latter will probably move towards a long-overdue economic *rapprochement* with the major world economic powers (such as the United States and Japan), as well as with non-Francophone African regional powers (notably Nigeria and South Africa). As Albert Bourgi cogently remarked, "The devaluation of the CFA franc will ultimately have a cathartic effect, that of mentally decolonizing the African leaders in their relations with France, thus finally cutting the umbilical cord which, for more than three decades, has tied them to their former metropole."[44]

Endnotes

1. Quoted by Mort Rosenblum, *Mission to Civilize: The French Way* (San Diego: Harcourt, Brace, Jovanovich, 1986), p. 8 ("France is, above all, the French language").
2. See John Chipman, *French Power in Africa* (Oxford:Basil Blackwell, 1989), pp. 61-84; Max Liniger-Goumaz, *L'Eurafrique: Utopie ou Réalité* (Yaoundé: Editions CLÉ, 1972); and Guy Martin, "Africa and the Ideology of Eurafrica: Neo-colonialism or Pan-Africanism?," *The Journal of Modern African Studies,* vol 20, no 2 (June 1982), pp. 221-238.
3. Eugène Guernier, *L'Afrique: Champ d'expansion de l'Europe* (1933), quoted in Chipman, *op. cit.,* pp. 71-72.
4. For an analysis of the origin, substance and impact of the Lomé Conventions on African countries, see chapter 2 in this volume.
5. Georges Chaffard, *Les Carnets secrets de la décolonisation,* vol 2 (Paris: Calmann-Lévy, 1965), p. 197. See also Chipman, *op. cit.* pp. 85-110 and Francis T. McNamara, *France in Black Africa* (Washington, DC: National Defense University Press, 1989), pp. 67-93. In his memoirs, the then French Governor of Guinea (later to become Prime Minister under de Gaulle), reveals that

that country was deliberately made to suffer the consequences of its fateful decision; he personally gave specific orders for the speedy withdrawal of all French personnel (within two months), and the re-routing of two rice-cargo shipments and several thousand million newly-printed CFA francs from Conakry to Dakar. Pierre Messmer, *Après tant de batailles* (Paris: Albin Michel, 1992), pp. 240-242; see also P. Messmer, *Les Blancs s'en vont: Récits de décolonisation* (Paris: Albin Michel, 1998), pp. 214-220.

6. Albert Bourgi, *La Politique française de coopération en Afrique* (Paris: Librairie Générale de Droit & de Jurisprudence , 1979; Chipman, *op.cit*, 102-13; Guy Martin, "The Historical, Economic, and Political Bases of France's African Policy", *The Journal of Modern African Studies*, vol 23, no 2 (June 1985), pp.189-92; and McNamara, *op.cit.*, pp. 95-9.

7. See Xavier Deniau, *La Francophonie* (Paris: Presses Universitaires de France, 1983); Robert Aldrich and John Connell, "Francophonie: Language, Culture, or Politics?" in Aldrich & Connell (eds.), *France in World Politics* (New York: Routledge, 1989), and Michel Guillou, *La Francophonie: nouvel enjeu mondial* (Paris: Hatier, 1993).

8. Some serious concerns have recently been expressed in France about alleged "American activism" in francophone Africa, following the appointment of George Moose (former Ambassador to Senegal) as Assistant Secretary of State for African Affairs; Washington's discreet support of pro-democracy forces in Cameroon, Congo, and Togo; the signature of the Congo-Oxy purchase agreement of 27 April 1993; and the resounding success of the second African/African-American summit in Libreville, 24-28 May 1993, attended by 18 francophone heads of state and government. See "France-États-Unis: George Moose inquiète," *Jeune Afrique* (13-19 May 1993), p.19; Géraldine Faes, "États-Unis-Afrique: les conseilleurs ne sont pas les payeurs," in *ibid.* (10-16 June 1993), pp.22-6; Philippe Triay, "Deuxième sommet africain/africain-américain: la consécration

d'une idée," in *Jeune Afrique Économie*, vol 109 (July 1993), pp.17-33; and Claude Wauthier, "Appétits américains et compromissions françaises," *Le Monde diplomatique* (October 1994), p.10.

9. Televised interview of Valéry Giscard d'Estaing, quoted in T. Jallaud, "La Coopération militaire," *La France contre l'Afrique* (Paris: Maspéro, 1981). Author's translation from the French, as elsewhere in this volume .

10. Jean-Pierre Cot, *À l'Épreuve du pouvoir* (Paris: Éditions du Seuil, 1984), p. 63. On the patrimonial character of Franco-African relations, see also Jean-François Médard, "France-Afrique: des affaires de famille," in Y. Mény & D. Della Porta (eds.), *Démocratie et corruption en Europe* (Paris: La Découverte, 1995), pp. 29-41; Antoine Glaser & Stephen Smith, *Ces Messieurs Afrique: Le Paris-Village du continent noir* (Paris: Calmann-Lévy, 1992); Glaser & Smith, *Ces Messieurs Afrique 2: des réseaux aux lobbies* (Paris: Calmann-Lévy, 1997); and François-Xavier Verschave, *La Françafrique: le plus long scandale de la République* (Paris: Stock, 1998).

11. Much the same argument was made by Jean-François Bayart, who goes so far as to assert that it was, in fact, Mitterrand himself who initiated a new deal for Africa when he became minister for overseas France in 1954: "The real continuity actually starts with Mr. Mitterrand and was passed on to General de Gaulle and to his successors; " see J.F. Bayart, *La Politique africaine de François Mitterrand* (Paris: Karthala, 1984), p. 52.

12. Lynn K. Mytelka, "A Genealogy of Francophone West and Equatorial African Regional Organisations", *The Journal of Modern African Studies*, vol 12, no 2 (June 1974), pp. 297-320; see also Abdul A. Jalloh, *Political Integration in French-Speaking Africa* (Berkeley: Institute of International Studies/University of California, 1973).

13. The 17th summit was held in Libreville, Gabon, 5-7 October 1992, with 13 Heads of State and Government in attendance.

The same city hosted the interim ministerial conference, 29-30 July 1993, attended by some 30 Ministers of Foreign Affairs. The 18th summit was held in Biarritz, France, 8-9 November 1994. The 19th summit was held in Ouagadoubou, Burkina Faso, 4-6 December 1996, with 45 African countries represented and 26 Heads of State and Government in attendance. The 20th summit was held in Paris, France, 26-29 November 1998, with 49 African countries represented (including 25 non-francophone) and 34 Heads of State and Government (including 16 non-francophone) in attendance.

14. See "Jean-Christophe Mitterrand, le conseiller," in A. Glaser and S. Smith, *Ces Messieurs Afrique: le Paris-village du continent noir* (Paris: Calmann-Lévy, 1992), pp. 209-235; and François Soudan, "Le 'vrai-faux' départ de Jean Christophe," in *Jeune Afrique* (28 April 1992), p. 10.

15. For an interesting overview of the foreign policy of *francophonie* from the perspective of one of its first ministers, see Alain Decaux, *Le Tapis rouge*. Paris: Perrin, 1992.

16. The Presidents of Ethiopia, Eritrea, and Zimbabwe, as well as the Vice-President of South Africa, attended the 18th franco-African summit in Biarritz, France, 8-9 November 1994.

17. See Zaki Laidi, *The Superpowers and Africa: the constraints of rivalry, 1960-1990* (Chicago: The University of Chicago Press, 1990); Guy Martin, "France and Africa", in Aldrich and Connell (eds.), *op. cit.*, pp. 170-193, and "The Theory and Practice of Non-Alignment: the case of the francophone West and Central African states", in L. Adele Jinadu and Ibbo Mandaza (eds.), *African Perspectives on Non-Alignment* (Harare: AAPS, 1986); see also chapter 5 in this volume.

18. The classic *exposé* of this argument is to be found in Jacques Marseille, *Empire colonial et capitalisme français: histoire d'une divorce* (Paris: Albin Michel,1984). See also Chipman, *op. cit.*, pp. 186-92. Cartierists (and their contemporary supporters, the neo-Cartierists) are those who, following French journalist

Raymond Cartier's series of articles in the early 1950s in the weekly *Paris-Match*, believe that French economic assistance should be primarily directed within (to underdeveloped French regions) rather than without (overseas), according to the famous motto, "*La Corrèze avant le Zambèze!*"

19. Louis de Guiringaud, "La Politique africaine de la France," *Politique étrangère*, vol 2, (June 1982), p. 443.

20. Statistical data are from Jacques Adda and Marie-Claude Smouts, *La France face au Sud: le Miroir brisé* (Paris: Karthala, 1989), p. 98, table 10.

21. Pierre Lellouche and Dominique Moisi, "French Policy in Africa: a Lonely Battle against Destabilization', *International Security*, vol. 3 (Spring 1979, no. 4), p. 116, n. 15.

22. "Rapport Prouteau, 1994: Les Entreprises françaises et l'Afrique", *Jeune Afrique* (27 October-9 November 1994), pp.19-21. Jean-Pierre Prouteau is president of the *Conseil des investisseurs français en Afrique*.

23. On Franco-African trade relations, see Elsa Assidon, *Le Commerce captif: les Sociétés commerciales françaises de l'Afrique noire* (Paris: L'Harmattan, 1989), and Adda and Smouts, *op. cit.*, pp. 81-103.

24. Trade statistics are taken from "France-Afrique: l'afro-pessimisme ne passera pas,",*Jeune Afrique* (14-27 August 1991), pp. 128-41; François Dorce, Géraldine Faes, and Rémi Godeau, "France-Afrique: le Temps du réalisme," in *ibid.* (13-26 August 1992, pp.130-35; "Rapport Prouteau, 1992: les Entreprises françaises et l'Afrique", in *ibid.* (22-28 October 1992), pp. 47-55; "Rapport Prouteau, 1993", in *ibid.* (28 October-10 November 1993), pp. 53-98, and "Rapport Prouteau, 1994".

25. On French aid to Africa, see Adda and Smouts, *op. cit.*, pp. 27-60. French aid statistics are taken from "Rapport Prouteau, 1992," pp. 13-22 & 37-44; "Rapport Prouteau, 1993,", pp. 94-8; OECD, *Development Assistance Committee Report, 1991* and *1992* (Paris: OECD, 1991 & 1992); and "Coopération: le budget de la déval-uation," *Jeune Afrique* (27 October-9 November 1994), p. 8.

26. See Adda and Smouts, *op. cit.*, pp. 50-60, and Zaki Laidi, *Enquête sur la banque mondiale* (Paris: Fayard, 1989), pp. 313-337.
27. See Neil B. Ridler, "Fixed Exchange Rates and Structural Adjustment Programmes: Côte d'Ivoire", *The Journal of Modern African Studies*, vol 31, no 2 (June 1993), pp. 301-8, which analyses "an economy which cannot meet an essential SAP condition for success, namely: the devaluation of its currency. The country is Côte d'Ivoire, but the illustration could come from any of the 13 African members of the franc zone where a fixed exchange rate precludes a major policy instrument for ending prolonged recession," p. 301.
28. See Patrick and Sylvianne Guillaumont, *Zone franc et développement africain* (Paris: Economica, 1984); Guy Martin, "The Franc Zone: underdevelopment and dependency in francophone Africa," *Third World Quarterly*, vol 8, no 1 (January 1986), pp. 205-35; Olivier Vallée, *Le Prix de l'argent CFA: heurs et malheurs de la zone franc* (Paris: Karthala, 1989); Adda & Smouts, op. cit. pp.62-79; and Shantayaran Devarajan and Jaime de Melo, "Relative Performance of CFA Franc Zone Members and Other Countries," in I. William Zartman (ed.), *Europe and Africa: the New Phase* (Boulder: Lynne Rienner, 1993), pp. 121-137. On recent developments in franco-African economic relations, see François Gaulme, "France-Afrique: une crise de coopération," *Études*, vol. 3801 (January 1994), pp. 41-52, and Philippe Leymarie, "Inexorable effritement du 'modèle' franco-africain," *Le Monde diplomatique*, no 478 (January 1994), pp, 4-5.
29. *Africa South of the Sahara, 1994.* London: 1994.
30. On French military presence in Africa, see Lellouche & Moisi, *loc. cit.*, pp. 108-33; Robin Luckham, "French Militarism in Africa," *Review of African Political Economy*, no 24 (May-August 1982), pp. 55-84; George E. Moose, "French Military Policy in Africa," in William J. Foltz and Henry S. Bienen (eds.), *Arms and the African: military influences on Africa's international relations* (New Haven: Yale University Press, 1985), and John

Chipman, *French Military Policy and African Security* (London: International Institute for Strategic Studies/IISS, 1985), Adelphi Paper No 201, and *French Power in Africa*, pp. 114-67. The statistical data are from P.M. de la Gorce, "Pourquoi la France est sur tous les Fronts," *Jeune Afrique* (14-20 May 1992), pp. 30-31, and Philippe Leymarie, "Les Voies incertaines de la Coopération franco-africaine," *Le Monde diplomatique*, no 463 (October 1992), pp. 22-23, and "La France et le Maintien de l'Ordre en Afrique," in *ibid.* No 483, (June 1994), p.28.

31. Secrétariat général du Parti socialiste, *Le Parti socialiste et l'Afrique sub-saharienne* (Paris: Secrétariat général du PS, 1981). French military interventions during the period 1981 to 1994 include Chad (1983, 1986-9), Togo (1986), Comoros (1989), Côte d'Ivoire and Gabon (May 1990), Rwanda (October 1990-December 1993, June-August 1994), and Zaïre (September 1991).

32. Leymarie, *loc. cit.* (October 1992).

33. On the concept of the "second independence," see Georges Nzongola-Ntalaja, *Revolution and Counter-Revolution in Africa* (London: Zed Books, 1987), pp. 92-120 and on the "second liberation," see George Ayittey, *Africa Betrayed* (New York: St. Martin's Press, 1992), pp. 305-334. The term 'Springtime of Africa' was coined by Albert Bourgi and Christian Casteran, *Le Printemps de l'Afrique.* (Paris:Hachette, 1991).

34. Quoted in Christian Casteran and Hugo Sada, "Sommet de La Baule: l'Avertissement," *Jeune Afrique* (27 June-3 July 1990), p. 15.

35. Data provided by Jean-Pierre Alaux, "Les Contradictions de la coopération française en Afrique," *Le Monde diplomatique*, no 456 (March 1992), p. 4.

36. See Elimane Fall, "Le Sommet des désillusions," *Jeune Afrique* (15-21 October 1992), p.4, and "La Coopération et les processus démocratiques en Afrique," an interview with French Minister of Co-operation Marcel Debarge, *Le Monde* (17 February 1993), pp. 1, 6.

37. This revealing story is chronicled in some detail in Francis Kpatindé, "La Guerre du pétrole", *Jeune Afrique* (27 May-2 June 1993), pp. 12-15, and "La Guerre du pétrole est-elle finie?", in *ibid.* (9-15 September 1993), pp. 52-55. Apparently under intense French pressure, President Lissouba later reneged on the April 1993 Congo-Oxy agreement by retroactively recognising, through a special law passed in December 1993, *Elf-Aquitaine*'s exclusive exploitation rights over the new Nkossa off-shore oil fields. See Francis Kpatindé, "Lissouba dit tout", in *ibid.* (24 February-2 March 1994), pp. 68-9.

38. See, in particular, J.P. Alaux, loc. cit.; Mongo Béti, *La France contre l'Afrique* (Paris: La Découverte, 1993); and Leymarie, *loc. cit.* (June 1994), p. 28.

39. Edouard Balladur's statements as reported in *Le Monde* (23 September 1993), and *Le Point* (16 October 1993). See also P. Leymarie, "Inexorable effritement du 'modèle' franco-africain," p. 5, and Gaulme, *loc. cit.*, pp. 46-7.

40. Interview of Bernard Debré by François Soudan, *Jeune Afrique* (24-30 November 1994), p. 8.

41. Quoted in J.P. Bechtold, Zyad Limam, and François Soudan, "Balladur: ce que veut la France," *Jeune Afrique* (23 December 1993-5 January 1994), p. 55.

42. Pierre Messmer, "Il faut dévaluer le franc CFA," in *ibid.* (20-26 May 1993), pp. 26-7. See also Géraldine Faes, "Franc CFA: comment éviter l'inévitable, " in *ibid.* (12-25 August 1993), pp. 47-50; Rémi Godeau, "La Dévaluation en douze questions," in *ibid.*, pp. 50-58; and Jones Dowe, "Du rififi à CFA City," in Serge Michaïlof (ed.), *La France et l'Afrique: Vade-mecum pour une nouveau voyage* (Paris: Karthala, 1993), pp. 461-68.

43. See Patrick and Sylvianne Guillaumont, "La Zone franc à un tournant vers l'intégration régionale," in Michailof (ed.), *op.cit.*, pp. 411-22, and Marie-France l'Hériteau, "Intégration régionale en Afrique et coopération monétaire euro-africaine," in *ibid.*, pp. 449-58. On the CFA franc devaluation of 12 January 1994, see,

in particular, "Franc CFA: la déchirure," *Jeune Afrique* (20-26 January 1994), pp. 36-52; George Ola Davies, "The Devaluation Bombshell," *West Africa* (24-January 1994), pp. 116-17; and "Dévaluation du franc CFA: plus pauvres que jamais!," *Jeune Afrique Économie*, no 176 (February 1994), pp. 10-34. The argument of continued Franco-African cooperation under the euro regime is made by Philippe Hugon, *La zone franc à l'épreuve de l'euro* (Paris: Karthala, 1999), pp. 219-228.

44. Albert Bourgi, "Dévaluation, émancipation...," *Jeune Afrique* (20-26 January 1994), pp. 46-7.

Chapter 4

France's African Policy in Transition: Disengagement and Redeployment

Introduction

This chapter examines current French policy towards Africa. Is France's African policy truly in transition between old-style neo-colonial and patrimonial type of policies characterized by intimate and quasi-familial relations between the French and francophone African elites—*le village franco-africain*,[1] or *la Françafrique*[2] —and a new policy in which francophone Africa is subsumed within a broader Third World policy? is France resolutely moving away from its traditional policy of *domaine réservé* and *chasse gardée* (private domain) toward a politico-diplomatic, military and economic and financial disengagement from and redeployment in, Africa? In brief, are we witnessing a decolonization of Franco-African relations?

A number of symbolic events clearly show that a new French African policy is taking shape, leading to a progressive divorce between France and Francophone Africa. In a changing world environment characterized by the end of the Cold War and globalization, French policy towards Africa is no longer determined by politico-diplomatic and geo-political factors but by purely economic and financial considerations, namely the search for new African and Third World markets, and a renewed focus on European integration. At the same time, built-in structural factors tend to favor a status quo policy. Thus, while some observers point to a genuine French disengagement and redeployment, others stress France's tendency to preserve the *status quo*.

TOWARDS A NEW FRENCH POLICY IN AFRICA? SIX SYMBOLIC EVENTS

Six separate (though interrelated) events are symbolic of France's new African policy: the passing away of Houphouët-Boigny and Foccart; the *La Baule* doctrine; the Abidjan doctrine and the devaluation of the CFA franc; French setbacks in the Great Lakes region; the Democratic Republic of the Congo *débacle*; the Franco-South African *rapprochement*; and French immigration policy.

The death of Houphouët-Boigny and Foccart: The End of an Era?

The passing away of two key figures of the Franco-African family (*La Françafrique*), Félix Houphouët-Boigny (December 1993) and Jacques Foccart (May 1997) signaled the end of an era in Franco-African relations.

When he died in December 1993, Félix Houphouët-Boigny had been president of Côte d'Ivoire since 1960 and was unquestionably the *doyen* of francophone Africa and a key ally of France. His close personal ties with several generations of French leaders were reflected in the level and size of the French delegation to his state funeral in Yamoussokro (February 1994), which included the late president Mitterand, then prime minister Balladur, former president Giscard d'Estaing, six former prime ministers, and more than 70 other dignitaries. As the *New York Times* remarked, "Houphouët-Boigny's death is not only the end of a political era here, but perhaps as well the end of the close French-African relationship that he came to symbolize."[3]

Jacques Foccart was the personal embodiment of continuity in Franco-African relations. A trusted adviser on African affairs and close confidante of the founder of the Fifth Republic, Charles de Gaulle, and of his successor, Georges Pompidou, Foccart was called back to duty by president Jacques Chirac in May 1995, and remained active until his death on May 19, 1997.

As he reveals in his memoirs, he carefully nurtured close personal relations with the francophone African élite, and through a closely knit network of public and private individuals, organizations and interests (*les réseaux*), single-handedly managed to determine France's African policy in what he perceived to be France's best interest.[4]

French policy setbacks in the Great Lakes Region

From the October 1990 military intervention to rescue the Habyarimana regime to *Opération Turquoise* (June 14-August 21, 1994) designed to allow the *forces armées rwandaises* (FAR) to retreat into eastern Zaire, France provided diplomatic, military, technical and financial support to the *génocidaires* extremists of the *Hutu Power* (*Interahamwe* and FAR) who, in April 1994, planned and carried out the genocide of some one million Tutsis and moderate Hutus in Rwanda. As François-Xavier Verschave has noted, "In Rwanda, France has backed a racist regime intent upon moving towards a "final solution." As acknowledged in the final report of the French Parliamentary Information Committee on Rwanda [*Mission d'information parlementaire française sur le Rwanda*] published in December 1998, France has largely contributed to finance, train and arm the military and security units which later executed the geno-cide."[5] As Jean-François Bayart has remarked, this has considerably tarnished French prestige in Africa: "Having been unable to prevent the RPF's [Rwanda Patriotic Front] victory, France became alienated from one of the major regional actors who later played a key role in the Zaïre/DRC crisis, discredited itself as an honest broker in the region and found itself compromised in the genocide. The resulting net loss of influence is enormous."[6] The replacement of Mobutu Sese Seko's Zaïre—which France supported until the bitter end—by Laurent-Désiré Kabila's Democratic Republic of the Congo—supported by Rwanda's Kagame and Uganda's Museveni—in May 1997 further aggravated French loss of influence in the subregion. It also exacerbated France's "Fachoda syndrome" of an Anglo-Saxon plot to permanently evict it from its central African *chasse gardée*.[7] The fact that France proved unable to put together a coalition for a "humanitarian" intervention in eastern Zaire in late 1996, the fall of Mobutu two months after Foccart's death and France's impotence in the face of the upheaval in June 1997 in Brazzaville (where French troops simply evacuated French nationals) were all symptomatic of a major loss of French power and influence in central Africa.

France and South Africa: towards a new engagement in Africa?

Coming in the wake of French foreign affairs minister Hubert Védrine's one-day visit to Cape Town in October 1997, French president Jacques Chirac's state visit to South Africa in June 1998 and to Angola, Mozambique and Namibia, was meant to demonstrate France's resolve in opening a new chapter in Franco-African relations while resolutely turning a page in the neo-colonial relations that have traditionally characterized its relations with its former colonies in Africa. As France progressively disengages politically, economically and militarily from francophone sub-Saharan Africa, it can only view favorably South Africa's parallel involvement in France's former *domaine réservé.* Thus, South Africa's diplomatic involvement in the final stages of the DRC/Zaïre crisis, South African firms' active involvement in gold mining in countries such as Burkina Faso, Guinea, Mali and Niger, or South African farmers' new northern Trek to Congo-Brazzaville or the DRC, which would have never been allowed by *La Françafrique,* are now tolerated (if not actively encouraged) by France. In search of new trading partners and new outlets for both public and private investments in Africa, France increasingly looks up to South Africa as an ideal intermediary and power broker to penetrate Southern African markets, which have for many years been firmly situated within South Africa's traditional sphere of influence.

With the end of apartheid, economic relations between France and South Africa have progressed steadily. In 1997, the sale of French goods on the South African market increased by more than 27 per cent in real terms compared to 1996, reaching a record U.S. $1 billion in value. South Africa has since become France's main trading partner in sub-Saharan Africa, before Côte d'Ivoire and Nigeria. Altogether, the French market share in South Africa has increased to nearly 3 billion rands since 1994. Over 125 French firms now have a subsidiary in South Africa (a three-fold increase since 1993). In 1997, French development aid to South Africa amounted to 230 million francs, and French cultural, educational and scientific aid (governed by a special protocol since February 1995) reached 42 million francs.[8] Following the visit to South Africa of French foreign affairs minister Hubert Védrine, a formal agreement setting up a Franco-South African Forum for Political Dialogue—conceived as a permanent mechanism for consultation in international affairs—was concluded between the two governments in October 1997. Other signs of Franco-South African *rapprochement* include Vice-President Thabo Mbeki's participation in the 20th Franco-African summit meeting in Paris (November 1998); the inclusion of South Africa's in France's newly defined *Zone de solidarité prioritaire* for purposes of French aid; and France's allocation of FF 3.5 million to the South

African Development Community's *Blue Crane* war games conducted in April 1999 in South Africa. While South Africa would officially prefer—for historical and political reasons—not to be seen as too closely associated with France, considerations of *realpolitik* dictate that it agrees to a marriage of convenience with France while the latter acknowledges the former's status as an ascending subregional power with budding continental ambitions, as evidenced by its vocal advocacy and active promotion of a pan-African policy of African Renaissance.

French immigration policy

During the *cohabitation* régime in which a socialist president (François Mitterand) co-existed with a rightist government (with Charles Pasqua as minister of home affairs)—between 1986 and 1988, and between 1993 and 1995—France enacted extremely restrictive immigration policies specifically targeting francophone Africans (including *Maghrébins* from north Africa). Taking various forms—drastic reduction in the delivery of entry visas in France; multiplication of administrative obstacles and extreme bureaucratization of the visa issuance process; forced expulsion on charter planes of "illegal" immigrants in degrading conditions; forced expulsion of the African protesters at the Saint-Bernard Church in Paris—this policy succeeded in antagonizing many francophone Africans (including students, businessmen and politicians) and further contributed to a significant degradation of France's image in Africa. This led some observers to remark that France actively promoted a policy of *Francophonie* while at the same time busily engaged in chasing the *francophones* away from France.[9]

HOW "NEW" IS FRANCE'S NEW AFRICAN POLICY? BETWEEN A SECOND DECOLONIZATION AND MAINTAINING THE *STATUS QUO*

There are two opposing viewpoints on the evolving Franco-African relationship. According to the first view, we are witnessing a real French disengagement from francophone Africa and a simultaneous redeployment of French politico-diplomatic, strategic and economic interests away from francophone Africa and into new countries in Africa (Nigeria, Angola, Namibia, Zimbabwe and South Africa) and other Third World countries (Brazil, India, Vietnam etc.). The second view argues that this decolonization policy is a mere smoke screen behind which the traditional *status quo* policy of *La Françafrique* is maintained.

A new African policy of disengagement and redeployment: towards a second decolonization?

While direct French presence had always been a hallmark of French cooperation policy in Africa, there has been a significant decrease in the number of civilian and military technical assistants in Africa. The number of French civilian *coopérants* in Africa has decreased from 7,669 in 1988 to 2,919 in 1998 while that of their military counterparts decreased from 954 to 570 during the same period.[10] This trend clearly indicates a move away from what the French call a *coopération de substitution* (aid substituting for local manpower) to a medium to long-term project-based type of assistance.

Its renewed European focus, its economic and financial crisis, and setbacks experienced in the Great Lakes region have led France to reassess its security policy in Africa. This new policy is characterized by military disengagement (from 8,000 to 5,600 troops over the period 1997-2002); concentration of these troops in only five locations (Abidjan, Dakar, Djibouti, Libreville and N'Djamena), and closure of two bases (Bangui and Bouar, in the Central African Republic); financial, material and logistical support to subregional and pan-African peace-keeping forces (in cooperation with Britain and the United States.); and relocation of military training from France to four subregional training centers in Africa (Thiès in Senegal, Koulikoro in Mali, and Bouaké in Côte d'Ivoire, where the Zambakro subregional peacekeeping training center was inaugurated in June 1999).[11]

A distinct French disengagement from Africa is taking place at the economic and financial levels as well. Following the general trend of "donor fatigue," French ODA has decreased from FF 42.1 billion in 1995 to FF 34.7 billion in 1998 while the budget of the ministry of cooperation was reduced from FF 8 billion. in 1993 to FF 6.4 billion. in 1998.[12] This French disengagement also takes the form of a gradual process of multilateralization of French ODA whereby the provision of French aid to francophone African states is henceforth made conditional to the conclusion of agreements between the latter and the IM F and World Bank. Clearly, France no longer has the means to pursue an ambitious African policy.

Defending *La Françafrique* and maintaining the *status quo*

At the official level, pronouncements by key *décideurs* of France's African policy (notably President Chirac and foreign minister Védrine) indicate that France does not intend to change its African policy, let alone to disengage from Africa, and that it remains faithful to its traditional African allies. As for the observable signs of change, they are rationalized as being a mere adaptation to changing circumstances.[13] Looking beyond the official discourse emphasizing continuity in Franco-African relations within the *longue durée*, one may observe the survival of certain attitudes and of various individuals, networks, firms and institutions that have a vested interest in preserving *La Françafrique* for a few more years. These would include:

a cross-section of the French political and military elite; the *cellule africaine* (African affairs unit) at the *Élysée* Palace, manned by two *Foccartiens* (Michel Dupuch and Fernand Wibaux); the French oil major Elf Aquitaine (now Elf-Total) which, for years, has conducted its own autonomous African policy in its central African *chasses gardées* (notably Gabon and Congo); the francophone African political and military elite from the core countries of *Françafrique* (Cameroon, Chad, Côte d'Ivoire, Gabon, Senegal, and Togo), linked to their French counterparts through various official and occult networks, such as the freemasons;[14] various firms, experts and consultants who benefit from French ODA; and some non-governmental organizations benefitting from the provision of humanitarian assistance to Africa.

France's African policy has, indeed, entered a *transitional phase* in which clear signs of change co-exist with *status quo* policies. Thus, while the edifice shows some cracks, it still stands. As we review the concrete manifestations of France's "new" policy in Africa, we must keep in mind the fact that in the gray areas of policy, new orientations may very well coexist with old habits for some time.[15]

How "new" is the new French African policy?
Plus ça change, plus c'est la même chose...

What is really "new" in France's African policy? Not much, as a closer examination of that policy reveals.

French military and security policy in Africa

The restructuring of the French military announced in mid-1997, which resulted in the reduction and redeployment of French forces in Africa, is the logical outcome of a strategy of intervention from bases located in France (through a 44,500-men strong *Force* *d'action rapide/*FAR)—as opposed to a strategy of direct military presence—which was initiated in the late seventies. Thus, while the number of troops based in Africa is being reduced (from 8,000 to 5,600 between 1997 and 2002), their capacity to intervene will be maintained and even improved. Furthermore, as Albert Bourgi rightly observes, "In spite of the reforms undertaken, French military presence in Africa retains a colonial character, as demonstrated by the decision to maintain bases in countries considered as strategic for the perpetuation of French political, economic and strategic influence on the continent, namely Senegal, Côte d'Ivoire, Gabon and Chad." And he adds: "French military presence in Africa appears more than ever as the symbol of an outdated imperial policy which is meaningless in the post-Cold War world..."[16]

In the same way, one can view the new French policy of assistance to multinational and subregional peace-keeping forces in Africa within the context of continuity in French military policy in Africa. Thus, the *Mission interafricaine de stabilisation à Bangui* (MISAB) set up by France in the Central African Republic in early1997, while made up of African contingents, has been armed, equipped, trained and managed by France. Similarly, the new French military policy of RECAMP (*Renforcement des capacités africaines de maintien de la paix*) was tested during the *Guidimakha* inter-African military war games conducted in Senegal in early 1998, which benefitted from significant technical, logistical and financial support from France, as well as from symbolic assistance from the United States. and Great Britain. Thus, in spite of an official French military policy of disengagement and redeployment, African technical, logistical and financial military dependency on France persists.

The management of the 1997 crisis in Congo-Brazzaville

Throughout the civil war in Congo-Brazzaville (June-October 1997) between the forces of incumbent president Pascal Lissouba and those of former president Denis Sassou-Nguesso, France officially maintained an attitude of strict "neutrality" excluding any military intervention (except for the evacuation of French nationals in June 1997) and actively supporting the mediation effort initiated by president Omar Bongo of Gabon. However, official French neutrality was quickly superseded by the "benevolent neutrality" of the French state, notably the military establishment, the *Elysée* Palace and Elf Aquitaine, all of which, in effect, actively supported Sassou-Nguesso, who fought his way back into power on October 25, 1997 with the assistance of Chadian troops backed by French logistical support. Elf appears to be the common denominator of the assistance which Sassou-Nguesso got from Angola and Gabon in his reconquest of power. Indeed, in early1998, Elf agreed to provide him with $310 million as the cost of rescheduling the Congo's debt. President Chirac continues to support his old friend Sassou-Nguesso, and General Jeannou Lacaze—former chief-of-staff of Mitterand and Mobutu—now serves as adviser to the Congolese army.[17] The management of the Congolese crisis clearly reveals a tension between the *anciens'* policy of "benevolent neutrality" (in fact, of active support), and the *modernes'* official posture of non-interference and strict neutrality (as advocated by Prime Minister Lionel Jospin), resolved to the benefit of the former.

France's 'non-intervention' in the December 1999 military coup d'état in Côte d'Ivoire

On December, 24 1999, General Robert Guei took power in a bloodless military coup d'état which toppled the authoritarian and unpopular regime of Houphouët-Boigny's political heir, Henri Konan Bédié. The latter ended up in France on January 3. 2000, after having been whisked to safety under French military escort to Lomé, Togo. As Bédié left, 300 French paratroopers stood by in Dakar (Senegal) to enter Côte d'Ivoire in the name of protecting the

22,000 French nationals there, but were dissuaded by General Guei's warning that sending in French reinforcements would be unwise under the circumstances. France's 'sober' reaction to the coup in Côte d'Ivoire must be viewed within the context of the new European Union's coordinated foreign policy under which France's bilateral African policy must henceforth be subsumed. French Cooperation Minister Charles Josselin said France's approach to the coup reflected a "new policy" of non-intervention in Africa. As he put it, "We will no longer intervene in internal political debates. Maintaining a leader against the people's will is out of the question. What has happened in Côte d'Ivoire reflects France's new policy in Africa."[18] Similar feelings were expressed by French Minister of Foreign Affairs Hubert Védrine, when he remarked that "Disengagement from Africa is not on the agenda; nor is intervention in internal conflicts, which now belongs to a bygone era," adding: "This being said, we remain firmly opposed to any forcible removal of a legitimate government." Thus, according to him, France's main objective is to "promptly arrive at an electoral time table leading to a return to democracy and the rule of law." To encourage this process, France threatened to get the European Union's economic and financial assistance to Côte d'Ivoire suspended.[19] Indeed, the fact that the French government might simply be making virtue out of necessity seems to be confirmed by its January 2000 decision to partially suspend its military cooperation with Côte d'Ivoire by asking 16 of its 37 technical military assistants posted there to stop working.[20]

This episode shows that French African policy is progressively moving out of the exclusive domain (*domaine réservé*) of the presidency (*L'Elysée*) and into an area of increasingly shared responsibility with the prime minister's office (*Matignon*) and the government, to the advantage of the latter. The management of the Ivoirian crisis clearly shows that *Matignon* and the government—in the person of Prime Minister Lionel Jospin and foreign minister Hubert Védrine—were opposed to any intervention to help Henri Konan Bédié stay in power, while the *Elysée*—particularly President Jacques Chirac and his

African affairs adviser, Michel Dupuch, a former ambassador to Abidjan—clearly wanted to rescue him under the usual pretense of the protection of French nationals. In the event, the *modernes* went through the motions of sending to Abidjan two helicopters and 40 men from the French military base at Libreville, Gabon and of pre-positioning 300 *légionnaires* of the 2ème *Régiment étranger parachutiste* in Dakar, Senegal, but firmly resisted the *Elysée*'s (*anciens*) pressure to actually send these helicopters and troops into Côte d'Ivoire to rescue the beleaguered Bédié, who had urged the Ivoirian people to rise against the insurgents on *Radio France Internationale*. As foreign minister Hubert Védrine remarked on this occasion, "The Bédié case clearly demonstrates that France is now friendly without being complacent. Even our closest associates no longer have *carte blanche*...Our new policy is now firmly set between 'interventionism' and 'withdrawal.'"21

The reform of the French cooperation system

Initiated by Prime Minister Lionel Jospin in February 1998 with the full backing of the *Elysée*, the reform of the French cooperation system is an attempt to adapt aging institutions to a changing world environment characterized by globalization and the multilateralization of ODA. The former secretariat of state for cooperation has become a unit within the ministry of foreign affairs (*le Quai d'Orsay*). Henceforth, the minister of foreign affairs is responsible for all aspects of France's external relations. The new system revolves around two pillars: the *Quai d'Orsay* and *Bercy* (the ministry of economy and finance), who jointly supervise a new structure, the *Comité interministériel de la Coopération internationale et du développement* (CICID). The CICID determines the cooperation policy and its geographical priorities. The renamed *Agence française de développement* (French Development Agency), has overall responsibility for the management and disbursement of French ODA. To maintain a degree of consistency between French ODA and unofficial assistance, a *Haut Conseil de la Coopération Internationale* with consultative status, which brings together representatives of NGOs, municipalities, academics and experts, has been set up. Henceforth, the main target of French ODA is a "solidarity priority area" (*Zone de solidarité prioritaire*: ZSP) made up of the least developed countries falling within the purview of the deputy-ministry of cooperation (basically all the African, Carribean and Pacific states signatories of the Lomé Convention, plus South Africa).

Does this structural reform represent a substantive change in France's cooperation policy? To some observers, it is merely an administrative rationalization rather than a structural transformation. Thus, President Bongo of Gabon alluded to a mere semantic change when he remarked: "I don't care whether you call the person in charge of cooperation minister, secretary or messenger; what matters is that the cooperation policy is maintained."[22] Indeed, the *Elysée* maintains its *cellule africaine*; the military cooperation agreements are still in force; the ZSP includes all the 36 countries of the former *domaine réservé* (*pays du champ*); and deputy-minister of cooperation Charles Josselin takes part in cabinet meetings, which constitutes a real advantage in the eyes of the francophone African heads of state. Ultimately, this reform perfectly illustrates the transitory nature of France's African policy.

Conclusion

France's African policy is in a transitional phase in which clear signs of change and new orientations co-exist with old habits and *status quo* policies. The growing influence of the French Socialist Party (PS) in determining France's African policy is symptomatic of this phase. Indeed, the *Monsieur Afrique* of the PS, Guy Labertit—who travels frequently to francophone Africa and entertains good relations with all major opposition leaders there—, reports both to Prime Minister

Lionel Jospin and to deputy-minister for cooperation Charles Josselin, with whom he meets every two months.[23]

Ultimately, the extent to which real change takes place in Franco-African relations depends on two main factors. The first is a genuine political will for change among the main actors involved: the French and African political, military and business elites; representatives of key NGOs; and French and African citizens organizations. The second factor is the increasing tendency of Africa's "new leadership"—such as Uganda's Yoweri Museveni and Rwanda's Paul Kagame –to reject French presence and intervention in Africa (particularly in central Africa and the Great Lakes region) in favor of purely African solutions to African problems within appropriate regional (e.g. Organization of African Unity) or subregional (e.g. Southern African Development Community) institutional frameworks. More than 40 years after independence, the time has really come for Africa's "second decolonization" and for Franco-African relations to be truly decolonized. As eloquently stated by the CFA coalition (*coalition Citoyens France Afrique*), "What we do not want is an African policy devoid of any democratic control and focused on short-term political and economic interests...African democratic aspirations must become a key component of renovated Franco-African and Euro-African relations built on the principles of equity and reciprocity."[24]

Endnotes

1. See Antoine Glaser & Stephen Smith, *Ces messieurs Afrique 1: Le Paris-village du continent noir* (Paris: Calmann-Lévy, 1992); and A. Glaser & S. Smith, *Ces messieurs Afrique 2: Des réseaux aux lobbies* (Paris: Calmann-Lévy, 1997).

2. François-Xavier Verschave, *La Françafrique: le plus long scandale de la République* (Paris: Stock, 1998). The term of *Françafrique* has now gained wide currency through frequent usage, notably in the *Dossiers noirs de la politique africaine de la France* pub-

lished at regular intervals by the French non-governmental organization advocating a new African policy, Agir ici-Survie.

3. Kenneth B. Noble, "Ivory Coast Buries its Father of Freedom," *The New York Times* (8 February 1994), pp. A1, A5.

4. Philippe Gaillard (entretiens avec), *Foccart Parle* (Paris: Fayard/Jeune Afrique); vol. 1 (1995); vol. 2 (1997); Jacques Foccart, *Tous les soirs avec de Gaulle* 1 (Paris: Fayard, 1997). For a concise and informative overview of Foccart's role and legacy in *Françafrique*, see Kaye Whiteman, "The Man Who Ran Françafrique," *The National Interest* no. 49 (Fall 1997), pp. 92-99. For another perspective on Foccart , see Pierre Péan, *L'Homme de l'Ombre* (Paris: Fayard, 1990). Interestingly, a close associate of Foccart, Fernand Wibaux, retains, since 1995, an office at 14, rue de l'Elysée which duplicates that of the "official" adviser to the Presidency on African affairs located at 2, rue de l'Elysée (Michel Dupuch).

5. François-Xavier Verschave, *Complicité de génocide? La politique de la France au Rwanda* (Paris: La Découverte, 1994), p. 7; see also Agir ici-Survie, "Rwanda: la France choisit le camp du géno-cide," [Dossiers noir de la politique africaine de la France no. 1] (Paris: L'Harmattan, 1995), pp. 7-64; Agir ici-Survie, *La sécurite au sommet, l'insécurité à la base* [Dossiers noirs de la politique africaine de la France no. 12] (Paris: L'Harmattan, 1998), pp. 121-142. On the genocide, see Colette Braeckman, *Rwanda: his-toire d'un génocide* (Paris: Fayard, 1994); and Gérard Prunier, *The Rwanda Crisis: History of a Genocide* (New York: Columbia University Press, 1995). On *Opération Turquoise*, see G. Prunier, *op. cit*, pp. 281-311. Agir ici-Survie reveals that as early as 1992, the French state bank *Crédit Lyonnais* acted as collateral for a $6 million Rwandan arms purchase from Egypt and that on the day following the outbreak of the genocide (8 April 1994), a heavily armed French brigade (*Amaryllis*) landed in Kigali, one of its planes carrying ammunition for the FAR (Agir ici-Survie, Dossiers noirs no. 12, *op. cit.*, pp. 206-7). See also: *Rapport de la*

Mission d'information parlementaire française sur le Rwanda, 15 décembre 1998 [Pierre Brana & Bernard Cazenave, Rapporteurs].

6. Jean-François Bayart, "*Bis repetita*: La politique africaine de François Mitterand de 1989 à 1995," Colloque sur *La politique extérieure de François Mitterand à l'Épreuve de l'après-guerre froide*, Centre d'études et de recherches internationales (CERI), Paris (13-15 May 1997), p. 20.

7. On recent developments in central Africa, see Colette Braeckman, *L'Enjeu Congolais: L'Afrique centrale après Mobutu* (Paris: Fayard, 1999).

8. Economic and financial data provided by the Economic & Trade Development Office [*Poste d'expansion Économique*], French Embassy in South Africa, Pretoria (May 1998).

9. Mentioned in Philippe Marchesin, "La politique africaine de la France en transition," *Politique africaine* no. 71 (October 1998), pp. 93-4.

10. Data provided in the French National Assembly parliamentary financial committee's report on foreign affairs and cooperation for 1998 [A. Adevah-Poeuf, rapporteur], quoted in P. Marchesin, *art. cit.*, p. 97.

11. See Jean-Dominique Geslin, "Quels gendarmes pour l'Afrique?" *Jeune Afrique* (15-21 June 1999), pp. 27-8, who notes that the Zambakro training center is financed by France to the tune of 15 million francs.

12. French National Assembly, *Adevah-Poeuf Report*, 1998, pp. 9, 23; P. Marchesin, "L'aide publique au développement en 1997," *Observatoire permanent de la coopération française*, Rapport 1997 (Paris: Karthala, 1997), p. 17.

13. For a representative sample of such French official pronouncements, see P. Marchesin, "La politique africaine de la France en transition," *op. cit.*, pp. 99-100.

14. On the resilience of Franco-African freemason networks in Africa, see in particular Claude Wauthier, "L'étrange influence des

francs-maçons en Afrique francophone," *Le Monde diplomatique* (September 1997), pp. 6-7.

15. This point is eloquently made by P. Marchesin, "La politique africaine de la France en transition," *op. cit.*, p. 101.

16. Albert Bourgi, "La fin de l'épopée coloniale?" *Jeune Afrique* (13-26 August 1997); A. Bourgi, "Centrafrique: la tentation impériale." *Jeune Afrique* (15-21 January 1997), p. 15.

17. See Agir ici-Survie, *La Sécurité au Sommet, l'insécurité à la base* [Dossiers noirs de la politique africaine de la France no. 12] (Paris: L'Harmattan, 1998), pp. 81-112.

18. Quoted in Ruth Nabakwe, "Ivory Coast: Lessons from Africa's latest coup d'etat," *Panafrican News Agency* (30 December 1999).

19. All the quotes are from Vincent Hugeux, "La France et le test ivoirien," *L'Express* (30 décembre 1999).

20. Since its independence from France in August 1960, Côte d'Ivoire and its former president Félix Houphouët-Boigny have traditionally been considered a core country and key ally in terms of French presence and policy in Africa. The French expatriate community numbers 22,000 in all, with 300 French firms operating there. In addition to the 37 French technical military assistants, another 200 French civilian technical assistants are posted there. In 1998, 51 Ivoirian military officers underwent advanced training in various French military academies. As a result of the recent redeployment of French military personnel and bases in Africa, 550 French troops [43rd *bataillon d'infanterie de marine*] remain stationed at Port-Bouët, a base adjacent to Abidjan's international airport from which former president Henri Konan-Bédié was whisked to safety from the French Ambassador's residence to Lomé, Togo (figures from *Radio France Internationale/ MFI*, "Afrique/France: Les habits neufs de la coopération militaire," No. 931 (30 October 1998); "Afrique/France: La France recentre son engagement africain sur le maintien de la paix," No. 967 (9 November 1998); and V.

Hugeux, "La France et le test ivoirien," in *op. cit.*

21. This situation is chronicled in some detail in Stephen Smith, "L'Elysée perd sa chasse en Afrique," *Libération* (10 février 2000), which also includes Védrine's quote.

22. Quoted in Philippe Gaillard, "Feu la 'Coopé'," in *Jeune Afrique* (10-16 February 1998), p. 9.

23. François Soudan, "Les certitudes de Guy labertit," *Jeune Afrique* (7-13 décembre 1999), p. 24; see also F. Soudan, "Le tour d'Afrique de Charles Josselin," in *Ibidem*, pp. 22-24.

24. Agir ici-Survie, *Jacques Chirac et la Françafrique. Retour à la case Foccart?* [Dossiers noirs de la politique africaine de la France no. 6] (Paris: L'Harmattan, 1995), pp. 108, 111.

Chapter 5

The Theory and Practice of Non-Alignment: The Case of the Francophone African States

Nonalignment is both a concept and a political movement. It is primarily a principle of foreign policy in individual countries. But it is also an informal grouping of nations sharing certain common principles and objectives. In a world system that was dominated by two superpowers (the United States and the Soviet Union), nonalignment was an expression of the resolve of the smaller nations of Africa, Asia, Europe, Latin America, and the Pacific to maintain a reasonable degree of political, military, and economic independence in foreign policy decisions and actions. It was quite natural for the former French colonies of Africa to join the movement when they became independent in the early 1960s. Some of these countries retained close political, military, and economic ties with France throughout the following decades while others moved away from France towards closer ties with socialist countries. Can any of the Francophone African states still be characterized as "nonaligned" today, using such criteria as diplomatic and military alignment, voting in the United Nations, and economic relations (trade and aid) with developed countries? By the time of the Eighth Non-Aligned Summit Meeting (Harare, August-September 1986), very few, if any, Francophone African states remained nonaligned in the original sense of the term.

PRINCIPLES AND EVOLUTION OF THE NON-ALIGNED MOVEMENT

As a principle of foreign policy, nonalignment is essentially an assertion of freedom of judgment and action enabling smaller powers to "deal with each problem as it occurs, and on its own merits."[1] The essence of nonalignment is the ability to exercise a reasonable degree of independence of policy and action in world affairs. Nonalignment started out as a solidarity and protest movement for moderation in East-West relations and is now a commitment to global reform in North-South relations.[2] The genesis of non-alignment, as a concept and as a political movement is tied to the post-World War II international system. This system is characterized by decolonization, the Cold War, economic and social underdevelopment, and the development of international organizations.[3] The 1970 *Lusaka Declaration* adopted at the Third Non-Aligned Summit Conference provides a good summary of the fundamental objectives of nonalignment:

> ...the pursuit of world peace and peaceful co-existence by strengthening the role of non-aligned countries within the United Nations so that it will be a more effective instrument against all forms of aggressive action and the threat or use of force against the freedom, independence, sovereignty, and territorial integrity of any country; the fight against colonialism and racialism which are a negation of human equality and dignity; the settlement of disputes by peaceful

means; the ending of the arms race followed by universal disarmament; opposition to great power military alliance and pacts; opposition to the establishment of foreign military bases and foreign troops on the soil of other nations in the context of great power conflicts and colonial and racist oppression; the universality of, and the strengthening of the efficacy of the United Nations; and the struggle for economic independence and mutual cooperation on a basis of equality and mutual benefit.[4]

This summary reveals a number of recurrent themes which have characterized the Nonaligned Movement (NAM) for most of its existence, namely: anti-colonialism; anti-racism; the preservation of small states' independence, sovereignty, and territorial integrity; the quest for world peace, security, and disarmament, and the peaceful settlement of disputes; the opposition to great power conflicts, military alliances and pacts; the promotion of multilateral diplomacy within the framework of the United Nations; and economic independence.

The Lusaka Summit Conference constitutes a watershed between the two main historical periods of the movement. From the First Summit Conference (Belgrade, September 1961) to the Lusaka Summit (1970), the nonaligned countries demonstrated a clear tendency to assert themselves as full-fledged actors in the international system. This may be characterized as the "political" period of the NAM. With the progressive realization in the early 1970s that political independence and national sovereignty are meaningless without economic independence, the main emphasis of the NAM's declarations and activities noticeably shifted from the political to the economic domain. What most nonaligned countries have in common is that they are small, weak, underdeveloped, and dependent in the contemporary world system. The economic weakness, underdevelopment, and dependency of the nonaligned countries is perceived as being as threatening to their independence as superpower military competition. In Julius Nyerere's words, "The real and urgent threat to the independence of almost all the non-aligned states thus comes not from the military, but from the economic power of the big states."[5]

The NAM has adapted the main emphasis of its objectives to the changing configuration of power within the world system. During the pre-*détente* Cold War era (1945-1960), diplomatic and military alignment with the great powers constituted the main criteria of definition and membership of the NAM. The *détente* between the USA and the USSR throughout the 1960s largely contributed to a decrease in politico-strategic issues and brought to light the more urgent and pressing issue of autonomous socio-economic development. Similarly, the "New Cold War" brought about by the aggressively anti-communist foreign policy of the Reagan administration in the early 1980s again brought to the fore politico-strategic issues within the NAM. The late 1980s and early 1990s witnessed the end of the Cold War, the demise of the Soviet Union, and a widening of the economic gap between North and South. This changing international environment substantially altered the nature and structure of the NAM, which evolved from a non-military, anti-colonial alliance to a trade union of and for the weak and poor nations. As they progressively acceded to international sovereignty, all Third World nations systematically sought (and obtained) membership in the NAM, just as they automatically became members of the United Nations. This resulted in a quadrupling of the membership of the NAM (from 25 to 101 member states) between the First Summit (Belgrade, 1961) and the Seventh Summit (New Delhi, 1983). Although three European states and an increasing number of Caribbean and Latin American states became members of the NAM,[6] most members are relatively small, weak, and poor Asian and Africa states. While the Jakarta summit (1992) made development and eradication of poverty a global priority, the eleventh summit in Cartagena (1995) promoted popular development, addressed global issues and promoted North-South dialogues.

This expansion inevitably brought a measure of diversity and heterogeneity within the NAM in terms of unequal political, military, and economic power among member states. To some extent, such diversity and heterogeneity has adversely affected the group's cohesion and effectiveness. As considerations of *realpolitik* and national interest tend to prevail over NAM solidarity, an increasing number of conflicts between NAM member states erupted during the organization's first twenty years, the most dramatic of which was undoubtedly the Iran-Iraq war. This has led some Western observers to categorically state that "there is no such thing as 'nonalignment', there are only non-aligned countries".[7] Such views are excessive. Ultimately, the NAM is only as strong as its members, and its influence, real and potential, will vary depending upon which issue or criterion its achievement is measured against.[8] The fact remains, however, that Third World countries must necessarily improve the domestic management of their vast economic resources and rationalize and reorient their domestic economic and social policies. This is essential for the nonaligned countries to gain a position of economic strength so they can make their influence felt in the contemporary international system.[9]

THE FRANCOPHONE AFRICAN STATES IN THE NONALIGNED MOVEMENT

As the 14 constituent territorial units of the French West and Central Africa Federations became independent in the early 1960s,[10] the context and conditions in which such independence was granted ensured the perpetuation of France's political, military, economic, and cultural dominance over its former colonies.[11] Yet as early as 1958, a marked cleavage began to appear among these countries between those who eagerly accepted and exploited this situation and those who tried to somewhat mitigate its most negative aspects. The latter (Guinea and Mali) soon joined the "Casablanca Group", a group of radical, socialist-oriented African states who took a militant stance over the burning political issues of the time, notably the Congo/Zaïre affair. The Casablanca Group also advocated Pan-Africanism, namely the immediate and total political *and* economic integration of the African continent. The former, the other 12 African countries, known as the "moderates,", constituted successive groupings between 1960 and 1965, whose common objectives were the preservation of sovereignty and territorial integrity, loose economic cooperation (rather than political integration), and the promotion of regionalism as a stepping-stone towards African unity.[12]

With the May 1963 Addis-Ababa Summit Meeting which led to the creation of the Organization of African Unity (OAU), this radical-moderate cleavage among the Francophone African states (FAS) temporarily abated in the face of pressing decolonization issues, only to reappear at regular intervals, and with various degrees of intensity, in the following decades. Furthermore, French neo-colonialism remained a persistent and crucial factor in the foreign policy of these states. To this day, France continues to wield substantial power and influence in the core Francophone African countries—CAR, Cameroon, Côte d'Ivoire, Gabon, Senegal and Togo—politically, economically, socially, and culturally, thanks to a tightly knit network of formal and informal relations.[13] Yet, all these countries without exception are members of the NAM. This raises the delicate issue of the degree and extent to which the FAS can be said to be truly non-aligned in the face of continuing French influence on their political and economic systems. Such an evaluation will, of necessity, depend on the definition or criteria used to measure the degree of alignment, or nonalignment. Hveem and Willetts and Willetts have developed four indexes of alignment.[14] These criteria are: diplomatic alignment; voting in the United Nations General Assembly (UN-GA); military alignment; and economic alignment (that is, trade and aid) with developed countries.[15] I attempt to evaluate the degree and extent of nonalignment of the Francophone African States members of the NAM in the light of these various criteria.

THE PRACTICE OF NON-ALIGNMENT BY THE FRANCOPHONE AFRICAN STATES

Diplomatic Alignment

A nation cannot be considered "non-aligned" if it has any permanent diplomatic identification with a great power. Did the Francophone African states identified themselves with either side of the Cold War in the 1960s? During the decade 1960-1970, four countries of the world were split between the opposing camps of the East-West conflict: China, Germany, Korea, and Vietnam. The pattern of relations with these divided states gives an indication of the extent of diplomatic alignment. On the basis of an elaborate index of diplomatic alignment, Hveem and Willetts and Willetts[16] conclude that from 1964 to 1970, nine of the fourteen Francophone African states were either moderately or highly (Cameroon, Gabon, and Togo) aligned to the West; two (Guinea and Mali) were consistently aligned to the East; two others (Congo and Mauritania) progressively became pro-East; one (the Central African Republic/CAR) was nonaligned. A close scrutiny of the general diplomatic behavior of the Francophone African states between 1970 and 1990 reveals a number of significant changes during that period. Nine states were either moderately (Cameroon, Chad, Mauritania, and Niger) or highly (CAR, Gabon, Côte d'Ivoire, Senegal, and Togo) aligned to the West; three (Congo, Guinea, and Mali) have consistently been aligned to the East; and two others (Benin and Burkina Faso) became moderately aligned to the East. The end of the Cold War and the demise of the former Soviet Union and Eastern bloc in the late 1980s-early 1990s signalled the end of ideologically-based conflict (and thus, of political nonalignment) and the resurgence of the North-South economic divide between rich and poor countries (that is, of economic alignment).

Voting in the United Nations General Assembly (UNGA)

As emphasized in the *Lusaka Declaration*, the United Nations is of great importance to the nonaligned countries. Since these countries are generally small, weak, and poor, the UNGA provides them with a convenient forum and a useful arena of activity where they can actively participate in the debates and decisions relating to major world issues on an equal footing with the big powers.

A quantitative analysis of the voting pattern of the Francophone African states in the UNGA reveals that between 1964 and 1970, seven states were Western-aligned, three (Cameroon, Chad, and Senegal) were nonaligned, and three others (Guinea, Mali, and Mauritania) were Eastern-aligned.[17] These findings are, on the whole, consistent with those relating to diplomatic alignment for the same period. A global analysis of the general voting pattern of these states in the UNGA since 1970 reveals, by and large, a close correspondence with the changing pattern of diplomatic behavior noted above. Taking voting in the UNGA on the issues of Afghanistan and Kampuchea as an indicator of Eastern alignment, one observes that during the period 1980 to 1984 when these issues were raised yearly, countries such as Benin, Burkina Faso, Congo and Madagascar have consistently abstained on the Afghanistan vote, while casting negative votes (i.e. favourable to the Soviet position) on the Kampuchea issue.[18] The period 1984 to 1990 was characterized by a progressive realignment of Francophone African states on the West, culminating with the broad anti-Iraki coalition during the Gulf War (1990-91) to which Senegal contributed a small military contingent. A similar, broad, pro-American and anti-Taliban front emerged following the terrorist attack on the United States of September 11, 2001.

Military Alignment

A fundamental dimension of nonalignment includes opposition to the arms race and to the establishment of foreign military bases and foreign troops in Third World countries. The June 1961 Cairo preparatory meeting to the First Non-Aligned Summit put forward the most widely accepted definition of nonalignment still recognized to this day. Among the main criteria of nonalignment outlined were the abjuring of multilateral military alliances concluded in the context of great power conflicts, the refusal to conclude a bilateral alliance with a great power, and the refusal to permit the establishment of foreign military bases for purposes related to great power conflicts.[19] Thus, any NAM member state who concludes any such bilateral or multilateral military alliance, or allows the establishment of foreign military bases on its soil would automatically disqualify as a *bona fide* member of the movement. Yet when one takes a close look at the pattern of bilateral and multilateral military alliance of the Francophone African states, the global picture which emerges is one of a high degree of military alignment with the West in general, and with France in particular. Between 1960 and 1965, all Francophone African states (except Guinea and Mali) were militarily linked to France. This was done within the framework of fairly loose "Regional Defence Councils" set up within each region as a multilateral military alliance designed to harmonize and integrate the military infrastructure of the various countries of the region under the overall authority and supervision of France.[20] More importantly, France has, since 1960, concluded a number of bilateral defence agreements and military technical assistance agreements with most Francophone African states. These agreements were renegotiated and extended several times since the mid-1970s without significant changes. In addition, France maintains a number of military bases, troops, and military advisors in those countries, with which she occasionally conducts joint military war games. Finally, France remains the single most important arms exporter to these countries. As of 1985, all the

Francophone African states (except Guinea) maintained military technical assistance agreements with France. While a number of these states (Benin, Burkina Faso, Congo, Guinea, Mali, Mauritania, and Niger) seem, on the whole, to remain on the periphery of this military alliance system, a nucleus among them (Cameroon, CAR, Gabon, Côte d'Ivoire, Senegal, and Togo) have also concluded defence agreements, harbor French military bases, are host to a number of French troops and military advisors, and procure the bulk of their arms from France. This elaborate network of defence and military assistance agreements and logistical support structures has enabled the French army to intervene about 20 times in Africa between 1963 and 1983. The basic objective of this network is the continued integration of the Francophone African states within the framework of French geo-strategic planning and, ultimately, within the Western defence system of NATO. More generally these security arrangements are part of the dense network of economic, political, and cultural cooperation agreements through which these states are tied to France.[21]

A survey of the main sources of arms deliveries to the Francophone African states over the period 1976 to 1980 shows that those states that remained on the fringe of the French military alliance system got the bulk of their arms requirements from the USSR (Benin, Congo, Guinea, and Mali) or, exceptionally, from West Germany or the United Kingdom (Burkina Faso, and Togo). The same data reveals that the Francophone African states got 46.3 percent of their arms requirements from the West (including 42 percent from France alone) and 26.6 percent from the Soviet Union. Out of a total expenditure of US $ 940 million over the period 1976 to 1980 for all 14 Francophone African states (which represents 11.2 percent of total arms deliveries to sub-Saharan Africa), the heaviest spenders (in percentage of total expenditure) are Côte d'Ivoire (26.6 percent), Mali (12.8 percent), and Gabon (11.7 percent). Finally, it noteworthy that the Congo is the only country in the region with which the USSR has concluded a Friendship and Cooperation Treaty

(May 1981) which does not include a military assistance clause.[22]

The general picture which emerges from this survey is that between the years 1976-1980 five Francophone African states (Cameroon, CAR, Gabon, Côte d'Ivoire, and Senegal) demonstrated a high degree of military alignment with France and the West. Another five (Burkina Faso, Chad, Mauritania, Niger, and Togo) were moderately aligned in the same direction, while the remaining four (Benin, Congo, Guinea, and Mali) were distinctively aligned with the East. This predominantly Western-aligned military pattern did not prevent the existence of tensions and the outbreak of conflicts among the states of the region. Thus a brief but violent armed conflict erupted between Burkina Faso and Mali over the Agacher border area in December 1985, causing 300 casualties. This conflict between two West African states, members of the NAM, occurred within a context of shifting alliances in which Mali apparently obtained military and logistical support from France while Burkina Faso progressively turned to the socialist countries for military assistance.[23]

Economic Alignment: Trade and Aid

The 1970 Lusaka Summit Conference constituted a watershed between the political and economic periods of the NAM. The latter came with the realization by the member states of the absolute necessity to achieve economic independence, in addition to political independence, in order to give its full meaning to the concept of "sovereignty." Hence the quest for autonomous, self-reliant development at the national level and for a New International Economic Order (NIEO) at the international level, as priority objectives pursued by the NAM. The question arises as to whether and to what extent the Francophone African states were truly nonaligned economically, that is, able to pursue a relatively independent strategy of development without being overly dependent on one bloc or the other. In a world system characterized by increasing economic interdependence, Third World nations need to engage in commercial relations with, and to resort to the economic assistance of, developed countries if they are to survive and develop economically and socially. In so doing, during the Cold War years they had to endeavour to strike a delicate balance between the two blocs so as not to fall into the dependency trap.

In the area of trade, the destination of exports and origin of imports are generally accepted as reasonable indicators of dependency. As of 1984, Francophone African states are still overwhelmingly dependent on the West in this area, both for their exports and for their imports. One notes a high degree of Western dependence in such countries as Cameroon, CAR, Gabon, and a lesser, but still significant, degree of Western dependence in Benin, Congo, Guinea, Mauritania, and Togo. Trade between the Francophone African states and the socialist countries was negligible. Commercial transactions between the two groups of states remain at a symbolic level. It is noteworthy that such staunchly capitalist countries as Gabon, Côte d'Ivoire, Senegal, and Togo conducted a small, but not insignificant, proportion of their trade with socialist countries. The available data reveals a surprising pattern of trade alignment. While such avowedly socialist countries as Benin, Congo, and Guinea were Western-dependent to a significant degree, a number of capitalist countries also trade with the East. The analysis of aid patterns provides a more balanced view of these economic relations.

On the whole, during the period 1980-1984, the Francophone African states remained highly dependent on Western aid. Aid to these states by 17 member states of the OECD's Development Assistance Committee (DAC) consistently represented, on average, over 60 percent of total disbursements to these countries between 1980 and 1984. While a number of states' dependency in 1980 exceeded 80 percent (Côte d'Ivoire, Benin, and Cameroon), this dependency was, on the whole, reduced in 1984 but remains significant (above 70 percent on average) for some states (Gabon, Senegal, Benin, and Cameroon). The global amount of aid by the DAC countries to the African countries substantially decreased (by about 60 percent)

114

between 1980 and 1984. During the same period, aid by the socialist member countries of the Council for Mutual Economic Assistance (CMEA) to the Francophone African states was negligible. This aid—US $2 million in 1980 and 18.6 million in 1984—represented only one percent of total Western aid for 1984. Regular beneficiaries of Eastern aid were Benin, Congo, Guinea, and Mali. The greatest beneficiaries of such aid in 1984 were Guinea (US $8 million) and Congo (US$7 million). Zaki Laïdi indicates that in 1984, Guinea obtained Soviet aid amounting to US $230 million, over twice the amount of aid received by this country from other sources during that year (i.e. US $129 million).[24] Overall, the pattern of socialist aid to African countries was consistent with the politico-ideological orientation of these countries, the bulk of this aid going, except in special circumstances (Mali, Mauritania, and Senegal), to socialist-oriented countries. It is noteworthy in this regard that Burkina Faso, which had never been a beneficiary of socialist aid, received US$ 200 000 in 1984 following the coming to power of the populist revolutionary regime of Captain Thomas Sankara in August 1983.[25] However, a number of socialist-leaning African countries such as Benin and Congo remained highly dependent on Western aid.

CONCLUSION: HOW "NON-ALIGNED" ARE THE FRANCOPHONE AFRICAN STATES?

What follows is a summary of our findings on the degree and extent to which the Francophone African states conform to the various criteria of non-alignment which have been identified in this study during the period 1980-1984.On the diplomatic/UN voting dimension, a fairly consistent pattern emerges whereby five states (CAR, Gabon, Côte d'Ivoire, Senegal, and Togo) were highly aligned to the West; four other states (Cameroon, Chad, Mauritania, and Niger) were moderately Western-aligned, while the remaining five (Benin, Burkina Faso, Congo, Guinea, and Mali) were either consistently or progressively aligned to the East. On the military dimension, it was found that five states (Cameroon, CAR, Gabon, Côte d'Ivoire, and Senegal) were highly Western-aligned, another five (Burkina Faso, Chad, Mauritania, Niger, and Togo) were moderately Western-aligned, while the remaining four (Benin, Congo, Guinea, and Mali) were distinctly aligned to the East. On the economic dimension, in the area of trade, there was a greater degree of Western dependence in some states (Cameroon, CAR, and Gabon) than in others (Benin, Congo, Guinea, Mauritania, and Togo), while trade between the Francophone African states and the socialist countries was negligible. Finally, aid dependency on the West was greater for some states (Benin, Cameroon, Gabon, Côte d'Ivoire, and Senegal) than for others. The main beneficiaries for the limited amounts of Eastern bloc aid available were Benin, Congo, Guinea, and Mali. The economic dimension reveals an unusual alignment pattern. Thus, a number of socialist African countries such as Benin, Congo, and Guinea are moderately to highly Western dependent in trade and aid, while various capitalist countries (Gabon, Côte d'Ivoire, Senegal, and Togo) have some trade relations with the East.

The overall conclusion that might be drawn from these findings is that on the politico-diplomatic and military dimensions, all Francophone African states but four (Benin, Congo, Guinea, and Mali) are either moderately or highly Western-aligned, the others being Eastern-aligned. On the economic dimension, all these states (except Guinea) are moderately to highly Western-aligned. On the basis of this evidence, one might conclude that while the Francophone African states are all members of the NAM, the majority were, in fact, according to our criteria, aligned to the West, and four were aligned to the East. Consequently, they could not be considered to be genuinely "non-aligned." Such a conclusion, however, is somewhat disputable in that it is based on criteria which, on the whole, are more rigid than those used by the NAM itself for admission in the movement. Since France was not one of the "great" powers, its bilateral and multilateral military arrangements with the

Francophone African states cannot be considered, strictly speaking, as constituting a Cold War alliance. Ultimately, it all boils down to which criteria are being used to measure the degree of the Francophone African states alignment or nonalignment, and to how strictly these criteria are applied. Thus, while the Francophone African states might qualify as *bona fide* nonaligned countries when using the loose and permissive membership criteria of the NAM, they certainly do not meet these tighter and more stringent criteria.

Through their tight and continuing political, military, and economic relations with the Western countries in general (and with France in particular) the majority of the Francophone African states were indeed distinctly Western-aligned during the Cold War era, their denials notwithstanding. In other words, these states were merely pretenting to be nonaligned while in actual fact they were clearly Western-aligned.

Similarly, one might argue that such states as Benin, Burkina Faso, Congo, Guinea, and Mali were unquestionably aligned to the East and did not, therefore, belong in the NAM. The case of the socialist Francophone African states should, however, be viewed in its proper historical, politico-strategic, and economic context. Thus while these states (except for Mali) openly adhered to the Marxist-Leninist ideology and proclaimed their resolve to build socialism in their countries, their external economic relations were in fact heavily Western-oriented. This situation therefore introduced some kind of balance, or equilibrium, between their Eastern-oriented politico-strategic relations and their Western-oriented economic relations. While this might have had serious implications for their ability to maintain genuine and consistent socialist policies at home and abroad, it did place them in a convenient position of 'equidistance' between East and West, which is the essence of nonalignment. On this account, these five countries might be viewed as having been more genuinely nonaligned than the other, Western-aligned francophone African states.

What, then, was the status of the Francophone African states within the Non-Aligned Movement during the Cold War era? As long as they remained steadfastly aligned to the West, they could only, at best, have a very limited impact on the movement. Because their room for manoeuver was extremely limited, and their credibility seriously affected, they were actually not in a position to take meaningful initiatives and to significantly influence decisions within the movement. Because of their greater degree of equidistance between the two blocs, the socialist Francophone African states were in a better position to take such initiatives and to be more active and influential within the NAM, though there is no evidence-except for Guinea and Mali during 1960-1970—that they actually did that (presumably because of their overall weakness, dependency and lack of power and influence in the world system).

The NAM now has to adapt to the changing environment of the post-Cold War era. In that perspective, the achievement of a reasonable degree of power and influence by all the Francophone African states in the Non-Aligned Movement, as well as in the wider international system, will depend on these states' capacity to significantly decrease their overall dependence on Western powers in general, and on France in particular, and thus to progressively become more autonomous and self-reliant in all areas. France's new African policy characterized by a weakening of bilateral relations with Francophone Africa, an increasing multilateralization of aid and the progressive demise of the franc zone (in the context of the new link to the euro) might help them cut the umbilical cord that still ties them to the former metropole.[26] In the final analysis, the Francophone African states will have to build a much stronger and healthier domestic economic base—particularly through such Francophone African regional organizations as the *Union Économique et monétaire ouest-africaine*/UEMOA and the *Communauté Économique et monétaire d'Afrique centrale*/CEMAC—[27] if they are to ever gain their rightful place in the concert of nations.

Endnotes

1. Julius K. Nyerere, "Policy on Foreign Affairs," in J.K. Nyerere, *Freedom and Socialism* (New York: Oxford University Press, 1968), p. 368.
2. Ali A. Mazrui, in Peter Willetts, *The Non-Aligned Movement: The Origins of a Third World Alliance* (London: Frances Pinter, 1978), p. xiii.
3. S. Boutros Farajalla, "Non-Alignment: Ideological Pluralism," *India Quarterly* vol. XL, no. 2 (April 1984), p. 199.
4. *Lusaka Declaration on Peace, Independence, Development, Co-operation and Democratisation of International Relations* adopted by the Third Conference of Heads of State and Government of Non-Aligned Countries, Lusaka, Zambia (10 September 1970), pp. 67-8.
5. Helge Hveem & Peter Willetts, "The Practice of Non-Alignment: On the Present and the Future of an International Movement," in Yashpal Tandon & D. Chandarang (eds.), *Horizons in African Diplomacy* (Nairobi: East African Literature Bureau, 1974), p. 4.
6. The three European founding member states of the NAM are Yugoslavia, Malta and Cyprus. In addition, there are now 7 Caribbean and 10 Latin American NAM member states.
7. Jean Lacouture, in Philippe Braillard & Mohamed R. Djalili, *Tiers Monde et Relations Internationales* (Paris: Masson, 1984), p. 110.
8. Fred Halliday, "The Maturing of the Non-aligned Perspectives from New Delhi," *Third World Affairs* (1985), p. 51.
9. F. Halliday, *art. cit.*, p. 52; Dewan C. Vohra, *Economic Relevance of Non-Alignment* (New Delhi: ABC Publishing House, 1983), pp. 338-9.
10. The present study focuses exclusively on the following 14 francophone West and Central African states: Benin, Burkina Faso, Cameroon, Central African Republic/CAR, Chad, Congo, Côte

d'Ivoire, Gabon, Guinea, Mali, Mauritania, Niger, Senegal, and Togo.

11. Guy Martin, "Francophone Africa in the Context of Franco-African Relations," in John W. Harbeson & Donald Rothchild (eds.), *Africa in World Politics: Post-Cold War Challenges* (Boulder: Westview Press, 1995), pp. 166-7; see also chapter 3 in this volume.

12. The most significant of these groupings were the *Brazzaville Group* (December 1960), the *Monrovia Group* (May 1961), the *Conseil de l'Entente* (1959), and the *Organisation commune africaine et malagache* (OCAM, February 1965).

13. See Guy Martin, "Francophone Africa in the Context of Franco-African Relations," in *op. cit.*, pp. 163-188; and chapter 3 in this volume.

14. H. Hveem & P. Willetts, "The Practice of Non-Alignment," in *op. cit.*, pp. 7-30; Peter Willetts, *The Non-Aligned Movement: The Origins of a Third World Alliance* (London: Frances Pinter, 1978).

15. It should be noted (a) that Hveem and Willets (p. 7) use only trade, to the exclusion of aid, as an economic indicator of alignment; and (b) that I present here a much simplified version of the Hveem/Willetts and Willetts models, which leaves out the more mathematical and statistical elements of these models. The quantitatively-minded reader might wish to refer to the original models as outlined by these authors in their respective works.

16. Hveem & Willetts, "The Practice of Non-Alignment," in *op. cit*, p. 13; Willetts, *op. cit.*, pp. 116-127.

17. Hveem & Willetts, "The Practice of Non-Alignment," in *op. cit.*, pp. 36-40.

18. Zaki Laïdi, *The Super-Powers and Africa: The Constraints of a Rivalry, 1960-1990* (Chicago: The University of Chicago Press, 1990), pp. 186-190.

19. Braillard & Djalili, *op. cit.*, p. 102; Vohra, *op. cit.*, p. 144.

20. Pascal Chaigneau, *La Politique militaire de la France en Afrique*

(Paris: CHEAM, 1984), p. 23.

21. Guy Martin, "The Historical, Economic and Political Bases of France's African Policy," *The Journal of Modern African Studies* vol. 23, no. 2 (June 1985), pp. 204-7; Robin Luckham, "French Militarism in Africa," *Review of African Political Economy* no. 24 (May 1982), p. 58.

22. The absence of a military clause in the Soviet-Congolese friendship treaty seems to be due to the fact that—in the true spirit of nonalignment—Congo adamantly refused to accede to Soviet pressures for granting access rights to the naval facilities at the Pointe-Noire harbor (Z. Laïdi, *The Super-Powers and Africa*, pp. 183-4).

23. Guy Martin, "Ideology and Praxis in Thomas Sankara's Populist Revolution of 4 August 1983 in Burkina Faso," *Issue: A Journal of Opinion* vol. 15 (1987), pp. 86-7.

24. Z. Laïdi, *The Super-Powers and Africa*, p. 178.

25. G. Martin, "Ideology and Praxis in Thomas Sankara's Populist Revolution of 4 August 1983 in Burkina Faso," *op. cit.*

26. See chapter 4 in this volume.

27. See chapter 6 for further details on these and other African regional organizations.

Chapter 6

African Regional Cooperation and Integration

INTRODUCTION

Ever since they became independent in the early sixties, African states have consistently pursued policies of regional cooperation and integration as a means of promoting socioeconomic development and of reducing their dependence on the West. While African scholars and policy-makers generally agree on the need and desirability of African unity, they seriously disagree on the level, strategy, and ultimate goal of unification, as well as on the scope of cooperation.

While many institutions for regional cooperation and integration were created soon after independence, progress toward integration has been disappointingly slow. Thus, the East African Community (EAC) survived for only ten years (1967-1977). West and central African regional integration schemes, such as the *Union douanière et Économique de l'Afrique centrale* (UDEAC; December 1964), and the Economic Community of West African States (ECOWAS; May 1975) have been generally unsuccessful. The Southern African Development Coordination Conference (April 1980)—later . transformed into the Southern African Development Community (SADC; August 1992) and the Preferential Trade Area for Eastern and Southern Africa (PTA; December 1981), which has since become the Common Market for Eastern and Southern Africa (COMESA; November 1993), have been somewhat more promising. Eventually, the five key African subregional organizations (Arab Maghreb Union/AMU, ECOWAS, *Communauté Économique des États de l'Afrique central*/CEEAC, EAC and SADC) are scheduled to merge into a single *African Common Market* (ACM) as the core element of an *African Economic Community* (AEC) by 2025.

This chapter provides an overview on this subject. Part one states the case for regional coöperation and integration in Africa; part two reviews contending approaches and perspectives on regional cooperation and integration; part three surveys the aims and activities of 13 African regional cooperation and integration schemes; part four identifies the problems of, and assesses the prospects for, regional cooperation and integration in Africa.

THE CASE FOR REGIONAL INTEGRATION IN AFRICA

Of all the developing regions of the world, Africa is by far the poorest, least developed and most heterogeneous. Africa is the only continent where the number of the poor is increasing, with close to 350 million people (out of a total of 765.6 million) living on $1 a day or less, and up to 150 million children living below the poverty line. Of the 54 African countries, 32 have fewer than eight million inhabitants and 34 are in the low-income category, with an average annual rate of growth of 2.7 per cent for the period 1991-1999. Africa's overall GDP grew by 3.5 per cent during 1995-99, compared with 4.5 per cent during 1965-69. In 1999, Africa accounted for only 1.6 per cent of world exports and imports (compared to 4.6 per cent in 1980). In 1998, Africa's total exports amounted to US $106 billion, a decrease of 16% over the preceding year, while its imports reached 129 billion, a 1.5% decrease over 1997. Africa's terms of trade weakened by more than 12 per cent between 1995-96 and 1999, while the index of agricultural commodity prices declined by 14 per cent between 1998 and 1999. Overall, intra-African trade has barely increased, as a proportion of total trade, in recent years: 6.6 per cent in 1997, as opposed to 3.1 per cent in 1980. Between 1970 and the early 1990s, intra-regional trade as a proportion of total exports of member countries, has actually declined in all major regional groupings except AMU, ECOWAS and the West African Economic Community (CEAO). In the past two decades, sub-Saharan Africa has not received any net transfer of real resources from the rest of the world; the available data rather suggests a net transfer of real resources from sub-Saharan Africa to the rest of the world. Africa's total external debt reached US $336 billion in 1999, a 16 percent increase during the 1990s.[1] Africa is not only the poorest developing region, the most foreign-trade dependent economy and the most dependent on the markets of the developed countries; it is also the least regionally integrated and the slowest growing in terms of mutual interdependence.

This appalling economic situation has convinced African scholars and policy-makers that regionalism (or collective self-reliance) is the most appropriate strategy to achieve autonomous, self-reliant, and self-sustained development. Thus, the 1979 OAU Monrovia Symposium on the future development prospects of Africa called for "the creation of an African common market based on progressive coordination and integration, which would evolve in the form of concentric circles reflecting the economic areas that currently exist on the continent." Similarly, the 1980 OAU *Lagos Plan of Action* and *Final Act of Lagos* proposed the eventual establishment of an African Common Market (ACM) as a first step towards the creation of an African Economic Community (AEC) by the year 2000. *Africa's Priority Programme for Economic Recovery 1986-1990* (APPER), adopted in July 1985 by the 21st OAU Assembly of Heads of State and Government, acknowledges that "Economic integration through sub-regional, regional, and continental cooperation is today a top priority which will enable the economies of the African countries to be viable within a system of international relations characterised by inequality in the balance of power."[2] Similarly, the *United Nations Programme of Action for Africa's Economic Recovery and Development* (UN-PAAERD) adopted at the UN General Assembly's Special Session on Africa in June 1986 states that "The international community reaffirms its belief in the strategy for collective self-reliance among developing countries and reiterates its conviction that economic and technical cooperation among these countries should constitute a key element in the economic recovery of Africa and to the mutual benefit of developing countries..."[3]

The Lagos Plan of Action's proposed African Economic Community aims "to promote collective, accelerated, self-reliant and self-sustaining development of Member States; cooperation among these States; and their integration in the economic, social, and cultural fields."[4] This goal was to be achieved in two stages. During the first stage (decade of the 1980s), the objective was to strengthen the existing regional economic communities and to establish economic groupings in the other regions of Africa, so as to cover the continent as a whole (north, west, central, eastern, and southern Africa); to effectively strengthen sectoral integration at the continental level; and to promote coordination and harmonization among the existing and future economic groupings for the gradual establishment of an African Common Market. During the second stage (decade of the 1990s), sectoral integration was to be further strengthened, and measures towards the progressive establishment of a common market and an African Economic Community were to be taken. In this context, the following sub-regional organizations have been successively created: the 16 member states Economic Community of West African States: ECOWAS (Lagos, May 1975); the 16 member states Preferential Trade Area for Eastern and Southern Africa: PTA (Lusaka, December 1981), now Common Market of Eastern and Southern African States: COMESA; the 10 member states Economic Community of Central African States/ECCAS (Libreville, October

1983); the 10 member states Southern African Development Community: SADC (August 1992), as successor institution to the Southern African Development Coordination Conference: SADCC (April 1980); and the five member states Arab Maghreb Union: AMU (Marrakech, February 1989). This elaborate network of subregional organisations thus extends over the whole African continent.

CONTENDING APPROACHES AND PERSPECTIVES

Ever since the early days of independence, African scholars and policy-makers have been deeply divided on the issue of African unity. A first group (the Panafricanists) favoured political integration as a prerequisite to economic integration. Its members (Cheikh Anta Diop, Modibo Kéïta, Kwame Nkrumah, Sékou Touré) advocated the immediate and total integration of the African continent, and the setting up of a single continental government with common institutions. Another group (the Gradualists or Functionalists), anxious to preserve the African states' recently acquired sovereignty, favoured a more gradual approach to African integration. This group (Félix Houphouët-Boigny, Jomo Kenyatta, Léopold Senghor) held that economic integration should precede political integration. Its members favoured a loose cooperation in non-controversial (technical and economic) areas and viewed regional institutions as a stepping-stone to the progressive political and economic unification of the continent. With the progressive removal of the Panafricanists from the African political scene, neo-functionalism has become the dominant approach and serves as the model for most, if not all, current regional integration schemes in Africa. *Cooperation* and *integration* are two distinct concepts. Briefly stated, cooperation refers to joint action, by two or more states, in the form of common programs or projects in functionally specific areas, while integration implies the creation of new, supra-national institutions within which common policies are planned and implemented.

Another major distinction should be established between *market integration* and *production integration*. According to conventional neoclassical theory, market integration constitutes a means of expanding economic opportunities through specialization based on comparative advantage and economies of scale. This theory analyses the effects of integration essentially in terms of *trade creation* and *trade diversion*. Trade creation refers to a shift from the consumption of higher-cost domestic products to the lower-cost products of other member states. Trade diversion refers to a shift in the source of imports from lower-cost sources outside the regional bloc to a higher-cost source within it. A union that is on balance trade-creating is regarded as beneficial, whereas a trade-diverting union is regarded as detrimental.[5] The core of the argument for integration is that "so long as there are economies of scale to be obtained, or so long as there are possibilities for specialization between countries on the lines of comparative advantage, industrialization to serve the wider regional market will be more efficient than industrialization within the confines of each national market."[6]

Furthermore, neoclassical theory views market integration as a gradual process evolving through five successive stages. These are: the formation of a *free-trade area* (abolition of trade barriers among member countries); a *customs union* (establishment of a common tariff policy toward non-member countries); a *common market* (free movement of factors of production as well as of commodities within the area); a complete *economic union* (harmonization of national economic policies among the member countries); and total *economic integration* (unification of economic and social policies and setting up of a supra-national authority).[7]

AFRICAN REGIONAL COOPERATION AND INTEGRATION EXPERIMENTS, 1960 TO 2000

Many institutions for regional cooperation and integration were created soon after independence in Africa. There are at present more than 200 such organizations on the continent; more than 160 are inter-governmental and the rest non-governmental. There are some 40 inter-governmental organizations in West Africa alone. This institutional proliferation has resulted in multiple membership, duplication, a waste of human and financial resources, and lack of inter-institutional coordination.

A UN-ECA report has devised a useful typology of African intergovernmental organizations, based on their objectives. According to these criteria, one may distinguish between: economic communities, aiming at establishing an economic union via the stages of free-trade area, customs union and common market; development organizations, whose purpose is to harmonize policies in various economic sectors, such as agriculture, transport, and energy; technical/service organizations, which coordinate policies with respect to a particular sector or project; monetary and financial institutions, which are specialized technical/service organizations; professional organizations, which actually belong to the category of non-governmental organizations.[8]

Table 3-1 provides a synopsis of the various African organizations existing in each category. What follows is a brief survey of the aims and activities of a cross-section of African economic communities, development organizations, and monetary and financial institutions.

Table 3-1
Major African Regional Organizations

Organization	Founding date	Member states	Aims
CPCM-Maghreb Permanent Consultative Committee	October 1964	[4] Algeria, Lybia, Morocco, Tunisia	Common market
UAM-Union of the Arab Maghreb	February 1989	[5] Algeria, Libya, Mauritania, Morocco, Tunisia	Economic, social, and cultural
Organization	Founding date	Member states	Aims

Organization	Founding date	Member states	Aims
Entente Council	May 1959	[5] Benin, Burkina, CI, Niger, Togo	Economic, and technical cooperation
OCAM-Organisation commune africaine et mauricienne	February 1965	[9] Benin, Burkina, CAR, CI, Mauritius, Niger, Rwanda, Senegal, Togo	Economic, and technical cooperation
CEAO-Communauté Économique de l'Afrique de l'Ouest	April 1973	[7] Benin, Burkina, CI, Mali Mauritania, Niger Senegal	Common market
ECOWAS-Economic Community of West African States	May 1975	[16] Benin, Burkina, CI, CV, Gambia, Ghana, Guinea, Guinea-Bissau, Liberia, Mali, Mauritania, Niger, Nigeria, Senegal, Sierra-Leone, Togo	Common market and Economic Community
MRU-Mano River Union	October 1973	[3] Guinea, Liberia, Sierra Leone	Customs union
Senegambia Confederation	December 1981	[2] Senegal, Gambia	Political union
UDEAC-Union douanière & Économique de l'Afrique centrale	December 1964	[6] Cameroon, CAR, Chad, Congo, Equat. Guinea, Gabon	Common market
ECCAS-Economic Community of Central African States	October 1983	[10] Burundi, Cameroon, CAR, Chad, Congo, Equat. Guinea, Gabon, Rwanda, Sao Tomé and P., Zaïre	Common market
CEPGL-Communauté Économique des Pays des Grands Lacs	September 1976	[3] Burundi, Rwanda, Zaïre	Common market
EAC-East African Community	December 1967	[3] Kenya, Tanzania, Uganda	Common market
Organization	Founding date	Member states	Aims

PTA-Preferential Trade Area for Eastern and Southern Africa	December 1981	[16] Burundi, Comoros, Djibouti, Ethiopia, Kenya, Lesotho, Malawi, Mauritius, Mozam-bique, Rwanda, Somalia, Swaziland, Tanzania, Uganda, Zambia, Zimbabwe	Common market and Economic Community
SADCC-Southern African Development Coordination Conference	April 1980	[9] Angola, Botswana, Lesotho, Malawi, Mozam-bique, Swaziland, Tanzania, Zambia, Zimbabwe	Project-oriented Economic cooperation

Note: CAR=Central African Republic; CI=Côte d'Ivoire; CV=Cape Verde

The Arab Maghreb Union (AMU)

Created in February 1989 in Marrakech (Morocco), the Arab Maghreb Union (AMU) is the major regional integration arrangement in the North African region, comprising Algeria, Libya, Mauritania, Morocco, and Tunisia. After several unsuccessful attempts (including the 1964 Permanent Advisory Committee for the Maghreb/*Comité Permanent Consultatif du Maghreb*), the dream of Maghreb unity was finally realized. Together, these countries have an area of 5,784 million square kilometres., a population of about 60 million, and an average GNP per capita of US$1,874. The distribution of population and resources remains, however, very uneven. Algeria and Morocco between them have 46.4 million inhabitants, more than three-quarters of the union's total population. The combined GNP per capita of Algeria and Libya (US $8,140) is seven times greater than that of the other three member countries combined (US $1,230).[9] As a share of the total Maghreban foreign trade, intra-union trade declined from 3 per cent in 1962 to 1.5 per cent in 1985.

The main objectives of the AMU treaty are to strengthen all forms of ties among member states to ensure regional stability and enhance policy coordination, as well as to gradually introduce free circulation of goods and services, and factors of production among them. Common defence and non-interference in the domestic affairs of the partners are also key aspects of the treaty, which highlights the Union's broad economic strategy, namely the development of agriculture, industry, commerce, food security, and the setting up of joint projects and economic cooperation programs. The agreement does not view bilateral arrangements between the parties as an obstacle to the development of multilateral relations, and provides for the possibility of other Arab African countries joining the Union at a later stage.

Since 1990, the five member states have signed more than 37 multilateral agreements covering various economic, social and cultural areas. However, only five of these agreements have been ratified by all members of the union. These include agreements on customs and tariffs (covering all industrial products); trade in agricultural products; investment guarantee; avoidance of double taxation; and phytosanitary standards. The free trade area, which was scheduled to be operative before 1992, has not yet come into force. In December 1991, the five central banks of the AMU signed a multilateral agreement to help facilitate inter-state payments within the union. A number of specialized committees have been working in such areas as food security, economic and financial affairs, basic infrastructure, and human resources. In 1992, the AMU's Secretariat General was established permanently in Rabat (Morocco), with an annual operating budget of US $ 1.7 million.[10] Since 1994, the AMU has been at an institutional and operational standstill. Recent signs of progress include the appointment of Habib Boularès (Tunisia) to the post of Secretary General, effective February 2002; the Algiers summit meeting, scheduled for Spring 2002; and the revival of a number of transport and infrastructure projects, notably a railway linking the five capital cities, interconnection of the member countries electric grid, and construction of a Tripoli-Nouakchott highway.[11]

The reopening of the borders between Libya and Tunisia, and between Algeria and Morocco, has already demonstrated the potential for the growth of trade, as well as the benefits of a free movement of labor within the subregion. In spite of these favourable circumstances, the risk of failure of this new attempt at regional integration remains high for various reasons. These include: the relative lack of complementarity in the production structures of the various countries; the heavy dependence of the countries of the region on European markets for their external trade; the limited short-term gains that may be expected from integration; payments problems (adverse effect of the multiplicity of non-convertible currencies, heavy burden of indebtedness); the endemic economic difficulties of the Maghreb countries; and the resurgence of politico-ethno-religious conflicts linked to the rise of fundamentalist Islamic movements. A notable development in AMU is the association agreements recently signed by two of its wealthiest members, Morocco and Tunisia with the EU, which might impair AMU's progress toward integration.

The *Communauté Éonomique de l'Afrique de l'Ouest* (CEAO)

The *Communauté Économique de l'Afrique de l'Ouest* (CEAO) was the successor organization to UDEAO (*Union douanière et Économique de l'Afrique occidentale*), a free-trade area set up within the framework of the former French West African Federation. The organization was established through the Abidjan Treaty of April 1973, and its membership included seven Francophone west African states: Benin, Burkina Faso, Côte d'Ivoire, Mali, Mauritania, Niger, and Senegal. All CEAO states (except Mauritania) were also members of the franc zone system and of its affiliated institutions (*Banque centrale des États de l'Afrique de l'Ouest*/BCEAO, and *Banque Ousest-africaine de Développement*/BOAD).

CEAO was conceived as an *organized trade zone*, a type of free trade area with various tariff structures and customs regulations. It aimed to develop into a customs union within twelve years of its creation and, ultimately, into a full-fledged common market. CEAO also sought to promote cooperation and integration in such areas as agriculture, livestock, fishing, industry, transport and communications, and tourism. The two main instruments of this regional integration structure were the Regional Cooperation Tax (*Taxe de coopération régionale*), designed as an instrument of trade liberalization in industrial products within CEAO; and the Community Development Fund (*Fonds Communautaire de Développement*), designed to compensate the least developed, most geographically disadvantaged member states for losses incurred through the operation of the TCR. The Community Development Solidarity and Guarantee Fund (*Fonds de Solidarité et d'Intervention pour le Développement de la Communauté*), was set up in October 1978 as a loan guarantee and investment fund for the member states and for public and private firms operating in those states.

Since it started operating in 1974, CEAO achieved a measure of success toward integration. The number of firms whose products have been approved under the regional tax regime has increased from 91 in 1975 to 222 in 1980, a 143 percent increase. During the same period, the number of products traded under this regime has risen from 129 to 403, an increase of 125 percent. The value of manufactured goods traded within CEAO increased by 241 percent from US $14 million in 1976 to US $48 million in 1986.[12] Similarly, intra-community trade has increased in value from US $73 million in 1970 to $396 million in 1981, $406 million in 1983 and $300 million in 1986. Intra-community trade as a percentage of total exports has increased from 6.9 percent in 1980 to 11.6 percent in 1983, falling back to 6.5 percent in 1986.[13] Furthermore, CEAO established a common nomenclature and harmonized duties and sales taxes. Finally, in 1978, CEAO initiated a number of common projects in small-scale irrigation, fisheries, and solar energy, and common advanced training institutions in the fields of management, fisheries, geology and mining, and textiles.

According to the World Bank, "Among Africa's market integration schemes the CEAO has been most successful."[14] While this may be the case, the organization has also experienced various problems and difficulties. There was little or no progress towards implementing the measures of positive integration required to establish an economic community. The common external tariff, scheduled for January 1985, never came into effect. In addition, most member states continued to enforce certain trade restrictions in defiance of the treaty provisions. Furthermore, the absence of a regional industrial policy resulted in duplication of industrial development efforts. The industrial development of the CEAO countries remained heavily dependent upon investment by foreign multinational corporations. Intra-community trade (and the regional tax regime) mostly benefited these foreign corporations. Thus, CEAO was very much a "penetrated organization," externally-oriented and dependent.[15] CEAO was officially disbanded in March 1994, and was replaced by the West African Economic and Monetary Union (WAEMU).

The West African Economic and Monetary Union (*Union Économique et monétaire Ouest-africaine*) (WAEMU/UEMOA)

The seven member states of the now defunct CEAO—Benin, Burkina Faso, Côte d'Ivoire, Mali, Niger, Senegal and Togo—, plus Guinea Bissau, which were also members of the *Union monétaire Ouest-africaine* (UMOA, created in May 1962)—formed in January 1994 a new organization combining the long-term objectives of both institutions and superseding them: a common market (CEAO) and a monetary union (UMOA). Created in the context of the 50 percent devaluation of the CFA franc, the 8-member West African Economic and Monetary Union (WAEMU: Benin, Burkina Faso, Côte d'Ivoire, Guinea-Bissau, Mali, Niger, Senegal and Togo) demonstrates a rare determination to achieve economic and monetary union within a realistic time-frame. WAEMU covers a land area of over 3.5 million square kilometres and represents a market of 70 million consumers with an average per capita income of $390. The Union's main objectives are:

- to reinforce the competitiveness of the economic and financial activities of member states in the context of an open and competitive market and a rationalized and harmonized legal environment;
- to ensure the convergence of the macro-economic performances and policies of member states with the institution of a multilateral control procedure;
- to create a common market among member states based on the free circulation of the people, goods, services, and capital and on the right of people to exercise an independent or remunerated activity;
- to establish a common external tariff, as well as a common commercial policy by 1 January 2000;
- to create a single monetary zone by 1 January 2000;
- to coordinate national sector-based policies with common actions and common policies, especially in the following domains: community-based land reclamation, agriculture, environment, transport, infrastructure, telecommunications, human resources, energy, industry, mines, and crafts;
- to harmonize the legislation—especially the fiscal systems—of the member states for the proper functioning of the common market.

The Union's elaborate institutional infrastructure includes: the Authority of the Heads of States and Governments as the supreme decision-making organ (it held its inaugural meeting in May 1996); the Council of Ministers, responsible for the implementation of the general policies defined by the Authority; the Commission (executive organ), composed of eight commissioners who are nationals of the member states; a Court of Justice and a Court of Accounts (the Commission and Court of Justice were set up in January 1995, with headquarters in Ouagadougou, Burkina Faso; the Court of Accounts is operational since March 1998); a 40-member Inter-parliamentary Committee (as embryo of the future Union Parliament), headquartered in Bamako (Mali) and operational since March 1998, meeting at least once a year; and an advisory institution headquartered in Lomé (Togo) and operational since April 1998, the Regional Consular Board, which is composed of national consular boards, professional associations and employers' organizations of the member states, and which is responsible for the effective involvement of the private sector in the WAEMU integration process.

WAEMU deserves special attention for two reasons: it illustrates the advantages and constraints of a monetary zone (the franc zone) anchored on a convertible external currency (formerly the French Franc, now the Euro); and it provides some ideas as to the impact of the arrangements on the process of economic integration among the participating countries. Tariff rates on trade within the union have been reduced to zero as from January 2000, and between 1996 and May 2001, 1,845 industrial products have been cleared for intra-community trade.[16] WAEMU includes a compensatory financing scheme, which consists of resources levied on the revenues collected under the common external tariff. Between September 1998 and November 2001, 40.8 billion CFA francs were allocated to five countries under this scheme, the greatest beneficiaries in 2001 being Mali, Niger (4.9 billion each) and Burkina Faso (3.1 billion).[17] A common investment code and common budgetary expenditure nomenclature were recently adopted, and the system of multilateral surveillance is contributing to the convergence of budgetary policies. The challenge is to press ahead with the program of harmonization of domestic (indirect and direct) taxation, and to effectively implement the provisions for the free movement of people, goods, services, and capital throughout the union. Remarkably, the share of intra-community exports as a proportion of total union exports increased from 11 percent in 1996 to 15.4 percent in 1999.[18] Subject to the political will of Francophone African leaders, WAEMU could provide one of the building blocks to achieving greater integration within a broader West African integration scheme such as the Economic Community of West African States (ECOWAS).[19]

The Economic Community of West African States (ECOWAS)

The treaty establishing the Economic Community of West African States (ECOWAS) was signed in Lagos in May 1975 and entered into force in July of the same year. The organization now has 16 member states (Cape Verde, Côte d'Ivoire, Benin, Burkina Faso, Gambia, Ghana, Guinea, Guinea-Bissau, Liberia, Mali, Mauritania, Niger, Nigeria, Senegal, Sierra Leone, and Togo.) A revised treaty—compatible with the planned African Economic Community—was signed by the 16 member states in July 1993. The sheer size of this economic grouping, with a total population of about 250 million and a combined Gross Domestic Product (GDP) of US $122.4 billion augurs well for the economic potential and future of the community. More significantly, ECOWAS constitutes the first regional integration attempt to transcend the traditional historical and linguistic cleavage between French, English, and Portuguese-speaking African states. In 1999 the subregion's GDP growth of 2.7 per cent was lower than the 3.2 percent and 4.8 percent recorded in 1998 and 1996, respectively. Nigeria alone controls more than 50 percent of the subregion's GNP. Only four countries—Gambia, Burkina Faso, Mali and Côte d'Ivoire—recorded impressive annual growth rates of more than 6 percent in 1998. During the same period, some countries—Benin, Cape Verde and Senegal—registered growth rates of 5.5 percent each, while others—Ghana, Guinea and Mauritania—recorded growth rates of 4.5 percent each. Nigeria could only manage a growth rate of less than 3 percent during the same period.[20]

The main objective of the ECOWAS treaty, to be achieved in

stages, is the creation of an economic and monetary union. To this end, a regional trade liberalization scheme has been adopted for the creation of a free-trade area by the end of 1999, and a common external tariff is envisaged. A three-phase program for the free movement of West African persons and goods, and the right of residence and establishment of people throughout the community is almost completed. The community's development and modernization of regional highway and telecommunications networks is designed to facilitate the physical integration of its member states. ECOWAS member states have committed themselves to the coordination and harmonization of national economic and financial policies in order to enhance the effectiveness of national structural adjustment and economic reform programs. The monetary program adopted by the Community has the medium-term objective of achieving regional convertibility of the nine national currencies and, in the long term, the creation of a single monetary zone. The West African unit of account is convertible into any of the currencies in the subregion. In July 1999, ECOWAS travellers cheques were launched to facilitate regional travel and commercial transactions.

Furthermore, the community has been implementing a number of sectoral programs, notably: the inter-connection of national electric grids; a regional pipeline for the distribution of natural gas; community seed production and cattle breeding centers; agricultural research program; a regional master plan for industrial development; coordination of desertification control programs; rural water supply schemes; cooperation in health matters; and establishment of equivalence for degrees and diplomas. The Executive Secretariat is based in Abuja (Nigeria), with Lansana Kouyaté (Guinea) as Executive Secretary since 1997. Five specialized commissions deal with different aspects of cooperation. In addition, a Committee of Governors of West African Central Banks coordinates the implementation of the ECOWAS monetary program. The Treaty also provides for a Court of Justice, a West African Parliament and an Economic and Social Council, all of which have now been established.

The community's activities began slowly. The treaty officially became operational in March 1977, but its substantive implementation started only in May 1979. Progress was achieved in a number of areas. By 1997, some 450 industrial items produced by more than 150 industrial companies in 11 member states became eligible for the trade liberalization scheme. The first telecommunications program (Intelcom I) was officially completed in 1995, with the automatic interconnection of the capitals of the 16 member states. In August 1997, a second program (Intelcom II) was adopted at a cost of about US$ 100 million. Meanwhile, the three trans-regional highway projects made substantial progress. By mid-1997, the trans-sahelian highway running from Dakar to Ndjamena (2,790 miles) was 87 percent completed, while 83 percent of the coastal route between Lagos and Nouakchott (2,850 miles) was tarred. This was also the case for 70 percent of the highways (4,876 miles) due to connect the trans-sahelian and trans-coastal routes.

Some progress has also been made in respect of self-sufficiency in agriculture and energy. ECOWAS embarked on village and pastoral water schemes involving 200 water holes per member state, focussing first on the 10 Sahelian states. Formally adopted in November 1996, the new regional industrial master plan should enable the community to establish an industrial data bank as well as to plan realistically for industrial cooperation, including identification of possible regional industrial enterprises. In 1990, for the first time, the Fund for Co-operation, Compensation and Development made available the sum of US$350,000 as compensation for loss of revenue arising from trade liberalization. The Fund has also financed projects in less-developed ECOWAS member states in the field of infrastructure, transport and telecommunications; seven member states received $12.5 million for partial financing of their telecommunication programs.[21]

Over the last 10 years, as a result of civil wars in Liberia, Sierra Leone and Guinea-Bissau, ECOWAS activated its 1978 non-aggression and 1981 defence protocols. Under the active leadership of Nigeria, the ECOWAS monitoring group (ECOMOG) became instrumental in ending the seven-year civil war in Liberia and in managing the conflict in Sierra Leone. These are two instances in which security considerations have, exceptionally and temporarily, taken precedence over regional economic integration.

A number of important decisions were adopted at the 22nd ECOWAS summit meeting in Lomé, Togo in December 1999. These include: a draft protocol on conflict prevention, management, resolution, peacekeeping and security; the setting up of a mediation and security council; administrative reforms; accelerating the free movement of people and goods, and the right of establishment within the community; harmonizing individual member state's economic policies as a key factor in the integration process; accelerating the integration process with a view to establishing a single regional market in West Africa; deepening the process of convergence of macro-economic performance of member states (to be met by 2003) in order to enhance the credibility of the single monetary zone; and creating a single monetary zone by 2004.[22]

While institution-building has proceeded apace, no significant progress has yet been made towards positive integration in ECOWAS. Intra-community trade has remained low, and even shown a tendency to steadily decline. The value of intra-ECOWAS trade has decreased from US $1,056 billion in 1980 to $500 million in 1984 and $491 million in 1986. During the same time, as a percentage of total exports, intra-community trade decreased from 3.9 per cent in 1980 to 2.5 per cent in 1984-85, slightly rising to 3.2 per cent in 1986.[23] In 1998, intra-regional trade remains a mere 11 per cent of the member state's total external trade. Indeed, trade liberalization has made little progress: no common external tariff has yet been established, the 1981 deadline for the freezing of tariff rates was not met, and little progress has been made towards implementing the new time-table.

In addition, the less-developed ECOWAS member states feel that the support and compensation arrangements are inadequate in the face of the dominant position of Côte d'Ivoire and Nigeria.

Furthermore, ECOWAS' rule of product origin has become a source of serious disagreements. This rule promotes indigenous manufacturers (notably in Ghana and Nigeria) but restricts exports from Côte d'Ivoire and Senegal (since their industrial plants, which are French-owned, are considered foreign investment) , thus discouraging foreign investment. More significantly, the pattern of trade has not changed. Côte d'Ivoire and Nigeria still dominate the export of manufactures. Côte d'Ivoire is the dominant trading partner within the rival WAEMU, where trade liberalization has advanced considerably. Unwilling to lose this advantage, Côte d'Ivoire (along with the other WAEMU members) resisted absorbing the Francophone community into the larger ECOWAS. This has resulted in a deadlock.[24] On labor mobility, there has been setback rather than progress; in September 1982, Ghana closed its borders, and in 1983 Nigeria expelled an estimated 2 million "illegal aliens" (mostly Ghanaians). In 1979, the ECOWAS Authority adopted a protocol on the Free Movement of Persons, Right of Residence and Establishment. Although a protocol on the right of residence and establishment was signed in 1986, few states ratified it and the matter now appears to be in abeyance.

There is minimal movement of capital within the region because capital markets remain underdeveloped. Lack of progress in the payments system is due to the failure of ECOWAS (in spite of its declared long-term commitment) to establish a single monetary zone, with a common currency and a pooling of foreign exchange reserves. Designed to facilitate intra-regional transactions and to economize on the use of foreign convertible currencies, the former West African Clearing House (WACH) has, through ratification of the July 1993 protocol, been transformed into the West African Monetary Agency (WAMA), now a specialized institution of the community responsible for its monetary program. This monetary program aims at creating a single monetary zone by 2004, with the ultimate objective of replacing the 10 existing currencies (the CFA franc and the nine inconvertible currencies) with a single common currency. WACH accomplished little of substance and became practically defunct. The activities of WAMA, whose statutes were eventually signed in March 1996, have been delayed by lack of coordination with the WAEMU monetary integration schedule, which aims at creating a single monetary zone by January 1st, 2000.[25]

Finally, non-compliance of member states with community decisions, policies and programs is a feature of ECOWAS. Such non-compliance includes a failure of member states to fully contribute their agreed payments to the Community budget and their capital contribution to the Fund. For example, as of December 1999, only five member states (Benin, Burkina Faso, Côte d'Ivoire, Mali and Nigeria) were up to date in their annual contributions. With an annual budget of US $10 million, the community is owed arrears of $38.4 million by 11 member states. The council of ministers approved a budget of $10.3 million for fiscal year 2000, but financial constraint remains a hindrance to the secretariat, which is being restructured.[26] The current ECOWAS chairman, president Alpha Oumar Konaré (Mali), remarked at the close of the Lomé summit that "Efforts should be made to have the integration and unity ideal embraced not only by decision-makers, but also by the populations..."[27]

The *Union douanière et Économique de l'Afrique centrale* (UDEAC) and the *Communauté Économique et monétaire d'Afrique centrale* (CEMAC)

The treaty creating UDEAC, signed in December 1964 (and effective in January 1966) by five central African countries (Cameroon, Central African Republic/CAR, Chad, Congo, and Gabon) in fact constituted a revamping of the Equatorial African Customs Union (*Union Douanière Équatoriale*) set up in June 1959 between the four members of the former *Fédération de l'Afrique Équatoriale Française* (the same as above, minus Cameroon). The CAR and Chad withdrew from UDEAC in 1968, but the CAR rejoined the Union shortly thereafter, and Chad applied for readmission in December 1983. Equatorial Guinea became the Union's sixth member in December

1983. All UDEAC member states are also members of the franc zone system. UDEAC constitutes a grouping of 25 million people stretching over 3 million square kilometres.

The UDEAC treaty ultimately aims to create a common market (through the usual steps of a free trade area and a customs union), though no time limit has been set. In fact, UDEAC has been stillborn since 1966. Little or no progress has been made since then towards creating a customs union or in coordinating the development, transport and communication and telecommunication policies and projects of the member states. Barriers remain with respect to the free movement of persons and capital, and convertibility of currency exists not because of specific UDEAC policies but because of common membership in the franc zone. The value of intra-community trade has decreased from US $200 million in 1980 to $100 million in 1984 and $84 million in 1986. As a percentage of total exports, intra-UDEAC trade decreased from 5 percent in 1970 and 4.1 percent in 1980 to 2 percent in 1985 and 2.8 percent in 1986.[28] The existence of a monetary union has not been sufficient to increase trade flows. Low intra-regional trade is also the result of trade barriers as well as the narrow export basket of member countries. The pattern of trade in the region is highly influenced by that of the relatively better-off oil exporting countries in the group (Cameroon, Congo and Gabon). Some limited progress has been made in harmonizing statistical information and internal fiscal regimes. However, various studies have shown that implementation of the UDEAC treaty provisions and mechanisms has actually resulted in increased market dominance of foreign-owned companies operating within UDEAC, increased economic inefficiency, an uneven pattern of industrialization, and disarticulation of the regional economy.[29]

A reform of UDEAC was initiated by the World Bank in November 1989, with the strong support and active participation of the French ministry of cooperation. The Bank and the Union's secretary general concluded an agreement on a Regional Reform Program (RRP) which included fiscal and tariff reforms, financial policy, and transport and transit. This program was endorsed by the Libreville meeting of UDEAC heads of state in December 1991. Three years after the implementation of the fiscal and customs reforms, their impact remains difficult to assess. The program adopted by UDEAC's steering committee in June 1993 included: the restoration of a common external tariff based on four rates (from 5 percent for basic necessities to 50 percent for luxury products); a regional preference for locally produced goods; and a tax on the companies' turnover. Preexisting arrangements that discouraged competition within UDEAC were due to be eliminated within two years. Another component of the RRP was the *Transit Inter-États des Pays de l'Afrique Centrale*, a program for the establishment of a regional scheme for the transportation and transit of goods whose ultimate goal was to contribute to regional integration by rationalizing transport policies in central Africa; its implementation, however, has been severely hampered by political instability in the subregion.[30]

The transformation of UDEAC into a genuine economic and monetary union was prepared in consultation with the *Banque des États de l'Afrique Centrale* (BEAC), and discussed by the UDEAC heads of state in December 1992. Two treaties were drafted to cover the monetary and economic aspects of regional integration. The treaty on the *Union Monétaire de l'Afrique centale* (UMAC) was designed to promote among the BEAC member states the convergence of macroeconomic policies and improved financial and monetary management through a system of multilateral economic monitoring. The second treaty was due to transform the UDEAC into a Central African Economic and Monetary Community (*Communauté Économique et monétaire d'Afrique centrale/* CEMAC) based on common economic and monetary policies. The treaty establishing CEMAC was signed in March 1994 and came into force in February 1998, officially superseding the UDEAC treaty.[31]

CEMAC's objective is to create a common market through trade liberalization and the elimination of tariffs and non-tarrif barriers. CEMAC is the fusion of two separate entities: the Economic Union of Central Africa (*Union Économique de l'Afrique centrale*/UEAC) and the Monetary Union of Central Africa (*Union monétaire de l'Afrique centrale*/UMAC). The institutions of the community include: the Conference of Heads of States (the supreme policy organ), the Council of Ministers, the Executive Secretariat, the Inter-State Committee (preparing the decisions of the Council of Ministers), the Court of Justice and the Inter-parliamentary Committee (future Parliament, the last two set up in 2001). UMAC also includes BEAC. CEMAC recently adopted a series of measures designed to consolidate the integration process, notably: a tourism development plan; a code of conduct for merchant shipping; community road guidelines and customs regulations; and a community passport (effective July 31, 2002). A Development Fund (*Fonds de Développement*), designed to finance community projects and to provide compensatory financing to the most disadvantaged member states was also set up and started operating in January 2002.[32]

However, effective implementation of the treaty is bound to remain ineffective as long as regional security is not restored. Congo-Brazzaville and the DRC are experiencing open or latent armed conflict. Political instability—caused by authoritarian rulers pitched against a vibrant civil society fighting for human rights and democracy—prevails in Cameroon, the CAR, Chad, Gabon and Equatorial Guinea. The crisis in which the UDEAC/CEMAC countries presently find themselves precludes any meaningful progress toward integration.

The Economic Community of Central African States (*Communauté Économique des États d'Afrique centrale*/CEEAC)

In accord with ECA policy and the Lagos Plan of Action recommendations, the December 1982 UDEAC enlarged summit of heads of state and government of the region proposed to create a region-wide central African economic union. In October 1983, 10 central African states meeting in Libreville (Gabon) adopted the treaty creating the

Communauté Économique des États de l'Afrique centrale/CEEAC. Like ECOWAS, CEEAC includes, and attempts to co-exist with other, pre-existing integration schemes like UDEAC and the Economic Community of the Great Lake States. CEEAC, too, transcends traditional colonial cleavages by bringing together former Belgian, French, Portuguese, and Spanish colonies; it represents a market of 70 million inhabitants spread over a surface area of 5.4 million square kilometres.

This 10-nation grouping (Burundi, Cameroon, CAR, Chad, Congo, Equatorial Guinea, Gabon, Rwanda, Sao Tomé and Principe, and the Democratic Republic of the Congo/DRC) eventually aims at establishing a central African common market and economic community by 1995. This was achieved in three, four-year stages: (1) stabilization and harmonization of the existing customs and fiscal regimes, and elaboration of the tariff and non-tariff reduction/elimination schedule; (2) creation of a free-trade area; and (3) creation of a customs union, with a common external tariff.

Stressing the need for the rapid development of the less-developed, land locked and otherwise disadvantaged member states, the CEEAC treaty established two funds to contribute to equitable distribution of the benefits and costs of integration: The Cooperation and Development Fund to provide technical and financial assistance to promote development; and the Compensation Fund to provide financial compensation for revenue losses arising from the lowering of tariffs. Recognizing the inadequacy of an exclusive focus on market integration, the CEEAC Treaty seeks to promote cooperation in the major sectors of the economy (agriculture, industry, energy, transport and communication) through production integration mechanisms.

This relatively young organization has already experienced financial and institutional difficulties. Financial difficulties led to a five-month postponement of the third summit meeting, due to take place in January 1987 in Bangui (CAR). The fourth summit (Kinshasa, Februuary 1988) drew back from the progress already achieved by rescinding earlier decisions to consolidate customs régimes and to establish a clearing house. The stabilization and harmonization of the member states' customs and fiscal régimes, due to be completed by 1984, has yet to be achieved. Two important decisions were adopted at the sixth summit meeting (Kigali, January 1990): the creation of a CEEAC development bank by 1990; and the free movement of persons, goods, and capital, to be realized by January 1st, 1991. However, endemic instability, insecurity and civil war in Burundi, the CAR, Congo, Rwanda and the DRC have emerged as the greatest impediments to regional integration in central Africa and (as in west Africa) have pushed peace and security issues to the top of CEEAC's agenda. In September 1993, a Permanent Consultative Committee on Issues of Security in Central Africa held a meeting under the aegis of CEEAC in Libreville; its recommendations included the creation by all member states of specialized units trained for crisis management and the adoption of a non-aggression pact. Unfortunately, these recommendations were never implemented.[33]

By restricting their membership to the francophone central African states, UMAC and UDEAC/CEMAC exclude *de facto* Angola and the DRC, and thus seriously diminish the prospects for successful regional integration in central Africa. Such prospects are further negatively affected by the lack of complementarity between the central African economies. Cameroon, as the main exporter of agricultural produce, is progressively emerging as the new core-state in the subregion. Plagued by endemic civil strife, poor communications and lack of interconnection between telecommunication networks, the central Africa subregion remains territorially segmented, and its integration process is on hold.[34] Indeed, as one observer concludes, "The prospects for a voluntary policy of integration are certainly not good...the UDEAC and CEMAC do not exist anymore, except on paper."[35]

Monetary and Financial Institutions: The Franc Zone System

The Franc Zone was set up as a monetary cooperation arrangement between France and its former west and central African colonies following their independence in the early sixties. Characterized by a very centralized decision-making structure, the zone is organized around four major principles: free convertibility, at par, of the local (CFA franc) and French (French franc) currencies; free movement of capital within the zone; pooling of gold and foreign exchange reserves in a common French Treasury account (*compte d'opérations*); and common rules and regulations for foreign commercial and financial transactions.

Clustered around France, the Franc Zone system includes: (1) France; (2) seven west African member states of the West African Monetary Union (*Union monétaire ouest-africaine*/UMOA)— including the seven CEAO member states—Benin, Burkina Faso, Côte d'Ivoire, Mali, Niger, Senegal, and Togo –, plus Guinea-Bissau; (3) six central African member states of the *Banque des États de l'Afrique Centrale*—including all six UDEAC member states— Cameroon, CAR, Chad, Congo, Equatorial Guinea, and Gabon; and (4) the Comoros (14 African countries in total).

In addition to the two subregional central banks, the *Banque Centrale des États de l'Afrique de l'Ouest*/BCEAO, based in Dakar (Senegal), and *Banque des États de l'Afrique Centrale*/BEAC based in Yaoundé (Cameroon), the Franc Zone system includes two regional development banks: the West African Development Bank (*Banque ouest-africaine de développement*/BOAD, created in 1973 and based in Lomé (Togo); and the Central African Development Bank (*Banque de développement des États de l'Afrique Centrale*/BDEAC, created in 1975 and based in Brazzaville (Congo).

In exchange for the guaranteed convertibility of the French franc, the Franc Zone African member states have accepted limits on budget deficits and domestic credit expansion. More significantly, by accepting the strict membership rules and regulations of the union, they have entrusted all their monetary and financial responsibilities to

France in what amounts to a voluntary surrender of sovereignty. Indeed, France controls these states' issuance and circulation of currency, their monetary and financial regulations, their banking activities, their credit allocation and, ultimately, their budgetary and economic policies.[36]

In 1991, three ambitious programs were launched to promote integration through the harmonization of legal regulations (*intégration par les règles*)—but also to avoid a devaluation of the CFA franc—in insurance, social welfare and business law. This resulted in the creation of the *Conférence interafricaine des marchés de l'Assurance* in 1992, followed a year later by the *Conférence interafricaine de Prévoyance sociale* and the *Organisation pour l'Harmonisation du Droit des Affaires en Afrique*. As Daniel Bach rightly observes, "These ambitious programs...proved unable to avoid the devaluation of the CFA franc in January 1994, but may well have contributed to avoiding the break-up of the Franc Zone."[37]

The current process of European monetary integration has affected the structure, functioning and future of the Franc Zone in several ways. In March 1979, the European countries decided to reduce the fluctuations of their currencies in relation to one another to 2.25 percent, and the CFA franc became linked to the Deutsche Mark or the Belgian franc, with identical margins of fluctuation. Around that time, difficulties—due in part to the fall of commodity prices following a severe deterioration in the terms of trade—began to arise for the Franc Zone African countries. As the European Monetary System (EMS) was progressively put in place, the EU emerged as an attractive zone of prosperity at a time when the Franc Zone's economies were declining, thus reducing the incentive to invest savings locally. And since the CFA franc could be freely converted into French francs, the capital available in the zone took flight. Between 1987 and 1993, these outflows of capital increased considerably: in 1987, they accounted for 31 percent of the bank notes circulating in the BCEAO area; in 1988, 57 percent of the bank notes circulating in the BEAC area had to be redeemed by the *Banque de France*. Further capital outflows resulted in the drain of 59 percent of the notes issued by BEAC for 1992; CFA franc 230 billion within the UMOA the same year; and more than CFA franc 250 billion during the first six months of 1993. All this made the 50 percent devaluation of the CFA franc vis-à-vis the French franc which took place in January 1994 all but inevitable. And when, on January 1st, 1999, the French franc was replaced by the Euro, the CFA franc was automatically pegged to the new single currency. Based on the EU model, the UEMOA treaty was signed in Januray 1994, and the CEMAC treaty in March 1994. The key provisions that these treaties have in common are: the creation of a common market through the elimination of customs duties and quantitative restrictions; the establishment of a common external tariff and trade policy; common rules of competition; free movement of workers; and the right of establishment, and freedom of provision of services.

What are the consequences of the Euro for the Franc Zone and for Africa? Since the operations accounts are kept within the French Treasury, the latter will continue to supply Euros to the African central banks, and the French government's budget will still be able to finance the needs of the Franc Zone. France retains the right to determine the parity of the CFA franc. Within the framework of various subregional African clearing-house systems and payment unions, the Euro could be useful in three ways: it could become the unit of account in which these transactions are denominated; it could also be the currency in which balances are periodically settled; it could even become a reserve asset. The Franc Zone, which is already a *de facto* clearing-house and which guarantees the stability of currencies, should, in the future, be able to facilitate regional integration as the monetary union components of both UEMOA and CEMAC. The crucial issue is whether the Euro will eventually replace the Franc Zone in Africa, or whether the Franc Zone will remain a crucial link and central element in the system of Franco-African cooperation.[38]

The East African Community (EAC)

The East African Community (EAC) was formally established in December 1967 by the coming into force of the Treaty for East African Cooperation signed by the three partner states (Kenya, Tanzania, and Uganda) earlier that year. The community's demise can be dated to 1977, when the partner states failed to approve the 1977-78 EAC budget. Thus, the community died before its tenth birthday. Yet, it had been one of the most successful regional integration experiments in the developing world. What had gone wrong? As Arthur Hazlewood rightly observes, the three countries' economies had been even more closely integrated before independence. At that time, the integration arrangement comprised a customs union with a common external tariff and free trade between the countries, common customs and income tax administrations, common transport and communications services, a common university, common research services, and a common currency. By the time the treaty was signed, however, the common currency had been abandoned, and the operation of the customs union was being seriously inhibited by non-tariff barriers to trade.[39]

The treaty aimed to put cooperation between the partner states on a firm footing of mutual advantage. It set up a formal structure for administering community institutions and provided measures to achieve an acceptable distribution of the benefits of integration between the member states. The main features were: the introduction of a "transfer tax" to give limited protection for industries in the less-developed states against competition from those in the more developed states; the establishment of an East African Development Bank (EADB), which was to allocate its investments disproportionately in favor of Tanzania and Uganda; and, the relocation of the headquarters of some of the common services (including the community secretariat), so that they were not concentrated in Kenya. Formally, the main structure—including the common external tariff—stood until the final collapse, but the common market became increasingly a dead letter and some of the common services effectively disintegrated. The EADB survived the final collapse, but in a largely moribund condition.⁴⁰ Many scholars have studied the demise of the EAC, providing significant insights of relevance to the relative lack of success of other African regional integration experiments. Among the major problems identified by these authors are: the uneven distribution of benefits; institutional difficulties; politico-ideological factors; and, external dependence.⁴¹

After reviving the EAC's common services in 1994 and the secretariat in 1995, the presidents of Kenya, Tanzania and Uganda signed, on November 30. 1999, a treaty setting up a new version of an East African Community, 22 years after the first such entity was dismantled by the three states. The new EAC aims at promoting social, economic and political cooperation between the member states. An East African passport and a joint military force are among the community's first projects to be implemented.

The Preferential Trade Area for Eastern and Southern Africa (PTA) and Common Market for Eastern and Southern Africa (COMESA)

The Preferrential Trade Area for Eastern and Southern Africa (PTA)

The creation of the PTA grew out of the United Nations Economic Commission for Africa's (UN-ECA) long-term strategy to create two large sub-regional groupings, one in eastern Africa, the other in southern Africa; it also came about as a result of the collapse of the EAC in 1977. The PTA project was initiated in October 1977 within the Lusaka-based Multinational Programming and Operational Centre (MULPOC), one of five subregional centres established by the UN-ECA in Africa in March 1977. Negotiations on the PTA treaty lasted from March 1978 to October 1981, and the treaty was signed at the Lusaka meeting of heads of state and government on December 21, 1981. From 10 original signatories, the membership of PTA grew to 16 (Burundi, Comoros, Djibouti, Ethiopia, Kenya, Lesotho, Malawi,

Mauritius, Mozambique, Rwanda, Somalia, Swaziland, Tanzania, Uganda, Zambia, and Zimbabwe). The potential members of PTA—who, for various reasons, have not joined but enjoy observer status—are Angola, Botswana, Madagascar, and the Seychelles.

The PTA was initially conceived as a free-trade area as a first step towards the establishment of a customs union, a common market and, eventually, of an economic community. Thus, to the extent that it aimed at rapidly moving beyond the stage of a mere free-trade area to become a full-fledged common market by 1992, the PTA is somewhat of a misnomer. The PTA combines a market integration approach (trade liberalization measures, such as reduction of tariff and non-tariff barriers and customs facilitation) with a production integration approach (common projects in the agricultural, industrial, and transport and communications sectors).

Trade links among the PTA member countries are still weak. Between 1980 and 1985, intra-PTA trade constituted only about 6.5 percent of these countries' total trade. Naturally, one of the main objectives of the PTA treaty is to promote intra-PTA trade, notably through the gradual reduction and eventual elimination among member countries of customs duties and non-tariff barriers (NTBs) to trade on a common list of—initially 212—selected commodities which are of both export and import interest to the member states. The list is regularly amended to progressively include all the commodities traded within the subregion by 1992. Zero tariff levels and complete elimination of non-tariff barriers was achieved by September 1992. According to the PTA's rule of product origin, goods are accepted as originating in a member country only if they have been produced in that country by enterprises which are subject to management by a majority of nationals and to at least 51 percent equity holding by nationals of that country.

The multilateral clearing system for eastern and southern Africa set up under the PTA treaty aims to enhance cooperation and the settlement of payments for intra-regional trade in goods and services. Under this scheme, member countries are able to use national currencies in the settlement of payments during a transactions period of two calendar months, with only net balances at the end of this period requiring settlement in convertible currencies (through the Federal Reserve Bank of New York). Intra-regional settlements are expressed and recorded in terms of the PTA unit of account, which is equal to the Special Drawing Right of the International Monetary Fund (i.e. US $1.14). The PTA Multilateral Clearing Facility (or Clearing House) started operating in February 1984 in Harare (Zimbabwe). The Reserve Bank of Zimbabwe provisionally performed the functions of executive secretary of the Clearing House until January 1992, when the Clearing House became fully autonomous. The Trade and Development Bank (PTA Bank) was established in 1985. The PTA Bank's cumulative trade financing activity between 1992 and 1996 totalled $345 million.

In the sector of transport and communications, programs for the rehabilitation and upgrading of substandard interstate roads and railways systems, and for the construction of new links, were adopted in 1985. A Road Customs Transit Declaration Document, for a PTA-harmonized, customs-control transit system to facilitate uninhibited cross-border transit by PTA vehicles, was introduced in all PTA countries in July 1986. In July 1987, a PTA Motor Vehicle Insurance Scheme, the Yellow Card, came into effect to eliminate the costly and cumbersome practice of taking out insurance for every cross-border transit operation. Other subregional programs and projects were initiated in the areas of air transport, inland-water and coastal maritime transportation systems, telecommunications, agriculture, and industry and energy. Finally, the PTA regularly conducted trade promotion activities such as buyer/seller meetings and PTA trade fairs.

Because of the non compliance of most member states with the initially approved tariff reduction time table and tariff rates publication requirement, the PTA Council decided to postpone the deadline for the complete elimination of tariffs to the year 2000 (instead of 1992, as initially scheduled). Thus, the member states reduced their intra-PTA tariffs by 10 percent per year every year between October 1988 and October 1996; the remaining 50 percent having been eliminated in two steps: 20 percent in 1998, and 30 percent in 2000.

Three major points of contention surfaced between the economically more advanced member states—mainly Kenya and Zimbabwe—and the least-developed, geographically disadvantaged micro-states of the subregion—Comoros, Mauritius, Djibouti, Rwanda, and Burundi—over the equitable distribution of the benefits and costs of integration: These issues included: the restrictive definition of the rules of origin in terms of the 51 percent minimum national-equity holding rule; the reduction and elimination of customs duties and "other charges of equivalent effect" by Comoros and Djibouti; and the formula for contribution to the PTA budget. Admittedly, the overwhelming industrial and trade dominance of Kenyan and Zimbabwean manufacturers partly explains the persistent dissatisfaction of some of the smaller member states. A recent study which assessed the costs and benefits to PTA member states of implementing the treaty provisions and programs, recommended measures likely to enhance the equitable distribution of costs and benefits among the member states.

Monetary and financial cooperation within the PTA has, on the whole, been fairly successful. All the member states except Djibouti have used the multilateral clearing facility for payment of contributions to the PTA institutions and some of their intra-PTA trade. A total of UAPTA 217.7 million have passed through the Clearing House since it began operating in February 1984. Indeed, the volume of trade settled through the Clearing House progressed slowly, but steadily, from 9 percent of total intra-PTA trade in 1984 to 10 percent in 1985, 15 percent in 1986, and 20 percent in 1987.[42] Finally, it should be noted that contrary to the prevailing norm in most African regional organizations, the PTA's finances have always been basically sound.

The Common Market for Eastern and Southern Africa (COMESA)

The treaty establishing the Common Market for Eastern and Southern Africa (COMESA) was signed in Kampala (Uganda) on

November 5, 1993 by the member states of the PTA. The COME-
SA treaty entered into force in December 1994, after its ratification
by 11 signatory states (COMESA now has 21 member states). The
PTA was formally dissolved on that date, being replaced by COME-
SA. The establishment of COMESA was a fulfilment of the requirements of the PTA treaty, which provided for the transformation of
the PTA into a common market 10 years after its entry into force.
Considerable progress has been made in implementing regional inte-
gration in eastern and southern Africa, particularly in trade facilita-
tion and institution building. The institutions established include the
PTA Trade and Development Bank in Nairobi, Kenya (with a capital
of $540 million, to be increased to $5.5 billion); the COMESA
Clearing House in Harare, Zimbabwe; the COMESA Leather and
Leather Products Institute in Addis Ababa, Ethiopia; the PTA
Metallurgical Technology Centre in Harare, Zimbabwe; the COME-
SA Re-insurance Company in Nairobi, Kenya; the COMESA
Metallurgical Industrial Association in Kampala, Uganda; the
Federation of National Association of Women in Business in COME-
SA in Lusaka, Zambia; the Pharmaceutical Manufacturers of Eastern
and Southern Africa; and the COMESA Bankers Association.

The main priorities of COMESA are to achieve a Free Trade Area
(FTA) by October 2000 and a common external tariff by 2004.
Realization of the FTA was predicated upon the successful implementation of the trade liberalization and transport facilitation program over a 16-year period. Progress towards the FTA has so far been
behind schedule. By 1997, only two of the 21 member states had met
the target of an 80 percent tariff reduction on intra-COMESA trade.
By early 1999 the cumulative tariff reduction was to have been 90
percent, yet only Madagascar had reached this target.

The other objectives of COMESA are:

- to attain sustainable growth of the member states by
promoting more balanced and harmonious develop-

ment of its production and marketing structures;
- to promote joint development in all fields of economic activity and the joint adoption of macro-economic policies and programs to raise the standard of living of its peoples and to foster closer relations among its member states;
- to cooperate in the creation of an enabling environment for foreign, cross-border, and domestic investment and in the joint promotion of research and adaptation of science and technology to development;
- to cooperate in the promotion of peace, security, and stability among the member states in order to enhance economic development in the region;
- to cooperate in strengthening the relations between the Common Market and the rest of the world, and in the adoption of common positions in international forums;
- to contribute towards the establishment, progress, and the realization of the objectives of the African Economic Community.

Accounts of COMESA are denominated in the organization's Unit of Account (the Unit of Account of the Common Market), also known as the COMESA dollar, which replaced the Unit of Account of the PTA. One COMESA dollar is equal to US$ 1. The COMESA organs are: the Authority of Heads of State and Government (the supreme policy-making organ); the Council of Ministers (responsible for policy recommendations); the Court of Justice (established in June 1998); the Committee of Governors of Central Banks; the Intergovernmental Committee; 12 Technical Committees; the Consultative Committee (of the business community and interest groups); and the Secretariat, currently headed by Sindiso Ngwenya (acting Secretary-General) headquartered in Lusaka (Zambia). The

COMESA Regional Investment Agency was established in May 1999 to formulate a regional competition policy consistent with World Trade Organization's principles, so as to harmonize existing national competition policies, to avoid contradictions and to provide a consistent regional competitive environment. A computer-based COMESA-wide Trade Information Network has also been established. Overlapping memberships between COMESA, CEEAC, EAC, SADC and the Southern African Customs Union (SACU) leads to duplication of efforts necessary to meet the requirements of different arrangements and costs both time and resources; it also hinders progress towards the implementation of COMESA's objectives.[43]

The Southern African Development Coordination Conference (SADCC) and the Southern African Development Community (SADC)

The Southern African Development Coordination Conference (SADCC)

SADCC grew out of a political grouping, the Front Line States, whose objective was to bring about independence under majority rule in Zimbabwe, Namibia, and South Africa. SADCC came into being at the 1980 Lusaka summit meeting with a membership of nine states—Angola, Botswana, Lesotho, Malawi, Mozambique, Swaziland, Tanzania, Zambia, and Zimbabwe. It explicitly sought to reduce the member states' economic dependence on South Africa through cooperation on specific projects in priority areas such as transport and communications, food security, and energy.

Taking into account the failings of EAC and ECOWAS, SADCC has avoided the market integration approach and has, instead, adopted an incremental, project-oriented, regional cooperation approach. SADCC's relative success as a regional cooperation organization is partly due to its focus on actions rather than on institution-building.

Indeed, one way in which SADCC differs from other African integration schemes is in the manner in which responsibility for sectoral programs has been allocated to various member states: transport and communications (Mozambique), food security (Zimbabwe), industrial development (Tanzania), and mining development (Zambia). SADCC avoided the creation of a dominant regional bureaucracy. In that sense, it was a multinational, rather than supranational, organization.

SADCC gave transport and communications the highest priority. Other areas of cooperation which were part of the conference's regional program of action included: food security; industrial development; energy conservation; manpower training; forestry, fisheries and wildlife; mining development; and soil conservation and land utilization. Over 80 per cent of SADCC programs and projects were financed through foreign aid. Annual meetings between SADCC and its international development cooperation partners were a specific feature of SADCC's *modus operandi*. Thus, at the 1980 Maputo Pledging Conference, 97 projects, for a total estimated cost of US $1.9 billion (and a total amount pledged of US $650 million), were adopted as part of the transport and communications program.

The situation facing the SADCC states suddenly deteriorated in the years following its creation. Thus, between 1981 and 1986, SADCC member states experienced economic recession, increased external financial dependence, severe drought, and intensified South African-backed attacks on the rural population, transport and other facilities. In spite of SADCC's programs and activities, the subregion became more dependent on trade and transport links with South Africa. However, by 1988, the situation had substantially improved. The 1988 SADCC conference brought a large increase in the amount of aid pledged. In 1988, the improved security situation led to the reopening and upgrading of the Zimbabwe-Maputo railway line. On March 21, 1990, Namibia became independent and joined SADCC as its tenth member state. However, the process of gradual political change leading to majority rule which unfolded in South Africa severely undermined SADCC's counter-dependence strategy and ultimately threatened the very *raison d'être* of the organization, which had to be thoroughly overhauled in order to survive.

The Southern African Development Community (SADC)

On August 17, 1992, the nine SADCC member states meeting in Windhoek (Namibia), adopted the Declaration and Treaty establishing the Southern African Development Community (SADC). South Africa joined the organization in 1994, Mauritius did so in 1995, and the Seychelles and DRC joined in 1997, bringing the total membership to 13. The treaty identifies the principles to which the member states commit themselves. These are: peace and security; human rights, democracy and the rule of law; the peaceful settlement of disputes; the development of common political values, systems and institutions; the promotion and defense of peace and stability; and the harmonization of political policies. In June 1996 at the Gaborone summit, the Organ on Politics, Defense and Security was established as the successor to the Front Line States, with responsibility for regional security cooperation. The Inter-State Defense and Security Committee (ISDSC) is one of the organ's main institutions. The 19th ordinary session of the ISDSC (Lusaka, 1997) adopted six important regional policy documents that covered disaster management; a regional satellite communications network (now operational); action against coup makers; peacekeeping training (through a regional Peacekeeping Training Centre, created in 1997); peacekeeping doctrine; and standard operating procedures for peacekeeping operations (a peacekeeping brigade was initiated in 1998).[44]

When the Protocol on Trade was signed in August 1996, SADC committed itself to the creation of a Free Trade Area (FTA) by 2012, to pave the way for a customs union and eventually a common market. The southern African subregion has a potential market of 200 million people and a combined gross domestic product (GDP) of US $ 176 billion. There has been a significant increase in intra-SADC trade, estimated at over 22 percent (the highest intra-regional trade level in sub-Saharan Africa). As a result of the tariff reduction schedules that was negotiated, it is estimated that intra-SADC trade has increased to about 35 percent of total trade by 2000. The fact that by 1998 about 70 percent of intra-SADC trade took place at tariff levels below 10 percent pointed to the achievement of a partial FTA. The elimination of tariff and non-tariff barriers to intra-SADC trade has been phased out over a period of eight years for 85 percent of total intra-regional trade, and twelve years for all trade. Indeed, the SADC FTA was formally launched in Windhoek (Namibia) in August 2000 and became effective September 1st, 2000. In the transport sector, SADC is pursuing a policy of "spatial development corridor," which is meant to bring development to depressed areas through which the transport route passes. Work is in progress on the Maputo Corridor, Beira Corridor and Trans-Kalahari Highway (Maputo-Walvis Bay). Among those projected are Nacala (linking Malawi and Mozambique), Benguela in Angola, and the Trans-Caprivi Highway. In 1995, SADC created a Southern African Power Pool, through which the subregion has an integrated power grid into which the power generated is pooled and allocated to member states as required. SADC's extensive institutional network include the SADC Parliamentary Forum, the SADC Electoral Commissions Forum, the SADC Lawyers Association, the SADC Council of Non-Governmental Organizations, the SADC Association of Chamber of Commerce and Industry, the SADC Women in Business, and the Southern African Regional Police Chiefs Cooperation Organization.[45]

The reinsertion of South Africa in the post-apartheid subregional system has resulted in severe strains and tensions within SADC. First, a political tug-of-war between South Africa and Zimbabwe over control of the SADC Organ stretched it almost to the breaking point. Serious disagreements over SADC's military intervention in Lesotho (December 1998) and in the DRC further aggravated the tensions. Thus, while the August 1999 Maputo summit maintained Zimbabwean President Robert Mugabe as chairman of the organ for another six months, its management is under review, and a proposed reform aims at severely curtailing the organ's mandate and its chairman's powers.[46]

Economically, South Africa is undoubtedly the giant of SADC, accounting for almost 75 percent of its US $127 billion market. This has raised serious concerns on the part of other SADC member states over South African hegemony. In particular, concerns have been expressed over the potential negative impact of the recently concluded EU-South Africa Trade, Development and Cooperation Agreement (TDCA) on SADC's Free Trade Area (FTA). The most direct implication for SADC of the TDCA is that it would reduce the margin of tariff preference granted to SADC countries and therefore place them in direct competition with EU producers. Given that access to the South African market is viewed as the catalyst for the expansion and diversification of the economies of SADC member states, they perceive the EU-SA FTA as a threat to their industrial development. However, the extent to which SADC member states enjoy preferential access to the South African market vis-à-vis the EU hinges on the timing of implementation of the two FTAs. Whereas South Africa will dismantle its tariff barriers to EU imports over a period of 12 years, SADC member states will face zero duties for 70 percent of their current exports to South Africa upon implementation of the agreement. Within five years, 98 percent of their exports will enter South Africa duty free. Hence they will enjoy a margin of preference vis-à-vis the EU throughout the 12 years during which the SA-EU FTA will be implemented. However, for the preferential access enjoyed by SADC member states to exceed significantly the access offered to the EU, both agreements must enter into force at the same time, that is January 1st, 2000. Any delay in the implementation of the SADC FTA will result in the erosion of preferential margins for SADC member states vis-à-vis the EU. Thus, SADC negotiatiors were under intense pressure to conclude the agreement so that its implementation could commence promptly on January 1st, 2000.[47]

The African Economic Community (AEC)

During the 27th ordinary session of their assembly held in Abuja (Nigeria) on June 3rd, 1991, the heads of state and government of the *Organization of African Unity* (OAU) signed the treaty establishing the African Economic Community (AEC). Upon ratification by two-thirds of the member states, the Treaty entered into force in May 1994.

The objective of the AEC is, *inter alia,* to promote the economic, social and cultural development and integration of African economies; and to mobilize and utilize the human and material resources of Africa so as to achieve a self-reliant development. To that end the member states of the AEC—which concurrently belong to the OAU—have undertaken to ensure the liberalization of trade in order to create, eventually, Free Trade Areas and Customs Unions at subregional and regional levels, until they converge into a single African Common Market (ACM) by 2025. To attain that goal, the member states have committed themselves to the gradual removal of obstacles to the free movement of persons, goods and services and capital, and the attainment of the rights of residence and establishment in member states of the community by citizens of participating countries. To boost intra-community trade in goods and services, the AEC envisages cooperation in monetary and financial fields. To that end, it plans to promote and eventually establish an African Clearing and Payments House, an African Monetary Union, an African Central Bank as well as a Community Solidarity, Development and Compensation Fund. Cooperation is also planned in other economic sectors, such as transport and communications, agriculture, industry, and energy.

The secretariat of the AEC is the same as that of the OAU, which is being restructured to meet the requirements of the AEC. The time-frame for the establishment of the community spans over 24 years (2025), divided into six distinct stages. The institutions of the AEC are: (a) the Economic and Social Commission; (b) the Pan-African Parliament; (c) the Court of Justice; and (d) seven Specialized Technical Committees:

- Monetary and Financial Affairs;
- Trade, Customs and Immigration Matters;
- Industry, Science, Technology, Energy, Natural Resources and Environment;
- Transport, Communication and Tourism;
- Rural Economy and Agricultural Matters;
- Health, Labour and Social Affairs; and
- Education, Culture and Human Resources.

The Economic and Social Commission (ECOSOC) is a major organ of the community. The ECOSOC held its first ministerial session in November 1996 in Abidjan (Côte d'Ivoire) to set in motion the administrative and technical requirements for launching the effective implementation of the AEC treaty. This session approved the text of the *Protocol on Relations between the African Economic Community and the Regional Economic Communities (RECs)* and adopted the work program for the period 1997-2000 for the establishment of the AEC. The AEC held its inaugural session in Harare (Zimbabwe) on June 3rd, 1997, when the 33rd OAU Assembly of Heads of State and Government transformed itself into the Assembly of the AEC. The Assembly received formal reports on the implementation of the AEC by the chairmen of the different regional economic communities: AMU, CEEAC, COMESA, ECOWAS, the Inter-Governmental Authority on Development/IGAD, and SADC. One of the major decisions of the Assembly was the approval of the Protocol on Relations between the AEC and the RECs, authorizing the secretary general to sign it on behalf of all the member states.

The New Partnership for Africa's Development (NEPAD) and the African Union (AU)

Promoted by South African President Thabo Mbeki—as a realization of his ideal of an African Renaissance—and co-sponsored by Algeria's

Abdelaziz Bouteflika and Nigeria's Olusegun Obasanjo, the Millenium Action Plan for African Recovery (MAP) was launched in February 2001. The plan's central thesis is that Africa's development depends on its full involvement in the global economy, and that this requires a mixture of reform in Africa and assistance from other countries. The most important reforms are: establishing peace and democratic governance; respecting human rights; combating disease; providing health and education to African people; and encouraging trade (rather than aid).[48] Another plan was launched by president Abdoulaye Wade of Senegal in January 2001. Known as the Omega plan, it also aims at enabling Africa to take full advantage of globalization through long-term financing of priority projects in the areas of infrastructure, education, health, and agriculture at the subregional and continental levels.[49] Following a suggestion of the OAU Secretariat, the two plans were eventually merged in July 2001 into a single plan incorporating elements of both and renamed the New Partnership for Africa's Development (NEPAD, formerly known as the New African Initiative). The NEPAD commits African leaders to eradicate poverty and calls for a new partnership between Africa and donor countries and organizations, grouped within the Strategic Partnership with Africa (SPA). Each of Africa's five subregion is expected to identify projects in the eight priority sectors of the NEPAD, namely good governance, infrastructure, education, health, agriculture, new informationj/communication technologies, energy, and market access.

Conceived in Sirte (Libya) in September 1999 and adopted by the OAU Lomé summit in July 2000, the Constitutive Act of the African Union was signed by all the OAU member states at the 5th extraordinary summit of the OAU held in Sirte on March 2, 2001, formally came into being on May 26, 2001, after the required number of ratifications (by 36 states), and officially replaced the OAU at its 37th summit in Lusaka (Zambia) on July 11, 2001. Amara Essy of Côte d'Ivoire was then elected as interim OAU Secretary General, to preside over the transition to the African Union, due to be completed by May 2002. Modeled after the European Union, the 53-member states African Union will, like its European counterpart, be endowed with supranational powers and shall comprise the following institutions: an executive (the Commission, to be based in Addis Ababa, Ethiopia), a Council of Ministers, a Parliament, a Court of Justice, a Monetary Fund and a Central Bank. In effect, it will incorporate the NEPAD program outlined above. Evidently, this is a far cry from the United States of Africa project envisaged by Libyan leader Col. Muammar Qaddafi, complete with a Pan-African defense force, an African common market, and a common currency.

Problems and Prospects of Regional Cooperation and Integration in Africa

Critics have declared market integration a failure. Few, if any, of the various African integration schemes surveyed in this chapter have achieved their stated goals and objectives. The consensus seems to be that African regional organizations have not succeeded in expanding intra-African trade, increasing Africa's total trade or enhancing the regions's overall economic growth. This section attempts to identify the nature and extent of the problems and difficulties experienced by these schemes with a view to drawing lessons of general validity in terms of the viability and prospects of regional cooperation and integration in Africa. The purpose of this evaluation is to determine the extent to which regionalism (or collective self-reliance) is an appropriate strategy to achieve autonomous, self-reliant and self-sustaining development in Africa.

Table 3-2

Africa's Intra-Regional Trade

	(value in $ millions)				(% of total exports)								
	1970 value % ($mn)		1980 value % ($mn)		1982 value % ($mn)		1984 value % ($mn)		1986 value % ($mn)	
UDEAC	33	3.4	200	4.1	150	3.6	100	3.5	84	3.0
CEAO	73	9.1	296	6.9	374	10.7	306	7.4	300	6.5
ECOWAS	61	2.1	1056	3.9	900	4.1	500	2.5	491	3.2
M R U	—	—	2	0.1	3	0.1	4	0.4	4	0.4
CEPGL	2	0.2	5	0.2	7	0.2	10	0.7	8	0.6

Source: UNCTAD, Handbook of International Trade and Development Statistics, Supplement 1986, table 1.13; Handbook 1988, table 1.13.

Lessons from Experience: Problems of Regional Cooperation and Integration[50]

Among the major problems identified by students of African regional integration arrangements are: the uneven distribution of the benefits and costs of integration; institutional deficiencies; politico-ideological factors; external dependence; and ethno-regional conflict.

The uneven distribution of the benefits and costs of integration

Assuming that one accepts the premises on which market integration is based, and supposing that full economic union is achieved, member states will necessarily differ in size and capabilities. They will thus demonstrate dissimilar abilities to take advantage of specialization, economies of scale, augmentation of factor input, and opportunities to improve market structures. Economic integration, then, tends to yield unequal benefits. Consequently, deliberate policies designed to distribute more evenly, or acceptably, whatever net benefits might accrue to the partner states must be devised. Typically, redistributive mechanisms take the form of financial or fiscal compensatory schemes.

The fairly elaborate compensatory mechanisms set up within CEAO have resulted in a relatively satisfactory redistribution of benefits in favor of the least-developed CEAO member states. UDEAC's single tax scheme and solidarity fund have been less successful, and real or perceived unequal distribution of benefits has been a major bone of contention within the organization. Similarly, the functioning of the ECOWAS Fund, which started operating in 1980, has, from the beginning, been plagued with financial difficulties and institutional malfunctions which have undermined its efficacy. The CEEAC treaty duly takes into account the problem of unequal distribution of the benefits and costs of integration by stressing the need for the rapid development of the less-developed, landlocked and otherwise disadvantaged member states. The Cooperation and Development Fund (provision of technical and financial assistance to promote development), and the Compensation Fund (for revenue losses arising from tariff reduction) primarily focus their activities on such members.

The compensatory mechanisms of the EAC treaty (transfer tax and EADB) were inadequate to persuade the partner states that continued cooperation was worthwhile. Within the PTA, the smaller member states—Comoros, Djibouti, Mauritius, Rwanda, and Burundi—have expressed their serious concern about the tendency for the two subregional economic "giants," Kenya and Zimbabwe, to dominate the organization. Indeed, in spite of the numerous derogations to the treaty provisions granted to them, the Comoros and Djibouti, in particular, appeared to be very reluctant members of the PTA. They frequently tended not to implement the organization's decisions and threatened to withdraw whenever they felt that any particular community decision endangered their national interests. They were not convinced by the arguments of the study team on the Equitable Distribution of Costs and Benefits in the PTA that government revenue losses resulting from implementation of the PTA tariff reduction program were negligible, and that appropriate developmental policies could correct any real or perceived unequal distribution of economic benefits within the organization. Similarly, 28 percent of the 1998 project financing from the Eastern & Southern African Trade & Development Bank was allocated to Kenya, hardly the Community's poorest member state.

No compensatory mechanism can ensure an equitable (and acceptable) distribution of the benefits and costs of integration, if only because different member states' perceptions differ—as the cases of the EAC and the PTA clearly demonstrate. The distribution may lead some members to think that they are "giving" too much, while others think that they are "receiving" too little. Ultimately, the settlement of such an issue calls for a politico-diplomatic, rather than a strictly economic approach, and requires a political decision.

Institutional deficiencies

Institutional proliferation is one of the African regional organizations' major deficiencies. There are more than 200 regional cooperation and integration organizations in Africa; more than 160 are inter-governmental and the rest non-governmental. A UN-ECA report identified 32 inter-governmental organizations in West Africa alone. To a large extent, the activities of these organizations overlap and are not coordinated, resulting in duplication of functions and multiple membership. Thus, seven out of 16 West African countries belong to at least 17 of the 32 West African regional organizations; Niger alone belongs to 25; Mauritania belongs to three economic communities: UEMOA, ECOWAS, and AMU. Similarly, the UEMOA, Mano River Union and Senegambia Confederation member states are also members of ECOWAS; the CEMAC and UDEAC member states are also members of CEEAC; and, in Southern Africa, the SADC and SACU member states also belong to COMESA. Such overlapping membership inevitably leads to problems of incompatible and potentially conflicting objectives, and raises the issue of divided loyalties and primary allegiance; it also stretches to the limit the African countries' already-scarce human, administrative, and financial resources.

Over-centralization and over-politicization of these organizations' decision-making processes constitutes another major institutional problem of most African regional organizations. To the extent that this process requires agreement at the highest political level (heads of state and government), it is bound to create difficulties because of overriding concern with the preservation of sovereignty and the defence of national interests, to the detriment of supra-national and community interests. The experience of European integration suggests that sustained political will is necessary for acceptance of the constraints on national sovereignty that are involved in the harmonization of economic policies and the eventual transfer of political and economic power and authority to supra-national institutions.

Table 3-3
African Regional Organizations:
Typical Institutional Set-up

Organ	Members	Frequency of meetings	Functions
Authority	Heads of State	once a year	Supreme and Government policy-making body
Council of Ministers	Ministers responsible for regional cooperation	twice a year	Policy-coordinating body
Executive Secretariat	Executive Secretary; Experts and Administrators	permanent	Administrative body
Tribunal	ad-hoc judges	permanent	Judicial body
Development Bank/Fund	Manager; Experts and Administrators	permanent	Financing economic and social development

Politico-ideological factors

The variety of political ideologies and related development strategies found in Africa might account for the slow pace of cooperation and integration in the region. Thus, all the ideological tendencies have been represented in the AMU: Islamic fundamentalism (Libya, Mauritania); socialism (Algeria); liberal monarchy (Morocco); and liberal democracy (Tunisia). In ECOWAS, political regimes have ranged from socialist (Guinea, Guinea-Bissau, Benin, Burkina) to capitalist (Côte d'Ivoire, Nigeria, Senegal) via Islamic republic (Mauritania). The same ideological variety is to be found in other African regional organizations such as CEAO, MRU, UDEAC, and CEEAC. Similarly, the Kenya-Tanzania ideological conflict is generally cited as one of the main reasons behind the disintegration of the EAC. Within the PTA, political regimes have ranged from orthodox Marxism-Leninism (Ethiopia, Mozambique, Zimbabwe) to unbridled Capitalism (Kenya, Malawi), with moderate socialism (Uganda, Tanzania) somewhere in-between.

In north Africa, three out of the five member states of the AMU (Algeria, Libya, and Mauritania) are military regimes. In west and central Africa, the proliferation of military coups d'état (28 in 23 years: 1963-1986) has created a context of endemic political instability. In 1999, out of 16 ECOWAS member states, 12 were ruled by army officers, and only four (Cape Verde, Côte d'Ivoire, Mali, and Senegal) by civilian leaders. The situation is very similar in CEEAC and CEMAC, where Cameroon, the CAR and Gabon are the only remaining civilian regimes. This militarization of the north, west, and central African countries introduces additional instability in these subregions to the extent that military regimes are generally insecure (because of the permanent threat of counter-coups), and create a potentially dangerous civilian-military cleavage among the various states in the region.

External dependence

The play of extra-regional power politics is another factor seriously affecting the cohesion of African regional groupings. In particular, France's continuing economic and political dominance over its former colonies is a permanent irritant and a major obstacle to the progress of economic and political integration in west and central Africa.[51] Such institutions as UEMOA and CEMAC, engineered and supported by France, might have to be scrapped before any progress toward integration within ECOWAS and CEEAC can be realized. Similarly, all UEMOA and CEMAC member states (and the Comoros within COMESA) continue to be economically and financially dependent on France because of their common membership in the Franc zone system. The continued existence of this system will prevent any further progress towards monetary integration—a necessary precondition of economic integration—within both ECOWAS and CEEAC.

Equally divisive, from the point of view of the internal cohesion of African regional groupings, is the dual membership of all UEMOA, ECOWAS, ECCAS, and COMESA members. The Lomé IV Convention (1990-2000) links 71 African, Caribbean, and Pacific states (ACPs) with the EU through a 10-year contractual arrangement on trade and aid cooperation. This—as the case of the EU-SA FTA vs. SADC FTA demonstrates—raises a potential conflict of interest, notably in the area of trade liberalization and trade preferences. This problem is further compounded by the fact that intra-regional trade remains very low—around 5-6 per cent of total trade—while trade between Africa and the EEC remains significant—around 48 per cent of total trade. It could thus be argued that the African states' economic and political links with the EU through the Lomé Convention are incompatible with intra-regional cooperation and integration. This is because the Lomé Convention tends to perpetuate and institutionalize neo-colonial, North-South links to the detriment of the collective self-reliant South-South strategy of such organizations as ECOWAS, CEEAC, COMESA and SADC.

Ethno-regional conflict

During the past 10 years, ethno-regional and religious political conflicts have erupted throughout north, west, central, eastern and southern Africa. Such armed conflicts continue to plague Angola, Burundi, the DRC, Ethiopia/Eritrea, Somalia and Sudan. Low-intensity civil warfare persists in Algeria, Senegal, Gambia, Guinea-Bissau, Sierra Leone, Liberia, Chad, Congo, the CAR, Rwanda and South Africa (see chapter 7 in this volume). These conflicts have severely disrupted the normal functioning of such subregional organizations as ECOWAS, CEEAC, COMESA, IGAD and SADC, and they have significantly delayed their trade liberalization programs and tariff reduction schedules. Indeed, each of these organizations has been forced to activate their respective security and defence protocols, and at times to actively engage in subregional peacekeeping—as ECOMOG in Liberia and Sierra Leone and SADC in Lesotho—without a clear mandate and adequate resources and logistical support. As a result, peace and security issues tend to take precedence over economic and social development concerns in practically all African regional organizations, at least for the time being.

Table 3-4

Phased Time-table of Trade Liberalization in Selected African Regional Organizations

Organization	Entry into force of Treaty	Free Trade Area (1)	Customs Union (2)	Common Market (3)	Economic Commu- nity (4)
C E A O	January 1974	1980	1986	**	
M R U	October 1973	1981 (1977)	**		
ECOWAS	June 1975	1989	1992	*	**
U D E A C	January 1966	*	*	**	
E C C A S	October 1983	1992	1996	2000	
P T A	September 1983	2000 (1992)	*	*	**
SADC	August 1992	2012	*	*	**

(1)	Complete elimination of tariff and non-tariff barriers;
(2)	Common external tariff against third countries;
(3)	Free movement of factors of production/commodities;
(4)	Harmonization of national economic policies.

*	Intermediary stage of integration (date unspecified);
**	Ultimate goal of integration (date unspecified).

The Prospects for Regional Cooperation and Integration in Africa

What type of regional cooperation and integration?

What type of regional cooperation and integration scheme is best suited to the present African conditions? Should it be market-oriented or production-oriented? Should it be based on a comprehensive, continental approach or on a gradual, functional approach? Only policy-oriented research can help gather the information to answer these kinds of questions.

African market integration experiments have generally been unsuccessful. Critics argue that the model, taken from the experience of highly industrialized European countries that have a high level of trade among themselves, is not relevant to Africa, where trade among countries and the level of industrialization are low. These critics recommend abandoning market integration and adoption of a new approach that emphasizes broadening the regional production base. This would give priority to regional investment in heavy industries and transport and communication infrastructure. In the absence of market signals, the production approach—implying a state-led development of core industries such as steel, cement, and chemicals—could force the pace of regional integration. Further research could assess the validity of this argument, and, if it seems justified in the case of specific basic industries, the kinds of institutional changes that might contribute to its success.

Other authors are of the opinion that Africa is particularly ill-suited for regional integration: "In Africa, the low levels of development and the limited possibilities for profitable intra-regional exchange simply do not provide the basis for integration at the present time... The requisites for integration do not presently exist but must be created."[52] Such neo-functionalist authors caution against excessive politicization of issues in African regional organizations, and advocate cooperation in non-controversial—social, economic, scientific, and technical—areas. They call for concentration on specific programs and projects in the area of postal, transport, communication and telecommunication infrastructure, as well as in the service sector, namely training and research, control of foreign investment, and transfer, adaptation and development of technology.[53] Such a "realistic" and "pragmatic" approach is designed to prevent African leaders from "chasing inappropriate and largely illusory goals," that is from pursuing the "myth of African unity" in search of "the promised land of some kind of pan-African political kingdom or common market."[54] Again, research could help identify the policy measures and institutional changes which might initiate and sustain a regional integration dynamic.

A strategy for future regional cooperation and integration

The essence of the neo-functionalist approach is that an incremental, step-by-step approach based on common economic interests offers the best prospects for integration. Such an incremental approach should not involve further proliferation of organizations, but bilateral or multilateral agreements between governments that receive benefits from a mutual liberalization of product and factor markets. Phased programs addressing critical barriers to regional integration are essential. Each phase would include advances in harmonizing policy and maintaining and improving infrastructure. As an urgent first step, regional organizations need to be rationalized. They should be reformed and consolidated into lean and efficient institutions, with a clear mandate and capacity for making decisions. These institutions (AMU, ECOWAS, CEEAC, COMESA and SADC) could then spearhead the creation of a physical, technical, and legal infrastructure that would support regional exchange in goods, services, labor, and capital. Initiation of appropriate institutional measures to attain these goals requires in-depth research as to the constraints and resources of existing institutional arrangements.

It is generally agreed that one function which African governments must perform if economic integration is to progress is to create what might be called an enabling environment. The removal of tariff barriers is not sufficient to create an effective enabling environment in African regional schemes. Other man-made barriers to intraregional trade must also be reduced and eventually eliminated. These include: quantitative restrictions on imports customs and other administrative regulations; transport, communications and telecommunications bottlenecks; and foreign exchange controls. Beyond actions on policy, infrastructure, and institutions lies a more fundamental need: to mobilize public opinion and popular support to promote the concept that cooperation within Africa is likely to enhance the progress of all African societies. Ultimately, regional integration should benefit the broad masses of the African people. Research should produce the necessary background information to create a more appropriate enabling environment.

While disagreement on the strategy and ultimate goal of African regional unity persists, African scholars and policy-makers generally agree that some minimal degree of regional cooperation and integration must be achieved. In their view, such a strategy of collective self-reliance should contribute to the promotion of the socioeconomic development and to the reduction of the dependency of the African countries on the West. The question is whether the existing African regional organizations are likely to contribute to the achievement of this objective. There is no doubt that the exclusively francophone African organizations (such as WAEMU, CEMAC, and the Franc zone system) are one of the means by which France maintains its political, economic, military, and cultural dominance over its former African colonies. Such neo-colonial organizations constitute major obstacles on the way to further regional integration and should be dismantled in order to pave the way for genuine regional and continental African unity.

If this is the case, do such organizations as AMU, ECOWAS, CEEAC, COMESA and SADC foreshadow the wave of the future?

The fact that these institutions have succeeded in transcending the traditional historical and linguistic barriers is already a positive step in the right direction. However, if these organizations are to constitute the building-blocks on which the future African Common Market and African Economic Community are to be erected, they will have to demonstrate more dynamism and show greater tangible achievements. Research should enable policy-makers to determine the possibilities, as well as the obstacles, to making the necessary institutional changes.

Finally, one must assess the potential and chances of success of the African Union, formally adopted in July 2001 and which is to replace the OAU by May 2002. Skeptics would argue that 53 African states will be hard pressed to achieve in ten months what it took no less than 45 years for the six—now 15, soon to be 28—European Union member states to realize. It is our deep conviction that only a bold, ambitious and accelerated Pan-African project of comprehensive political and economic integration and institution-building , as originally envisaged in the early 1960s by Cheikh Anta Diop and Kwame Nkrumah—and as recently advocated by Edem Kodjo and Muammar Qaddafi—in the form of the United States of Africa, could extricate Africa from its present predicament.

Endnotes

1. *L'État du monde 2000: Annuaire Économique géopolitique mondial* (Paris: La Découverte & Syros, 1999), various tables, pp. 78-83; The World Bank, *Annual Report 1999* [Africa: regional context] (Washington, DC: The World Bank, 1999); African Development Bank, *African Development Report 2000* (New York: Oxford university Press, 2000), pp. 1-44; UNCTAD, *Economic Development in Africa: Performance, Prospects and Policy Issues* (New York & Geneva: United Nations, 2001), pp. 3-7, 26-36.

2. Organization of African Unity, *Africa's Priority Programme for*

Economic Recovery 1986-1990 (Addis Ababa: OAU, 1985), sect. 101, p. 44.

3. United Nations, *United Nations Programme of Action for Africa's Recovery and Development* (New York: United Nations, 1986).

4. OAU, *Lagos Plan of Action for the Economic Development of Africa, 1980-2000* (Addis Ababa: OAU, 1981), p. 6; OAU, *Final Act of Lagos* (Addis Ababa: OAU, 1980), p. 128.

5. Jacob Viner, *The Customs Union Issue* (New York: Carnegie Endowment for International Peace, 1950).

6. Arthur Hazlewood, *Economic Integration: The East African Experience* (London: Heinemann, 1975), p. 11.

7. Bela Balassa, *The Theory of Economic Integration* (New York: George Allen & Unwin, 1962), p. 2.

8. ONU-CEA (Commission Économique pour l'Afrique), *Propositions visant a renforcer l'Integration Économique en Afrique de l'Ouest* (Addis Abéba: CEA, 1983), pp. 22-24.

9. UNDP/World Bank, *African Economic and Financial Data* (Washington, DC: The World Bank, 1989), table 1.1.

10. See in particular African Development Bank/ADB, *African Development Report 2000: Regional Integration in Africa* (New York: Oxford University Press, 2000), pp. 68-78, 147-9.

11. Chérif Ouazani, "Quand l'UMA s'éveillera," *Jeune Afrique* (22-28 janvier 2002), pp. 11-12.

12. ONU-CEA, *op. cit.*, p. 28.

13. United Nations Conference on Trade and Development/UNCTAD, *Handbook of International Trade and Development Statistics* (Geneva: UNCTAD) , various supplements.

14. World Bank, *Sub-Saharan Africa: From Crisis to Sustainable Growth. A Long-Term Perspective Study* (Washington, DC: The World Bank, 1989), p. 149.

15. ONU-CEA, *op.cit.*, 28-30; Peter Robson, *Integration, Development and Equity: Economic Integration in West Africa* (London: George Allen & Unwin, 1983), pp. 41-2.

16. UEMOA, *Rapport d'Activités de la Commission de l'UEMOA Présenté à la 6ème réunion de la Conférence des Chefs d'État et de Gouvernement de l'UEMOA* (Dakar, 19 décembre 2001), p. 10
17. UEMOA, *Rapport d'Activités*, p. 10.
18. UEMOA, *Rapport d'Activités*, p. 10.
19. ADB, African *Development Report 2000*, pp. 159-161.
20. "ECOWAS Leaders continue meeting in Lomé," *Panafrican News Agency* (10 December 1999).
21. See in particular Olatunde B.J. Ojo, "Integration in ECOWAS: Successes and Difficulties," in Daniel C. Bach (ed.), *Regionalisation in Africa: Integration & Disintegration* (Bloomington: Indiana University Press, 1999), pp. 119-121; and ADB, *African Development Report 2000*, pp. 161-2.
22. ECOWAS Leaders tackle security at the expense of economy," *Panafrican News Agency* (9 December 1999); "ECOWAS Leaders continue meeting in Lomé," *Panafrican News Agency* (10 December 1999); and "2004 set as target for single ECOWAS zone," *Panafrican News Agency* (11 December 1999).
23. UNCTAD, *op. cit.*
24. On the ECOWAS-WAEMU dispute, see O.B.J. Ojo, "Integration in ECOWAS," in *op. cit.*, p. 122.
25. See Abass Bundu, "ECOWAS and the Future of Regional Integration in West Africa," in Réal Lavergne (ed.), *Regional Integration and Cooperation in West Africa: A Multidimensional Perspective* (Trenton: Africa World Press, 1997), pp. 32-36; see also O.B.J. Ojo, "Integration in ECOWAS," in *op. cit.*, pp. 123-4.
26. "ECOWAS Leaders continue meeting in Lomé" and "2004 set as target for single ECOWAS zone, " *Panafrican News Agency* (10 & 11 December 1999).
27. "Konaré determined to promote integration ideal," *Panafrican News Agency* (11 December 1999).
28. UNCTAD, *op. cit.*
29. Abdul Aziz Jalloh, "Regional Integration in Africa: Lessons from the Past and Prospects for the Future," *Africa Development*, vol

1, no 2 (September 1976), pp. 44-57; Lynn K. Mytelka, "Competition, conflict and decline in the UDEAC," in Domenico Mazzeo (ed.), *African Regional Organizations* (Cambridge: Cambridge University Press, 1984), pp. 139-146; Wilfred A. Ndongko, "The Future of the Central African Customs and Economic Union/UDEAC." in R.I. Onwuka & A. Sesay, *The Future of Regionalism in Africa* (London: Macmillan, 1985), pp. 96-109.

30. Roland Pourtier, "The Renovation of UDEAC: Sense and Nonsense in Central African Integration," in Daniel C. Bach (ed.), *Regionalisation in Africa: Integration & Disintegration* (Bloomington: Indiana University Press, 1999), pp. 133-4; ADB, *African Development Report 2000*, pp. 140-146.

31. R. Pourtier, "The Renovation of UDEAC," in D.C. Bach (ed.), *op. cit.*, pp. 134-5.

32. CEMAC, *Sixième session ordinaire du Conseil des Ministres de la Communauté Économique et monétaire de l'Afrique centrale*, Communiqué final (Douala, 3 août 2001), pp. 1-3.

33. Marc-Louis Ropivia, "Failing Institutions and Shattered Space: What Regional Integration in Central Africa?" in Daniel C. Bach (ed.), *op. cit.*, p. 126.

34. *Ibidem*, pp. 126-7.

35. R. Pourtier, "The Renovation of UDEAC," in D.C. Bach (ed.), *op. cit.*, pp. 135, 136.

36. Guy Martin, "The Franc Zone, Underdevelopment and Dependency in Francophone Africa," *Third World Quarterly*, vol 8, no 1 (January 1986), pp, 205-235; G. Martin, "Zone franc, sous-développement et dépendance en Afrique noire francophone," *Africa Development* vol. 12, ,no.1 (1987), pp. 55-100; Olivier Vallée, *Le Prix de l'Argent CFA: Heurs et Malheurs de la Zone franc* (Paris: Karthala, 1989).

37. Daniel C. Bach, "Revisiting a Paradigm," in D.C. Bach (ed.), *Regionalisation in Africa: Integration and Disintegration* (Bloomington: Indiana University Press, 1999), p. 7.

38. Michel Lelart, "The Franc Zone and European Monetary Integration," in Daniel C. Bach (ed.), *op. cit.*, pp. 139-149; see also the excellent study on the subject by Philippe Hugon, *La zone franc a l'heure de l'euro* (Paris: Karthala, 1999).

39. Arthur Hazlewood, "The End of the East African Community: What are the Lessons for Regional Integration Schemes?" in Ralph I. Onwuka and Amadu Sesay (eds.), *The Future of Regionalism in Africa* (London: Macmillan, 1985), p. 173.

40. Hazlewood, in *op. cit.*, p, 174.

41. Hazlewood in *op.cit.*, pp. 172-189; D. Mazzeo in C.P. Potholm and R.A. Fredland (eds.), *Integration and Disintegration in East Africa* (Lanham: University Press of America, 1980), pp. 81-122; D. Mazzeo, *op. cit*, pp. 150-170; John Ravenhill, "Regional Integration and Development in Africa: Lessons from the East African Community," *Journal of Commonwealth and Comparative Politics*, vol 27, no 3 (November 1979), pp. 227-246; J. Ravenhill in Potholm & Fredland (eds.), *op. cit.*, pp.37-61; ADB, *African Development Report 2000*, pp. 157-8.

42. Bax D. Nomvete, *A Brief to the Sixth Meeting of the PTA Authority on Problem-Areas that are Delaying the Implementation Activities of the PTA* [PTA/AUTH/VI/3/November 1987], 8-10; see also Guy Martin, "The PTA: Achievements, Problems and Prospects," in Peter Anyang' Nyong'o (ed.), *Regional Integration in Africa: Unfinished Agenda* (Nairobi: Academy Science Publishers, 1990), pp. 157-179.

43. ADB, *African Development Report 2000*, pp. 154-7.

44. Walter Tapfumanyei, "Regional security cooperation in southern Africa: a view from Zimbabwe," *Global Dialogue* vol. 4, no. 2 (August 1999), pp. 23-26, 35.

45. Kaire Mbuende, *Separating Fact from Fiction* (Gaborone: SADC Secretariat, 1999), pp.2-6; "Foreword" by President Sam Nujoma, Chairman of SADC (January 2001), and "The SADC Free Trade Area, " available at <http://sadcreview.com/>

46. Philippe Bordes, "Thabo Mbeki reprend en main la SADC,"

Jeune Afrique (19 octobre-1er novembre 1999), pp. 49-50.

47. Marina Mayer, "The EU-South Africa trade deal: implications for southern Africa," *Global Dialogue* vol. 4, no. 2 (August 1999), pp. 10-13, 34; see also ADB, *African Development Report 2000*, pp. 152-4.

48. See "Africa's plan to save itself," *The Economist* (July 7, 2001), p. 44; note that MAP is variously referred to as the Millenium Partnership for the African Recovery, the Millenium Partnership for the Revival of Africa, or the African Renaissance Plan.

49. Brigitte Breuillac, "Le président sénégalais propose un plan de développement pour l'Afrique," *Le Monde* (20 juin 2001).

50. This section draws on two of the author's previous studies, namely: Guy Martin, *African Regional Integration: Lessons from the West and Central African Experiences* (Lagos: Nigerian Institute of International Affairs [Lecture Series no. 50], 1989); and G. Martin, "African Regional Cooperation and Integration: Achievements, Problems and Prospects," in Ann Seidman & Frederick Anang (eds.), *21st Century Africa: Towards a New Vision of Self-Sustainable Development* (Atlanta & Trenton: African Studies Association Press/Africa World Press, 1992), pp. 88-93.

51. Guy Martin, "France and Africa," in Robert Aldrich and John Connell (eds.), *France in World Politics* (London: Routledge, 1989), pp. 101-113.

52. Ravenhill, in Onwuka & Sesay (eds.), *op. cit*, p. 210.

53. Mazzeo, *African Regional Organizations*, p. 237 .

54. John Ravenhill, "Collective Self-Reliance or Collective Self-Delusion: Is the Lagos Plan a Viable Alternative?" in John Ravenhill (ed.), *Africa in Economic Crisis* (London: Macmillan, 1986), p. 217; Domenico Mazzeo, "Conclusion: problems and prospects of intra-African cooperation," in D. Mazzeo (ed.), *African Regional Organizations*, p.239.

Chapter 7

Conflict and Conflict Resolution in Africa

O ver the last 40 years, Africa has been (and continues to be) one of the most conflict-ridden regions of the world, which has resulted in untold human suffering. Thus, it has been estimated that between 1955 and 1995 some 10 million people died as a result of violent conflict in Africa. In Central Africa and the Great Lakes region alone, the death toll is over six million, including two million in Sudan, about one million in the Rwanda genocide of 1994, 3 million in the Democratic Republic of Congo/DRC (1998-2001), and 200,000 in Burundi. Out of 48 recorded genocides in the world, 20 occurred in Africa. Out of 66 minorities at threat world-wide, 27—representing 37 percent of world population—are in Africa. Africa is responsible for about a third of the world's 22 million refugees. Ongoing conflicts in more than 15 countries on the continent forced at least two million people to seek asylum across borders in 1999. While African conflicts are typically internal rather than inter-state, many of these conflicts have taken (and continue to take) an increasingly subregional character, particularly in the Greater Horn, the Great Lakes region, and southern Africa. Furthermore,

African conflicts are becoming increasingly "civilianized": 90 percent of the victims of African conflicts are innocent civilians, mostly women and children.[1] As of January 2002, some form of (latent or open) conflict persists in over half of the African countries (30 out of 54): Algeria, Angola, Burundi, Central African Republic, Cameroon, Chad, Comoros, Congo-Brazzaville, Côte d'Ivoire, Democratic Republic of Congo/DRC, Djibouti, Equatorial Guinea, Egypt, Ethiopia, Eritrea, Guinea, Guinea-Bissau, Kenya, Liberia, Niger, Nigeria, Rwanda, Senegal, Sierra Leone, Sudan, Somalia, South Africa, Tanzania, Western Sahara and Uganda.

Luc Reychler has identified eight types of costs entailed by African conflicts. They are worth enumerating:

1. humanitarian cost: number of deaths, wounded, refugees, internally displaced persons and famine;
2. political cost: state collapse, anarchy, subversion of the democratic process, political corruption and criminalization of power;
3. economic cost: loss of revenues from trade and tourism, destruction of economic, transport and educational infrastructure, diversion of resources away from development;
4. ecological cost: loss of arable land, soil erosion, deforestation and desertification;
5. social cost: breakdown of family structures, female victims of sexual violence, war orphans;
6. cultural cost: breakdown of traditional socio-cultural values, institutions and life-styles;
7. psychological cost: psychological disorders, post-traumatic syndromes, fear and mutual hostility between groups in conflict;
8. spiritual cost: loss of values related to the sanctity of life, development of a culture of violence.[2]

In view of this appalling situation, a number of peace-making, peace-keeping and peace-building measures and policies should be adopted to mitigate, resolve and prevent violent conflict in Africa. After a brief overview of the way in which African conflicts should be analysed, this chapter will examine the impact of recent changes in the external environment on these conflicts and review new conflict management approaches. It concludes that subregional and federal frameworks are best suited for the resolution of conflict in Africa.

In Africa, as elsewhere in the world, conflicts are part and parcel of the dynamics of society. There is a perennial struggle among individuals, families, clans, ethnic groups and nations for control over scarce natural, economic and political resources. While conflicts are a constant in African history, African conflicts should be viewed within their specific historical context. According to this dynamic perspective, what changes is the nature and intensity of conflict as a function of internal societal factors (such as ethnicity, class and religion) and of changes in the (subregional, regional and international) environment, with various degrees and levels of influence on the internal situation. In other words, the nature and intensity of African conflicts is a result of a complex, dialectical relationship between internal societal factors and the structure of the external environment.

IMPACT OF RECENT CHANGES IN THE EXTERNAL ENVIRONMENT ON AFRICAN CONFLICTS

The end of the Cold War signalled the end of ideologically based and motivated conflicts between capitalism and socialism and ushered in a new, cooperative mood between East and West for the management and resolution of African conflicts. Thus, progress toward a peaceful transition to democratic governance was achieved in Namibia, Eritrea, Ethiopia, Mozambique and South Africa. At the same time, subregional, ethnic and religious conflicts have flared up not only in southern Africa, but also in Burundi, the two Congos, Eritrea/

Ethiopia, Liberia, Sierra Leone, Rwanda, Sudan and Somalia. Under the dual influence of the policy of "benign neglect" now pursued by the major world powers and of increased arms transfers to Africa, there has been, over the last ten years, an increase in the number and intensity of African conflicts. Old conflicts and long simmering disputes (as in. Liberia, Somalia and Sudan) came to the fore and ran their full course. At the same time, the democratization processes initiated in Africa in the early nineties have pitted the ruling autocrats against democratic movements arising from an increasingly vibrant civil society, resulting in a spiral of domestic violence. Lately, a number of African dictators have been able to subvert and manipulate the democratic process to their advantage, thus managing to stay in power or even to be reelected presidents (for example, Kérékou in Benin, Eyadéma in Togo, Bongo in Gabon, Moi in Kenya and Ratsiraka in Madagascar). In 1996 there were a spate of military coup d'états (Burundi, Niger, and Sierra Leone), a strange throw back to a frequent occurence in the late sixties. The years 1997 to 1999 witnessed the forcible removal from office of the incumbent presidents and seizure of power by military means of new leaders in Congo (Denis Sassou-Nguesso), DRC (Laurent-Désiré Kabila), and Sierra Leone (Ahmad Tejan Kabbah). In Niger, president Ibrahim Baré Maïnassara was killed in an attempted coup in April 1999. All this inevitably increases the potential for civil strife.

NEW CONFLICT MANAGEMENT APPROACHES

At the international level, sacrosanct principles such as sovereignty, territorial integrity, and the sanctity of existing borders are being challenged while new ones, such as international humanitarian intervention, are emerging. New conflict management approaches have involved the intervention of individuals, states, or international organizations (both governmental and non-governmental) as mediators or facilitators. From his base at the Carter Center in Atlanta, former president Jimmy Carter has acted in that capacity on several occasions, notably in Ethiopia, Liberia, and (more recently) in the Great Lakes region and the Greater Horn (Burundi, Rwanda and Sudan). After 10 years of efforts, Jimmy Carter coaxed into existence on December 8, 1999 an 11-point peace agreement between presidents Yoweri Museveni of Uganda, and Omar Hassan Bashir of Sudan who, *inter alia*, agree to reestablish diplomatic ties and desist from aiding groups hostile to the other.[3] So has ex-South African president Nelson Mandela acted as mediator in the final phase of the DRC conflict and in Burundi. Based on its experience in Namibia, the United Nations has now developed a multi-sectoral approach to assist in transition toward democratic governance, which involve humanitarian assistance, refugee repatriation, election monitoring, integration of the military in civil society, as well as policing and even administrative functions (as in Western Sahara, Angola and Mozambique).

Subregional Peace-making Initiatives

At the subregional level, regional hegemons have often acted as facilitators in some conflict management and resolution exercises (for example Nigeria and Côte d'Ivoire in Liberia; Kenya and Uganda in Rwanda and Burundi; South Africa in Lesotho). African subregional organizations initially created as economic integration groupings have increasingly been entrusted with security and peace-making functions. The three most notable examples of such a functional shift are the ECOWAS Monitoring Group (ECOMOG) involvement in the Liberian and Sierra Leone conflicts, the Inter-Governmental Authority on Development (IGAD) involvement in the Somali and southern Sudanese conflicts, and the SADC peacekeeping initiatives in Lesotho (see chapter 6 in this volume).

Since 1990, the ECOWAS states have made a substantial contribution to restoring peace in Liberia. Troops have been provided (mostly by Nigeria and Ghana) and innumerable mediation sessions have been assembled in an effort to find a formula for peace among Liberia's several warring factions. Since the initial period of success, ECOMOG has experienced many obstacles to achieving its mandate, including internal dissent among contributing states and military setbacks on the ground. Peacemaking efforts were repeatedly stalled, and the civil war remained stalemated until the general elections of July 1997, which brought Charles Taylor to power through the ballot box rather than through the barrel of a gun.

On February 12, 1998, an ECOMOG contingent of 15,000 composed exclusively of Nigerian troops toppled the military junta of Major Johnny Paul Koroma and reinstated Ahmad Tejan Kabbah as president of Sierra Leone. Over eight years, nearly the entire population of Sierra Leone—4.4 million people—had been uprooted, mutilated, raped, or abducted. At least 50,000 people were killed, and an estimated 30,000 civilians (including children) had limbs cut off. On July 7, 1999, a peace agreement was signed in Lomé (Togo) between the government of President Ahmad Tejan Kabbah and the two main rebel leaders, Foday Sankoh (Revolutionary United Front/RUF) and Johnny Paul Koroma (Armed Forces Revolutionary Council). Under this agreement, Sankoh and Kabbah agreed to form a power-sharing government and to quickly set up a Truth and Reconciliation Commission, a Human Rights Commission, and a Commission for the Consolidation of Peace. The peace accord also provides for an amnesty. ECOMOG, which was instrumental in bringing about this accord, will continue to be responsible for maintaining security in Sierra Leone; it is also responsible for the implementation of the peace agreement and the disarmament and demobilization of combatants. On October 22, 1999, the U.N. Security Council authorized a 6,000-member UN peacekeeping force—including 260 military observers—for Sierra Leone for an initial period of six months. The mandate of this force—known as UNAMIL—is to assist in the disarmament and demobilization, to monitor adherence to the cease-fire, and to encourage the parties to create confidence-building measures. Implementation of the accord has been slow, however. Rebel leaders continue to control strategic regions, notably the gold and diamond-producing areas. And in view of the forthcoming elections, the warlords are engaged in a bitter power-struggle over control of the government in Freetown. On October 3, 1999, Sankoh and Koroma arrived in the country's capital city and told their followers to disarm; this led observers to express a guarded optimism. UNAMIL—composed of 3,000 Nigerian troops from ECOMOG, plus another 3,000 troops from Kenya, India and other countries—will be deployed in the countryside, over which the government had no control for the last eight years, while the remainder of the ECOMOG contingent will remain in Freetown.

In spite of these signs of hope, however, the implementation of the Lomé peace agreement remains extremely problematic. The multipartite ceasefire and demobilization committees are not yet operational. The four existing demobilization centers are insufficient, and widespread insecurity has prevented opening six additional ones. Out of an estimated 45,000 combatants, only 2,000 have been disarmed so far (at a cost of $300 per soldier surrendering his weapon). Furthermore, it is not clear whether UNAMIL troops will be able to deploy in coming weeks to the country's northern and eastern provinces and begin to move into diamond-mining areas controlled by RUF rebels. And while the Lomé accords have been built around rebel leaders Sankoh and Koroma, the extent to which these leaders still effectively control their troops is in doubt. Such a volatile context has led a UN-HCR representative to characterize this period as "an extremely dangerous one, a void in which anything can happen."[4]

The ECOWAS meeting of ministers of Yamoussoukro in March 1998 agreed to treat ECOMOG as the embryo of a future West African peacekeeping force. The 22nd ECOWAS summit held in Lomé in December 1999 decided to set-up a Mediation and Security Council as a key regional instrument for conflict prevention, management, resolution, peacekeeping, and security under the revised Treaty of the Community. The Council is made up of 9 countries: five Francophone (including Togo and Mali) and four Anglophone.

The summit also adopted a draft protocol on conflict prevention, management, resolution, peacekeeping, and security. This provides for extensive conflict prevention and early warning mechanisms, and the development of democratic institutions with the subregional peacekeeping force, ECOMOG, designated as a "vehicle of last resort". The new protocol is to spell out the composition, mandate, chain of command, appointment, and functions of ECOMOG, which was adopted in 1998 as the standing force for the subregion. As an extension of this structure, the community's member states are expected to have standby units that could be deployed under the ECOMOG command.[5] In early December 1999, the U.S. allocated $6 million to the force. Thus, in spite of its initial failures and set-backs, the ECOMOG experience remains an important example of both the constraints and opportunities of regional peacekeeping and peacemaking initiatives in Africa.

The main subregional organization of the Greater Horn of Africa, the Inter-Governmental Authority against Drought and for Development (IGADD) was renamed Inter-Governmental Authority on Development (IGAD), the member states being Sudan, Somalia, Ethiopia, Eritrea, Djibouti, Kenya, and Uganda. IGAD's mission is to achieve regional cooperation and economic integration through the promotion of food security, sustainable environmental management, peace and security, intra-regional trade, and development of improved communications infrastructure. The mandate of IGAD is to coordinate the efforts of member states in the priority areas of economic cooperation, political and humanitarian affairs, and food security and environment protection. Article 18.A of the agreement establishing IGAD stipulates that "member countries shall act collectively to preserve peace, security and stability, which are essential prerequisites for economic development and social progress". The aim of IGAD's Division of Political and Humanitarian Affairs is to enhance the capacity of member states in the field of conflict prevention, management and resolution through dialogue, to facilitate the evacuation of people from disaster or conflict areas through peace corridors, and to assist in rehabilitating the areas that have been affected. Two medium-term projects are being pursued: capacity-building in areas of conflict prevention; and alleviation and mitigation of humanitarian crises. IGAD has also elaborated a five-year program in conflict prevention, management, and resolution.

In this regard, IGAD heads of state and government have made concerted efforts to resolve internal conflicts where they exist. Ethiopia was mandated to lead and coordinate the peace process for Somalia, and IGAD continues to lobby with partners to provide humanitarian assistance to that country. The 6th IGAD Summit (Nairobi, July 1997) formed a Peace Committee chaired by Kenya and composed of Eritrea, Ethiopia, and Uganda, to mediate in the Sudan conflict. Since then, the parties in conflict have accepted the 1994 Declaration of Principles as the basis for negotiations, and several ministerial meetings have been held and shuttle diplomacy missions undertaken as part of the peace process. IGAD also hosted and facilitated negotiating sessions between the Sudanese government in Khartoum and the rebel forces from southern Sudan to try to end the country's devastating civil war. The Ethiopia-Eritrea conflict—the first IGAD interstate conflict—posed new challenges for the Authority. The IGAD chairman (the president of Djibouti) attempted mediation at the beginning of the conflict and is also a participant in the OAU peace initiative. Other heads of state and government have held bilateral mediation meetings with both Eritrea and Ethiopia. These initiatives eventually led to a peace agreement.[6]

A new regional mediator has recently emerged: Djibouti President Ismaïl Omar Guelleh. Under the auspices of IGAD, Guelleh was able to broker a peace accord for Somalia and to reconcile two sworn Sudanese enemies: President Omar Hasan Ahmad al-Bashir and former prime minister Sayed Sadiq el-Mahdi. The Somalia peace plan proposed by Guelleh at the Djibouti IGAD summit in November 1999 includes the following elements: a general agreement to re-empower civil society; preservation of the country's territorial integrity; voluntary disarmament of the militias; national reconciliation; formal recognition of actual (Somaliland, Puntland) and potential new subregional states; a national referendum over new governmental structures; setting up (with UN assistance) of a provisional police force pending the creation of the new state. Al-Bashir and el-Mahdi concluded, on November 26, 1999 an "agreement for a global political solution in Sudan", including a cease-fire; a four-year transition period; a referendum over autonomy in southern Sudan; democracy; and respect for human rights.[7]

Institutionally, IGAD might seem ill-suited to serve as mediator, but considerable attention and effort have been paid to bolstering the organization's capability. IGAD is seen as the best vehicle to break the Sudanese impasse because the mediating parties—neighbouring states led by Kenya—have a vested interest in regional stability. Similarly, IGAD constituted the ideal framework for a negotiated settlement of the Ethiopian-Eritrean conflict.

The strong interest of neighborly mediators in achieving stability was also behind the third recent example of peacemaking by subregional organizations, when, in December 1998, members of SADC launched a campaign to reverse the decision by Lesotho's monarch and military to oust the elected parliament. South African president Nelson Mandela and Zimbabwean leader Robert Mugabe led campaigns to calm the situation in Lesotho and to keep a nascent democratization process there on track. Similarly, southern African regional leaders were extensively involved in the UN/OAU-mediated talks in Lusaka (Zambia) to broker a new peace in Angola. These talks, which were successful, produced a detailed settlement in late 1994 along with a commitment by regional actors—especially South Africa—to participate in a newly invigorated two-year UN peacekeeping operation in Angola. However, by early 1998, this peace process, wrecked by mutual mistrust, reached a dead end, and hostilities resumed. By mid-1999, the war raged on, and both parties were busily engaged in an arms race.

Rebels backed by president Laurent-Désiré Kabila's former allies, Rwanda and Uganda, took up arms in the Democratic Republic of the Congo (DRC) in August 1998, vowing to topple him. Other countries (Angola, Namibia, Zimbabwe) were drawn into the conflict and peace talks failed. In July 1999, African defence and foreign ministers meeting in Lusaka (Zambia) adopted a draft cease-fire document, which was formally signed on August 31, 1999. The main elements of this agreement are the following: the cessation of hostilities from July 10, 1999; the UN Security Council will be asked to send a peacekeeping force to the Congo; the parties to the conflict will set up a Joint Military Commission (JMC, comprising senior military commanders) which, together with a UN/OAU observer group, will be responsible for carrying out peacekeeping operations until the deployment of the UN peacekeeping force; the disarmament of all renegade forces in the region; a special task force under the JMC will track down mass killers and human rights abusers and bring them to justice; the final withdrawal of all foreign forces shall be carried out within nine months ; once the agreement is signed, the government of the DRC and all armed (Congolese Rally for Democracy/RCD), Congo Liberation Movement/MLC) and unarmed opposition groups will enter into open dialogue. These negotiations will be held under the aegis of a neutral facilitator.

On December 15, 1999, OAU Secretary General Salim Ahmed Salim announced in Addis Ababa that the parties to the conflict agreed that former Botswana president Ketumile Masire should mediate political reform negotiations aimed at ending the civil war in the country. On December 1st, 1999, the UN Security Council agreed to set up a 20,000 person UN peacekeeping force for the Congo. An advance party (from Algeria, Malawi and Senegal) has already taken position in Goma and Kisangani, in anticipation of the arrival of 500 military observers. In view of the numerous cease-fire violations (at least 50 according to MLC leader Jean-Pierre Bemba) and of the fact that none of the parties welcome it, the United Nations Observer Mission in the Democratic Republic of Congo (UNOMC) will have a daunting task. The US pledged to finance UNOMC to the tune of $1 million but failed to advocate a large-scale UN operation in Congo.[8]

The SADC Organ on Politics, Defence and Security was established in June 1996 at the Gaborone summit as the successor to the Front Line States, with responsibility for regional security cooperation. The organ spells out the various political and security functions of the organization, notably preventive diplomacy, conflict resolution, peacekeeping, and collective security. As one of the organ's main institutions, the Inter-State Defense and Security Committee adopted a number of important regional policy decisions at its 19th ordinary session held in Lusaka (Zambia) in 1997, notably on peacekeeping training (through a regional Peacekeeping Training Center, created in 1997), peacekeeping doctrine, and standard operating procedures for peacekeeping operations (establishment of a peacekeeping brigade, initiated in 1998).[9] The reinsertion of South Africa in the post-apartheid subregional system has resulted in severe tensions within SADC. First, a political tug-of-war between South Africa and Zimbabwe over control of the SADC organ stretched it almost to the breaking point. Serious disagreements over SADC's military intervention in Lesotho (December 1998) and in the DRC further aggravated the tensions. Thus, while the Maputo summit (August 1999) maintained Zimbabwean president Robert Mugabe as chairman of the organ for another six months, its management is under review, and a proposed reform aims at severely curtailing the organ's mandate, and its chairman's powers.[10]

Finally, mention should be made of two central African security initiatives. The first is the *Mission interafricaine de stabilisation à Bangui* (MISAB), an exclusively Francophone inter-African peacekeeping force deployed in the Central African Republic (CAR) in February 1997 composed of 700 African and 1,500 French troops. When MISAB's mandate expired at the end of March 1998, it was replaced by the United Nations Mission in the Central African Republic (MINURCA). The 1,400-men strong MINURCA was instrumental in ensuring peaceful, free, and fair presidential elections in the CAR in September 1999.

In central Africa, a treaty creating an Economic community of central African states *(Communauté Économique des États de l'Afrique centrale/*CEEAC) was adopted in October 1983 as an instrument for regional economic integration. However, endemic instability, insecurity and civil war in Burundi, the CAR, Congo, Rwanda, and the DRC have pushed peace and security issues to the top of the Community's agenda. Thus, in September 1993, a Permanent Consultative Committee on Issues of Security in Central Africa meeting under the aegis of the Community in Libreville (Gabon); called for the creation of specialized units trained for crisis management and the adoption of a non aggression pact. Unfortunately, these recommendations have yet to be implemented.[11]

These five experiences in subregional peacemaking demonstrate the promise of subregional organizations as peace makers, despite their principal role in fostering economic cooperation, integration and development. Because of an overriding interest in their neighbourhood's stability and their actual or potential leverage with disputants, subregional organisations such as ECOWAS, IGAD and SADC may be uniquely qualified to launch preventive diplomacy efforts and to effect change in attitudes that leads to viable and sustainable negotiated settlements in cases of civil war.

Regional Conflict Management: The Role of the OAU

At the Organization of African Unity's (OAU) summit in June 1992, African heads of state agreed that the OAU should establish a Mechanism for Conflict Prevention, Management and Resolution. At the 1993 summit the heads of state formally approved the Mechanism as it was proposed by the OAU secretary-general, Salim Ahmed Salim. Rather remarkably for an organization that hitherto has avoided involvement in internal conflicts, the new OAU Mechanism has a clear mandate to concern itself with such conflicts. As the secretary-general cogently remarked, "Given that every African is his brother's keeper, and that our borders are at best artificial, we in Africa need to use our own cultural and social relationships to interpret the principle of non-intervention in such a way that we are able to apply it to our advantage in conflict prevention and resolution."[12]

The OAU Mechanism is charged with anticipating and preventing conflicts, as well as engaging in peacemaking and peace-building activities. While the African heads of state are committed to this OAU initiative, the OAU obviously needs substantial assistance in training staff, developing systems, and financing peacekeeping operations. An African Peace Fund (APF), to which donors may contribute up to $400 million to assist the OAU's peacekeeping program, has been established. In the United States, the Clinton administration and Congress provided some support for African peace-making initiatives. In 1994, the United States gave the OAU $3.3 million to strengthen its peacekeeping and peace-making operations. In October 1994, President Bill Clinton signed the African Conflict Resolution Act of 1994 which authorized the disbursement of a total of $7.5 million from1995 to 1998 to assist the OAU's conflict resolution programme. This was supplemented by President Clinton's 1996 African Crisis Response Initiative. In 1999, Japan contributed US $ 250,000 to the APF. Additional funds from other multilateral sources were earmarked to provide equipment and training, to enable African states to participate in international and regional peacekeeping operations, and to pay for the demobilization and reintegration of African military personnel into civilian societies.

However, the operational limitations of the OAU Mechanism soon became apparent. In particular, it lacked an efficient system by which it could monitor incipient conflicts and take proactive action. In July 1995, the OAU heads of state decided to strengthen the preventive capacity of the Mechanism by establishing, within the OAU, an Early Warning System on Conflict Situations in Africa. To this end, a seminar was convened in1996 in Addis Ababa (Ethiopia) to determine how to establish such a system, which has now reached the second stage of its implementation.[13]

CONFLICT AND CONFLICT RESOLUTION IN CENTRAL AFRICA AND THE GREAT LAKES REGION

The Rwanda Genocide of April-June 1994 which resulted in an estimated one million deaths,[14] ten years of endemic conflict in Burundi which led to another 200,000 deaths and conflict in the Congo where some 3 million people have been killed since August 1998—including 200,000 Hutus in eastern Congo—have created tremendous instability, as well as a political, economic and social situation of catastrophic proportions in the central African/Great Lakes regions of Africa.

In addition to the horrendous death toll as a result of war, disease (notably HIV/AIDS), famine and malnutrition, the Congo conflict has resulted in over 600,000 refugees and 2 million internally-displaced persons. The Congo conflict has also led to a distinct regionalization of the war, in which in addition to the 55,000-men strong *Forces armées congolaises* (FAC), 62,000 foreign troops from six African countries (Rwanda: 20,000; Burundi: 15,000; Zimbabwe: 11,000; Uganda: 10,000; Angola: 4,000; and Namibia: 2,000) are involved.[15] After helping Laurent-Désiré Kabila overthrow Mobutu Sese Seko and take power in May 1997, Uganda and Rwanda (assisted by Burundi) turned against him on August 2, 1998, only two weeks after Kabila decided to send back home the Rwanda Patriotic Army [RPA] on July 17, 1998.

For geo-strategic and domestic political reasons, Angola, Namibia and Zimbabwe intervened in support of Kabila's FAC. On January 16, 2001, Laurent-Désiré Kabila was assassinated (in circumstances that have yet to be elucidated), and on January 26, 2001 his son Joseph Kabila succeeded him as president. Following high-level consultations in France, the U.S. and the United Nations (January 31-February 2, 2001), Joseph Kabila has indicated his determination to bring peace to the Congo by implementing the Lusaka Agreement, to liberalize the economy and to create a climate conducive to foreign private investment.

The Lusaka Agreement (July 1999) outlined both military and

political measures to bring peace to the Congo. In particular, it entrusted the task of policing the disengagement of forces to the belligerents themselves. This is to be done under the auspices of a Joint Military Commission (JMC), composed of two representatives from each signatory and a neutral OAU-appointed chairman that reports to a Political Committee made up of the combatants' foreign and defense ministers. Politically, the Lusaka Agreement envisions a National Dialogue that would set the stage for a new political dispensation in the Congo. Following a preparatory meeting in Gaborone (Botswana) that brought together for the first time all Congolese political and armed factions (August 22-23, 2001), the Inter-Congolese Dialogue began in September 2001 in Windhoek (Namibia). It is significant to note in this regard that—in a dramatic reversal of the late Kabila's demand for the "unconditional withdrawal of the foreign troops from Congo" and "non-recognition of the rebels as equal political actors"—the Congolese government has now accepted to participate in the inter-Congolese peace dialogue *before* the withdrawal of foreign troops from the Congo.[16]

The United Nations Security Council (UN-SC) passed Resolution 1341 (of February 22, 2001) to reconcile UN-SC Resolution 1304 (2000) with the Lusaka cease-fire agreement, thus de-linking the disengagement and withdrawal of foreign forces, the disarmament of armed groups, and the Inter-Congolese Dialogue from one another, in order to allow each to achieve the maximum progress. UN-SC Resolution 1355 (of June 15, 2001) notes that the cease-fire among the parties to the Lusaka Agreement has been respected, and reiterates its call on all the parties to implement this agreement; it also extends the mandate of MONUC until June 15, 2002. Thus, UN-SC Resolutions 1341 and 1355 should be viewed as firm collective decisions by the international community to revive, accelerate and actualize the Lusaka Accords.

The historical background, origins, manifestations and consequences of the conflict in the Great Lakes regions (here defined as Rwanda, Burundi, Uganda and eastern Congo) have, over the last seven years, been painstakingly documented in a number of thorough and perceptive studies.[17] Building on these and taking both a historical (Fernand Braudel's *longue durée*) and a geo-political and geostrategic perspectives, this section briefly examines the origins, types and characteristic features of the current conflict in the Congo, with particular attention to the intervention of various external state and non-state actors at the sub-regional (Rwanda, Burundi, Zimbabwe, Uganda, Angola, Namibia and South Africa), continental (OAU) and international (Belgium, France, the European Union, the U.S. and the U.N.) levels.

While the Great Lakes region is characterized by ecological, cultural and linguistic unity, (and also by a violent history), three irreducible realities have set the scene for subsequent confrontations, namely: the lack of coincidence between ethnic and geographical maps: Hutu and Tutsi are found not only in Rwanda and Burundi but also in North and South Kivu, southern Uganda, and Western Tanzania; the sheer density of population and resulting pressures on land throughout the region (336 inhabitants per square kilometer in Rwanda, 220 p/sq. km in Burundi); the presence of large refugee populations in all four countries of the region; indeed, "the dynamics of violence in the Great Lakes involves the transformation of refugee-generating violence into violence-generating refugee flows... The refugee problem is thus inextricably bound up with the dynamics of ethnic conflict throughout the region"[18]

At one level, the war in the Congo is a conflict between two regional alliances—a "Great Lakes" alliance of Rwanda, Uganda, and Burundi, versus an alliance of Angola, Zimbabwe, and Namibia. At another level, that war is a violent mixture of national civil wars (including those of Rwanda, Uganda, Burundi, and Angola), all of which are partly fought on Congolese soil. Finally, the Congo's own brew of local ethnic feuds has sparked an explosion of violence in the eastern part of the country. All of these conflicts feed and reinforce one another, and together constitute an explosive combination.[19]

The geo-strategic significance of the Congo derives from various factors, notably its population (50 million); size (2.3 million square km); geographical location at the heart of Africa (bordering on Angola, Zambia, Tanzania, Burundi, Rwanda, Uganda, Sudan, the Central African Republic, and Congo-Brazzaville); and its vast natural resources which have earned it the French characterization of *scandale géologique* (diamonds, gold, silver, iron, zinc, copper, cobalt, columbite-tantalite, cadmium, manganese, bauxite, uranium, and radium). It is significant to note in this regard that all the sub-regional actors involved, as well as the various rebel movements systematically exploit for their benefit the natural resources found on the vast portions of the country's territory that they control. Congo's vast mineral resources have become even more valuable in the context of the current world financial crisis.[20]

Hence a specific focus on the role of natural resources in the conflict and on the war economy seems appropriate. For example, in the first quarter of 2000, Uganda and Rwanda became the number one exporters of diamond and copper on the world market. Eastern Congo is home to some of the richest columbite-tantalite (col-tan) deposits in the world, a mineral whose price skyrocketed to $200 a pound at the end of 2000. A secret report to the Swiss government reveals that over the last three years, the sales of col-tan world-wide have grossed a total of $90 million, a small portion of which was retained by the Rwandese military and other foreign intermediaries.[21]

The various rebel movements are organically linked to various sub-regional powers, who provide vital military, logistical and financial support. These include the *Mouvement pour la Libération du Congo* (MLC), led by Jean-Pierre Bemba and based in the Équateur province; the Congolese Rally for Democracy (*Rassemblement Congolais pour la Démocracie*/RCD) which broke up into two (then later, three) factions in March 1999: the RDC-Kisangani (or ML) faction, led by Wamba dia Wamba; and the RCD-Goma, based in eastern Congo, supported by Rwanda and led by Jean-Pierre Ondekane. A Congolese liberation front (*Front congolais de libération*/ FCL unifying the MLC and two RCD factions (excluding the

RCD-Kisangani) has recently been created.[22]

The unstable and volatile security situation in Congo-Brazzaville also has a bearing on developments in Congo-Kinshasa. In October 1997, rebel forces loyal to the former Congolese president General Denis Sassou-Nguesso seized control of the capital city Brazzaville, effectively ending the 4-month revolt against the government of Pascal Lissouba, which had been democratically elected in August 1992 and re-elected in 1995. Sassou-Nguesso, who became the new president in October 1997 (after having ruled the country from February 1979 to August 1992), was able to prevail with military assistance from Angola (concerned about alleged support of Lissouba to the rebel UNITA movement), and French logistical and financial support. The war resulted in some 10,000 deaths, 40,000 refugees and 500,0000 internally displaced persons. With Brazzaville and much of the countryside in ruins, militias loyal to Lissouba and other political rivals (such as Bernard Kolélas) active in some areas and the economy in a state of near-collapse, the return of Sassou-Nguesso does not bode well for the future of Congo-B and the stability of the region. Renewed violence erupted in October 1998 in the Pool region around Brazzaville, involving various militias (notably Sassou-Nguesso's 'Ninjas' and Kolélas' 'Cobras'), resulting in another 1,000 deaths and further contributing to endemic instability. This does not augur well for the return of democracy in the country, though a constitutional referendum and elections have been scheduled for 2001. In terms of sub-regional alliances, the Congolese government signed a military cooperation agreement with Angola in August 1998, and a "Non-aggression Pact" with Congo-K on December 29, 1998.[23]

Various world powers (particularly Belgium, France and the U.S.) have plaid (and continue to play) an important role in the Great Lakes region and in the Congolese peace process. As a close ally of both Rwanda and Congo up until the mid-nineties, France's responsibility in the 1994 genocide—and its staunch support of the Mobutu regime to the end—has now been established and abundantly documented.[24] Belgium, the U.S. and the U.N. non-intervention in the Rwanda genocide have also been the object of some criticism. France, Belgium and the U.S. have recently warmed up to Congo's young new leader, Joseph Kabila and even provided humanitarian aid ($10 million from the U.S.). Finally, the role of the United Nations which, on February 24, 2000, formally committed a 5,537-strong peace-keeping force to the Congo which has now been deployed, is significant.

CONCLUSION

A number of recent developments seem to indicate that the issue of peace and security in Africa has, at last, been moved to the top of the agenda of intergovernmental regional and international organizations. In December 1999, the UN Security Council held a day-long discussion on practical ways of resolving conflicts and maintaining peace in Africa, especially through improved cooperation with regional organizations. Addressing the meeting, UN Secretary General Kofi Annan put forward a number of specific proposals, emphasizing in particular the need for the Security Council to show sustained and effective interest in African conflicts or potential conflicts; the need to use contact groups of interested members to follow up on proposed action on specific conflicts; the need to establish closer and more regular contact with the heads and staff of the various regional and subregional organizations; and the dispatch of goal-oriented missions. A broad consensus emerged in the Council for regular and more structured consultations with the OAU and subregional bodies. When the U.S. assumed the presidency of the Security Council in January 2000, it made Africa the priority of the month and held at least four public meetings of the Security Council to focus on the UN and the problems of the continent, with particular attention to Angola, Burundi, and Congo. Similarly, a meeting of ambassadors of the OAU's committee on conflict prevention, management and resolution called upon the international community—through the UN agencies—to declare the year 2000 as "the year of peace, security and solidarity in Africa."

Endnotes

1. All figures are taken from Luc Reychler, "Les conflits en Afrique: comment les gérer ou les prévenir?", in GRIP, *Conflits en Afrique: Analyse des Crises et Pistes pour une Prévention* (Bruxelles: GRIP/Éditions Complexe, 1997), pp.15-22.
2. Reychler, "Les conflits en Afrique," *op. cit.*, pp. 23-26.
3. Karl Vick, "Carter's Patience Pays Off in Africa: Sudan-Uganda Agreement Caps Long Years of Effort by Former President," *The Washington Post* (12 December 1999), p. A44.
4. "Sierra Leone's Path to Peace: Key Issues at Year's End," U.S. Committee on Refugees, *Press Release* (15 December 1999); Rémy Ourdan, "Les premiers 'casques bleus' arrivent en Sierra Leone où les rebelles tardent à déposer les armes," *Le Monde* (2 décembre 1999); Elizabeth Blunt, "Paix fragile en Sierra Leone," *Le Monde diplomatique* (décembre 1999), p. 14 (the quote is from Soren Jensen Peterson of the U.N. High Commissioner for Refugees, in E. Blunt, *art. cit.*); for a more detailed account of the ECOMOG intervention in Sierra Leone, see Robert Mortimer, "From ECOMOG to ECOMOG II: Intervention in Sierra Leone," in John W. Harbeson and Donald Rothchild (eds.), *Africa in World Politics: The African State System in Flux* (Boulder: Westview Press, 3rd edition., 2000), pp. 188-207.
5. Paul Ejime, "ECOWAS Leaders Tackle Security at the Expense of Economy," *Panafrican News Agency* (9 December 1999).
6. Peace Priorities for IGAD: Challenges and Opportunities for Development," *IGAD News* vol. 1, no. 1 (June 1999), pp. 1, 3.
7. Samir Gharbi, "Djibouti: Un nouveau médiateur régional," *Jeune Afrique* (7-13 décembre 1999), p. 25.
8. "Conflict in Africa and the Search for Peace in Congo," remarks by U.S. Permanent Representative to the U.N. Richard C. Holbrooke, Pretoria, South Africa (6 December 1999); Jean-Dominique Geslin, "RD Congo: Impossible paix," *Jeune Afrique* (7-13 décembre 1999), pp. 10-11.

9. Horst Brammer, "In search of an effective regional security mechanism for southern Africa," *Global Dialogue* vol. 4, no. 2 (August 1999), pp. 21-22; Walter Tapfumanyei, "Regional security cooperation in southern Africa: a view from Zimbabwe," *Global Dialogue* vol. 4, no. 2 (August 1999), pp. 23-26, 35.
10. Philippe Bordes, "Thabo Mbeki reprend en main la SADC," *Jeune Afrique* (19 octobre-1er novembre 1999), pp. 49-50.
11. Marc-Louis Ropivia, "Failing institutions and shattered space: what regional integration in central Africa?" in Daniel C. Bach (ed.), *Regionalisation in Africa: Integration and Disintegration* (Bloomington: Indiana University Press, 1999), p. 126; see also chapter 6 in this volume.
12. Organization of African Unity/OAU, *OAU Report of the Secretary-General on Conflicts in Africa* (June 1992), pp. 11-12.
13. See in particular S. Bassey Ibok & William G. Nhara (eds.), *OAU Early Warning System on Conflict Situations in Africa* (Addis Ababa: OAU, 1997); and William G. Nhara, *Early Warning and Conflict in Africa*, Institute for Defence Policy Papers no. 1 (February 1996).
14. Rather than the generally accepted estimate of 800,000 deaths (or 850,000 according to Prunier, 1995: 261-65) "for reasons which remain obscure," we retain the figure of one million deaths given by Philippe Gaillard, chief delegate, International Committee of the Red Cross, Rwanda, 1993-94, confirmed by Charles Petrie, deputy coordinator of the UN Rwanda Emergency Office (Melvern, 2000: 4, 222-23).
15. ICG, *Scramble for the Congo: Anatomy of an Ugly War*. Nairobi & Brussels: International Crisis Group [ICG Africa Report No. 26, 2000], p. 4.
16. "Peace Talks in Congo Hit Snag Over Troop Withdrawal," *The New York Times* (22 August 2001); UN Integrated Regional Information Network, "Government Agrees to Dialogue Before Withdrawal of Foreign Troops" (30 August 2001); posted on www.allAfrica.com (29 August 2001).

17. See in partcular Colette Braeckman, *L'enjeu congolais: l'Afrique centrale après Mobutu* (Paris: Fayard, 1999); Jean-Pierre Chrétien, *L'Afrique des Grands Lacs: Deux mille ans d'histoire* (Paris: Aubier, 2000); René Lemarchand, "The Crisis in the Great Lakes," in John W. Harbeson & Donald Rothchild (eds), *Africa in World Politics* (Boulder: Westview Press,3rd edition, 2000), pp. 324-352; and Gérard Prunier, *The Rwanda Crisis: History of a Genocide* (New York: Columbia University Press, 1995).

18. R. Lemarchand in J.W. Harbeson & D. Rothchild (eds), *op. cit.*, pp. 327, 330-31.

19. ICG, *op. cit.*, p. 1.

20. Annick Lambert, *Le Testament de Laurent-Désiré Kabila: son Application et ses Conséquences sur la Stabilité en Afrique des Grands Lacs* (Montreal: Global Multi-Cultural Dialogue, 2001).

21. Karl Vick, "Vital Ore Funds Congo's War," *The Washington Post* (10 March 2001), page A01; Jean-Philippe Rémy, "Dans l'est du Congo, les belligérants organisent le pillage et le trafic du coltan," *Le Monde* (20 août 2001); see also U.N., *Report of the Expert Panel on the Illegal Exploitation of Natural Resources and other Forms of Wealth in the DRC* [S/2001/357] (12 April 2001).

22. ICG, *op.cit.*, pp. 2-11.

23. François-Xavier Verschave, *Noir Silence: Qui arrêtera la Françafrique?* (Paris: Éditions des Arènes, 2000), pp. 15-44.

24. See in particular Jean-Paul Gouteux, *Un génocide secret d'État: La France et le Rwanda, 1990-1997* (Paris: Éditions sociales, 1998); Linda Melvern, *A People Betrayed: The role of the West in Rwanda's Genocide* (New York: Zed Books, 2000); and F.X. Verschave, *Complicité de génocide? La politique de la France au Rwanda* (Paris: Éditions La Découverte, 1994);

Chapter 8

International Solidarity and Coooperation in Assistance to African Refugees

As of December 31, 1993, Africa accounted for 5,825,000 (or nearly 36 per cent) of the 16,255,000 refugees and asylum seekers in need of protection or assistance identified world wide. Out of this total, 4,343,500 (or nearly 75 per cent) were located in 10 African countries (Côte d'Ivoire, Guinea, Kenya, Malawi, Rwanda, South Africa, Sudan, Tanzania, Uganda, Democratic Republic of the Congo/DRC). Refugees began to return home to Mozambique, Liberia and Somalia during the year, while large populations became newly uprooted in DRC, Angola, Burundi, and Togo. Sizable numbers of nationals from Sudan, Eritrea, Ethiopia, Rwanda, Sierra-Leone, Mali, and other countries remained refugees and internally displaced due to persistent conflicts. Nearly 20 African countries accounted for the overwhelming majority of refugees on the continent, and some 32 countries were hosting large refugee populations.[1]

At the end of 1998, there were 13.5 million refugees and asylum seekers in the world. At that time, 44 countries in the world (out of

217) accounted for an estimated 12,773,000 refugees and asylum seekers; 19 African countries together hosted 2,912,000 of these (representing 22.8 percent of the total). As of December 1998, the African countries hosting the greatest numbers of refugees and asylum seekers were: Sierra Leone (480,000), Somalia (421,000), Sudan (352,000), Eritrea (323,000), Liberia (310,000), Angola (302,000), Burundi (281,000), DRC (136,000), Western Sahara (105,000), Algeria (40,000), Ethiopia (40,000), Mauritania (30,000), Congo-Brazzaville (20,000), Chad (16,000), Rwanda (12,000), Uganda (12,000), Ghana (11,000), Guinea-Bissau (11,000), and Senegal (10,000). At that time, 41 countries in the world (out of 217) accounted for an estimated 18,792,000 civilians who have been internally displaced by persecution or armed conflict; 18 African countries together hosted 8,858,000 of these (representing 47.1 percent of the total). As of 31 December 1998, the African countries hosting the greatest numbers of internally displaced persons were: Sudan (4 million), Angola (1.5 million), Burundi (500,000), Rwanda (500,000), Uganda (400,000), DRC (300,000), Sierra Leone (300,000), Congo-Brazzaville (250,000), Somalia (250,000), Guinea-Bissau (200,000), Kenya (200,000), Algeria (200,000), Ethiopia (150,000), Eritrea (100,000), Liberia (75,000), Ghana (20,000), Senegal (10,000), and Nigeria (3,000).[2]

On April 6, 1994, the presidents of Rwanda and Burundi were killed when a plane they were returning in from a peace meeting in Tanzania was gunned down while approaching Kigali airport. The violence that erupted throughout Rwanda following this plane crash resulted in a devastating humanitarian crisis of almost unprecedented proportions. An estimated one million Rwandans were killed in indiscriminate massacres waged against the civilian population. This resulted in the mass exodus of over two million Rwandan refugees to neighboring countries while another two million became internally displaced within the country (from a total population estimated at 8.1 million). The sheer intensity, scale and magnitude of the Rwandan tragedy and the untold suffering it has brought on millions

of innocent men, women and children in urgent need of the fundamental necessities of life—food, shelter, clothing, physical security,
clean water, basic health care, and the integrity of the family—once
again brought into sharp focus the paramount moral duties of the
international community in terms of international solidarity and burden-sharing. Yet the hesitant, belated and inadequate response of
bilateral donor governments (notably the United States and France),
inter-governmental organizations (notably the United Nations and
the Organization of African Unity OAU), and of certain humanitarian non-governmental organizations (NGOs)—which placed an
unbearable burden on the African countries concerned—raises the
question of the actual commitment of the international community
to seeking permanent and durable (i.e., political) solutions to the
refugee problem in Africa. And it begs the question of whether we
are not witnessing a progressive evolution of international humanitarian policies from burden-sharing to what should be more appropriately called "burden-shifting."

Coming in the wake of U.S. and UN interventions in northern
Iraq, Bosnia, and Somalia, the UN, French and American intervention in Rwanda raises a more general issue, namely that of the justification and rationale for international humanitarian intervention, and
of the degree to which new international moral and legal norms and
obligations have effectively eroded the principles of sovereignty and
non-intervention in the internal affairs of states.

International Solidarity and Burden-sharing in Assistance to African Refugees: Principles and Practice

The principal legal sources of protection for African refugees and displaced persons are human rights law, which proclaims broad guarantees for the fundamental rights of all human beings; humanitarian
law, which applies to situations of armed conflict; and refugee law,
which generally applies only when a border is crossed.

African refugees are effectively protected by two main repository of international refugee law: the 1951 Geneva Convention Relating to the Status of Refugees (hereafter referred to as Geneva Convention) and 1967 *Protocol*, and the 1969 OAU Convention Governing Specific Aspects of Refugee Problems in Africa (hereafter referred to as OAU Convention). According to these conventions, refugees are victims of natural or man made disasters, or victims of actual or threatened racial, religious, ethnic or political persecution who have sought refuge outside the borders of their country of origin. Thus, African refugees can be divided into two main groups: people fleeing from war, persecution, religious or ethnic conflicts, drought, famine and other natural disasters; and political refugees, namely people who have "a well-founded fear of being persecuted for reasons of race, religion, nationality, membership of a particular social group or political opinion..."[3] The OAU Convention makes a further distinction between two categories of refugees: the "ordinary refugee" who is trying to create a normal and peaceful life; and the "subversive refugee", i.e. anyone who flees his country with the sole aim of provoking upheaval in it. Specifically, "subversive activities are such as to cause tension between member states [of the Organization], especially with armed force or through the press or broadcasts."[4] Internally displaced persons are generally those who have been forced to leave their homes and sources of livelihood but are still within the borders of a country undergoing violent internal conflict. While the fundamental rights and human needs of African displaced persons are at least as threatened as are those of refugees, the legal doctrine and institutional arrangements for protecting and assisting the internally displaced are far less developed that those that apply to refugees.[5]

This chapter seeks to identify some of the essential prerequisites for the operation of an effective international refugee policy in the context of the problems raised by the phenomenon of large-scale influxes of asylum seekers, taking Rwanda as a case in point. International burden-sharing becomes crucial if the system of even minimal protection is not to break down under the sheer weight of numbers for lack of proper appreciation of the demands of human solidarity and international obligation. One result of the increasing prevalence of large-scale refugee crises has been the gradual acceptance of the desirability of differentiating between the obligations of states in respect of the two phases of the protection function: emergency refuge and the provision of durable solutions. *Non-refoulement* (an obligation of non-expulsion upon states in relation to any individual whose life or liberty would be in jeopardy if denied refuge) has to that extent become divorced from the notion of *asylum* (a state's voluntary acceptance of political refugees on a long-term or permanent basis). Thus, while *non-refoulement* has achieved a mandatory status as part of general international law and now binds all states, asylum remains very much a discretionary prerogative of the state of refuge.[6] Adopted by the UN General Assembly in 1981, the Australian proposal on *temporary refuge*—i.e. emergency admission on a provisional basis, solely with a view towards the provision of a safe-haven and without commitment concerning permanent or long-term residence in the country of refuge—was conceived as a kind of intermediate level of protection appropriate in large-scale influx situations and as a way to link admission of refugees with international solidarity.[7]

A basic principle of refugee law is *international solidarity*. It is the principle of solidarity which establishes: that the refugee is a person of concern to the international community; the obligation to extend refugee status to those compelled to flee persecution or communal violence and to treat them with dignity; and that states have an obligation to share the responsibility of finding durable solutions for the people who have been deprived of a community. In cases of large-scale refugee movements, burden-sharing is a virtual prerequisite to the effective operation of a comprehensive *non-refoulement* policy intended to ensure safe havens for all fugitives from political persecution or other man-made or natural disasters. International cooperation, however, cannot stop merely at the provision of financial and technical assistance in the first stage to alleviate the social and economic problems a sudden mass influx of refugees may create for countries of first refuge. It should also extend to the second phase, that of providing durable solutions. Durable solutions may take one of three forms: voluntary repatriation, local settlement, or resettlement in a third country. Second-stage measures must be seen as part of a joint responsibility of the world community, in which each nation must share to the best of its abilities. There is thus a functional necessity for burden-sharing in both stages of refugee protection: through financial assistance to countries of first refuge, and through financial assistance and, where necessary, provision of resettlement opportunities for the achievement of durable solutions. In this context, burden-sharing must be viewed as an essential component of the legal framework upon which respect for the obligation of *non-refoulement* is based .[8]

While burden-sharing is a functional necessity for the proper operation of an effective international refugee policy, it is also based on a number of humanitarian and moral considerations steeped in both the UN Charter and in contemporary international law. Thus, recent developments in human rights law have led to a renewed injection of moral content in the legal norms governing the world community. A new philosophy of international cooperation in which the principles of equity and redistribution seem to have been elevated to the status of overriding moral or legal principles has emerged through UN legislation and practice. Viewed in this context, burden-sharing in refugee matters merely represents one more facet of the new principle of *global equity* whereby those nations that have the necessary means are expected to assist those that do not.

As is often the case in international relations, while states and other actors generally recognize that international solidarity and burden-sharing are morally and legally justified and necessary, the actual implementation of these lofty principles encounters many difficulties in practice. It might be useful at this point to make a distinction between the different actors involved in burden-sharing. A first distinction has to do with the countries directly involved in the refugee problem, namely countries of first asylum (temporary refuge); third (resettlement) countries; and countries of origin (or source countries). A second, more general, typology relates to the various actors involved in the international relief network, namely governments (both donor and recipient), global and regional inter-governmental organizations (IGOs), and local and international non-governmental organizations (NGOs). These will be examined successively.

Countries of first asylum are expected to grant at least temporary refuge and to provide the basic necessities of life (food, water, medicine, shelter, sanitation, health care) to refugees. A large number of mass exoduses during the past 30 years have occurred in the less-developed countries of the Third World, causing an unbearable burden on these chronically underdeveloped economies. A consensus has emerged that it is the responsibility of the international community—particularly of the most developed countries—to alleviate the burden of the neighboring countries where the mass influx usually takes place. Indeed, many developed countries have in recent years, either directly or through the United Nations High Commissioner for Refugees (UNHCR) or other humanitarian agencies, helped the first asylum states and shared their burden. A major international fund-raising conference was held in April 1980 to assist refugees in Africa which raised about $600 million, most of it used for emergency assistance. The practice in this regard differs depending upon the region of the world concerned. Thus, while South-east Asian countries have generally adopted a restrictive attitude, in breach of the principle of *non-refoulement,*' African states have adopted a relatively liberal practice, with the possibility of local assimilation and, ultimately, voluntary repatriation. In most of these assistance programs, the idea is to facilitate the temporary stay of the refugees in the country of first asylum; aid agencies and donor countries thus tend to focus on emergency assistance measures at the expense of long-term, durable solutions (such as the promotion of development projects). Some legal experts have even proposed recognition of the right of a country of asylum to claim compensation from the state of origin of the refugees, based on the economic, social and other burdens due to the presence of large numbers of refugees on its territory.[9]

The role of countries of resettlement (or third countries) is essential in guaranteeing a degree of protection and assistance in keeping with international standards. However, third countries vary greatly in their provision of resettlement places or of aid. Thus, most developed countries, claiming "compassion fatigue," saturated absorptive capacity," and the need to ward off "economic migrants," have introduced a wide range of restrictive legal and administrative measures—such as excessive visa requirements, stringent border controls, and narrower applications of the criteria for refugee status—designed to deny entry of refugees, and deter would-be applicants, from Third World countries. As Bill Frelick aptly remarked in his perceptive review of the world refugee situation in 1993, "The international community is now generally committed to keeping would-be refugees at home, saying at once that this is for their own good and for the good of countries increasingly reluctant to host foreigners uprooted by war and persecution...The goal, ultimately, appeared not to be to protect the persecuted, but rather to protect potential host countries from them, in effect, punishing the victims. With the U.S. often taking a negative lead, the 'solution' focused on preventing refugee flight". And he concludes: "Support for the concept of asylum is clearly—and tragically—waning."[10] While most less developed countries have adopted more liberal resettlement policies, some (like Pakistan which closed its borders in 1994 to a new wave of Afghan refugees fleeing communal violence) are not immune to resorting to the same "human deterrence" measures used in the West to deny refuge to Third World asylum seekers. Similarly, Bangladesh, Mexico and South Africa were among the worst offenders in terms of involuntary returns and expulsions of refugees from neighboring countries in 1993, with 16,000, 130,000, and 65,000 refugees *refoulés* to Burma, Guatemala, and Mozambique, respectively.[11] In Africa, competition over increasingly scarce resources in a context of recurrent economic and social crisis and endemic warfare has exacerbated tensions between indigenous communities and immigrants, often bordering on xenophobia and leading to mass expulsions. In Côte d'Ivoire—which is home to 1.7 million foreign immigrants—the issue of immigration figures prominently in the current presidential electoral debate, and several hundred immigrants from Burkina Faso were expelled from the country. Following the 1998 Ethiopian-Eritrean border clashes, some 50,000 Eritreans were expelled from Ethiopia. In South Africa, over 500,000 illegal immigrants have been expelled from the country since 1990.[12]

How should countries of origin (or source countries) share the burden of assistance to refugees? One could argue that they should try to prevent the outflow in the first place. However, given the complex interplay of factors involved (e.g., political persecution, civil war and natural disasters), this might prove difficult, if not impossible. Prevention of root causes implies respect for human rights, political pluralism and democracy, people-centered and participatory development, as well as the availability of foreign development aid. However, it is generally agreed that *voluntary repatriation* (i.e. the return home of refugees of their own volition), which involves the return of large numbers of refugees to their home country, is the most happy solution to the refugee problem . Thus in 1993, under the auspices of the UNHCR, 500,000 Mozambicans returned home from Malawi and other countries; 70,000 Liberians returned home from Guinea and Côte d'Ivoire; and 56,000 Ethiopians and 50,000 Somalis returned home from Kenya.[13]

The various international conferences held in the 1980s to help solve the problem of burden-sharing in Africa have emphasized the need to link relief, recovery and development assistance in order to promote self-sufficiency and reduce the burden imposed on host countries and countries of origin, and support the regional peace processes through projects designed to integrate refugees, returnees and displaced persons into national development schemes. Refugees come overwhelmingly from the rural areas of the poorer developing countries and find refuge in rural areas of other low-income countries. A massive refugee inflow into a low-income country can be a major burden to this host country and to the local population in the affected area. Yet, the burden of the low-income hosts is not being effectively shared by the rest of the international community. Refugees from less-developed countries are being aided by states and communities in less developed countries. This situation—dramatically illustrated by the Rwanda crisis—has prompted some observers to suggest that while the international community fully endorses the principle of burden-sharing, individual states tend to practice some form of *burden-shifting*.[14]

International Cooperation and Burden-sharing: the role of States, Inter-governmental Organizations (IGOs) and Non-governmental organizations (NGOs)

International relief (or humanitarian) assistance

Among the many situations that call for international relief (or humanitarian) assistance, the UN secretary-general has identified genocide, arbitrary and summary executions, armed conflicts, gross violations of human rights, refugees and disaster relief, mass exoduses and displacements, natural and man-made disasters, and racial and religious intolerance. In Africa, the growing number of "failed" states has produced an increasing level of chaos to which the international community has tried to respond. This instability does not respect any boundaries and frequently spills over into neighboring countries, many of which are themselves unstable. The spreading chaos does not appear to be subsiding and presents the international community with a major challenge, to which it has tried to respond by developing the concept of "complex humanitarian emergency." According to Andrew Natsios, complex humanitarian emergencies are defined by five common characteristics: the deterioration or complete collapse of central government authority; ethnic or religious conflict and widespread human rights abuses; episodic food insecurity, frequently deteriorating into mass starvation; macroeconomic collapse involving hyperinflation, massive unemployment and net decreasés in GNP; and mass population movements of displaced people and refugees escaping conflict or searching for food.[15] All of these situations, unfortunately, prevail to some degree in many African countries, Rwanda being the most extreme case in point. As suggested earlier, the impact of natural and man made disasters falls largely on those countries which are least able to bear it: the Third World countries. The proportional economic burden is also much higher in those countries because of the disruptive impact of disasters on already hard-pressed economies and societies. When a disaster exceeds the resources available to handle it within a country, an appeal for outside aid is made, which generates international relief (or humanitarian) assistance. International relief assistance falls into three basic categories: assistance in kind (supplies and materials needed for the relief operation, depending on the nature of the disaster); financial contributions; and trained personnel (doctors, nurses and other health specialists, logistics experts, and administrative staff). All categories of assistance are to meet the immediate needs of the victims. International humanitarian assistance is distinguished from foreign aid by its concentration on the relief of victims, and, in most cases, by its emergency character. A timely intervention is dependent on complex political, logistical, financial and human resources factors. The cases of Somalia and Rwanda have amply demonstrated the need for more effective coordination of relief aid in the recipient country and at the international donor level. The lack of coordination has caused the duplication of aid, waste, the delivery of unwanted products, competition of relief agencies, and in general an inefficient relief assistance and a loss of credibility for some of the relief agencies.[16] The challenges of complex humanitarian emergencies in Africa have forced the UN system and NGOs to collaborate more closely in dealing with civil conflicts and famines and to try to develop a single unified strategy in each complex emergency.[17]

There is no international relief system *per se*, as the diverse set of actors displays little structural interdependence and rarely share a set of common institutional goals. Yet an international relief network has emerged. This network is characterized by an intense web of communications between Inter-governmental Organizations(IGOs), between NGOs, and between IGOs and NGOs. It also exhibits a large degree of transnationalism and specialization of organizations. The actors of this network are: the recipient governments, authorities and peoples of the "afflicted" nations; the donor governments which provide bilateral and multilateral assistance either directly or through the IGOs and/or the NGOs; the global (e.g., UN, UNHCR) and regional (e.g., OAU) IGOs; the complex world of the NGOs .[18] The amount of funding provided by the U.S. Agency for International Development (US-AID) for relief interventions in complex humanitarian emergencies has risen dramatically beginning in the late 1980s. A complex response system has evolved to spend this money and respond to these emergencies, composed of NGOs, UN organizations and the International Red Cross movement. There is, however, no consensus among donor governments, NGOs, the International Committee of the Red Cross (ICRC) and UN agencies on the need for a unified strategy in each complex emergency, and the response system is now on the verge of breakdown.[19]

The United Nations High Commissioner for Refugees (UNHCR)

The mandate and activities of the UNHCR are wholly humanitarian in the specialized field of international refugees' protection and assistance. They are in part of a legal nature (international protection) and in part of an operational nature. The latter category of activities is carried out in close association with humanitarian NGOs. In view of its limited financial and human resources, the UNHCR needs and uses the complementary support and action of NGOs to fulfill its operational mandate. As a rule, the UNHCR cooperates with any organization if it considers that such cooperation is beneficial to refugees and provided that the cooperation is carried out for purely humanitarian and social—as opposed to political—purposes. Besides granting them consultative status, the UNHCR establishes contractual relationships with the NGOs under varying terms. Some contracts are financed entirely by the UNHCR, while in other cases, the NGO makes a contribution in personnel, relief supplies (medicine, foodstuffs) and/or in cash. The complementary role of the NGOs is more evident in material assistance. NGOs frequently distribute food, clothing and blankets, organize health and sanitation services, and initiate or assume full responsibility for the process of integration. The UNHCR, as well as the NGOs contracted by the organization, need the agreement of the recipient government to provide operational assistance. In Geneva, the UNHCR maintains regular contact with some 60 NGOs through various consultative channels.[20]

The UNHCR's budget is mainly dependent on member states' voluntary contributions which, in turn, depend mainly on the good will and interests of Western donors and on the capacity of the Commissioner to attract funds. Ending 1989 with an unprecedented $38 million deficit, the agency has since experienced chronic financial difficulties, with voluntary contributions of (mostly Western) states typically amounting to only 50 per cent of minimum budgetary requirements. Donors' "compassion fatigue" explains in part the organization's financial problems.[21] As is often the case, the most generous contributors to international refugee aid agencies are not necessarily the wealthiest countries in the world. Thus, in 1993, the top five countries in terms of such contributions per capita (in US $) were Norway (14.12), Sweden (11.31), Denmark (8.14), the Netherlands (6.46), and Switzerland (5.56). By contrast, the per capita contributions of the U.S., the United Kingdom, Japan and France only amounted to US $ 1.74, 1.48, 1.14, and 0.95, respectively during the same year.[22]

The Organization of African Unity (OAU), Refugee Problems, and Human and People's Rights in Africa

Since its birth in Addis Ababa on May 25, 1963, the Organization of African Unity (OAU) has proclaimed its commitment and competence as the primary agency in the field of protection and assistance to African refugees. To the extent that Africa bears part of the responsibility for the abuses perpetrated against individuals, the refugee problem is very closely tied up with efforts being made to restore, maintain, and guarantee human rights and human dignity in Africa. The promotion and protection of economic, social, and cultural rights of the Africans, however, was not a central concern of the organization during its first years of existence, because of strict adherence to the cardinal OAU Charter principles of sovereign equality, non-interference in the internal affairs of states, and respect for the African states' sovereignty, territorial integrity, and independence.[23]

Following the creation of the OAU Council of Ten to examine solutions to the refugee problem and that of the Office for Placing and Educating African Refugees (BPERA) in 1964, and in the wake of the 1965 Accra OAU Declaration on the Refugee Problem in Africa, the organization adopted in 1969 a Convention Governing the Specific Aspects of Refugee Problems in Africa (hereafter referred to as OAU Convention), which adopted a broader definition of "refugee" and a more liberal policy of voluntary repatriation than those contained in the 1951 Geneva Convention. In the area of burden-sharing, the OAU Convention creates the joint responsibility of the OAU member states in relation to the refugee problem in that, in the name of "African solidarity", those states endeavor to ease the burden of some of their members who have difficulty in coping with the refugees crossing their borders; it also states that voluntary and international organizations will jointly endeavor to assist refugees who have voluntarily decided to return to their country of origin.[24] Finally, in 1981, the OAU member states adopted an African Charter on Human and Peoples' Rights (ACHPR) which guarantees the African citizens' fundamental individual rights and freedoms (equality before the law, respect of dignity, liberty and security; freedom of opinion and association; freedom of assembly); and protection of basic peoples' rights, notably African peoples' right to their economic, social and cultural development.[25] The Charter emphatically guarantees the rights of free movement and residence, return, asylum, and *non-refoulement* of every legal resident or refugee in any African state.[26] It also specifically prohibits the mass expulsion (i.e., that aimed at national, racial, ethnic or religious groups) of non-nationals.[27]

Non-governmental Organizations (NGOs)

Besides governments and IGOs, non-governmental organizations (NGOs) play a significant and increasingly recognized role in the international humanitarian network. NGOs initiate humanitarian action independently, assess needs, call for funds, send relief teams, provide equipment, medicine, food and other material to recipient populations. NGOs also supplement or complement IGO-initiated and funded programs, as indispensable operational partners. International humanitarian NGOs—also referred to as "private voluntary organizations"—may be defined as "non-governmental, autonomous, non profit organizations, initiated by private citizens for a stated international relief assistance purpose, supported mainly by voluntary contributions in cash and kind from private sources."[28]

A distinction is usually made between national and international NGOs, although the latter may be more appropriately described as national NGOs that have developed international activities. Because of the close connection between relief assistance and development, due to the need to expand emergency assistance into mid-and long-term development plans, and in view of the fact that some relief organizations also have a development role, humanitarian and development NGOs must be considered jointly. The global growth of NGOs over the last 40 years has been spectacular, from 832 in 1951 to 16,208 in

1990. It is estimated that some 400 to 500 international NGOs are involved in humanitarian activities world-wide.[29] Building upon the spirit of cooperation and consultation which had been fostered by various Geneva-based bodies involved in refugee matters, the International Council of Voluntary Agencies (ICVA) was created in 1962 as an independent international association of (now 86) non governmental, non-profit organizations. ICVA is not an operational agency but provides services and support to its member agencies to enable them to cooperate and perform more effectively. One of ICVA's primary functions is to promote national and regional networks of voluntary agencies as an important way of strengthening voluntary action in the Third World. Thus, ICVA—which is now composed primarily of Third World organizations—has been involved in the promotion of an African NGO network.[30] In the early 1990s, ICVA and the UNHCR jointly created Partners in Action (PARinAC). PARinAC is intended to "enhance dialogue and understanding between UNHCR and ICVA; to facilitate closer collaboration and increase the combined capacity to respond to the global refugee problem and...the problem of internal displacement." PARinAC also aims to "enhance and improve future NGO/UNHCR collaboration," and is motivated by UNHCR's belief that NGOs have "a community-based approach [that] is an asset in bridging the gap between relief and development."[31]

International Cooperation and Burden-sharing between States, IGOs and NGOs: Operation Lifeline Sudan (1989-1990) and the Rwanda Crisis (1994)

Operation Lifeline Sudan and the Rwanda crisis perfectly illustrate the complex relationship between states and international organizations, as well as the problems of inter-agency cooperation in internal conflict situations involving large numbers of refugees and displaced persons. These two cases also illustrate the complex interaction between humanitarian concerns and political and military agendas.

Operation Lifeline Sudan (1989-1990)

Chronicled in fascinating detail by Larry Minear and his team, Operation Lifeline Sudan was launched by the international community in April 1989 (and later extended into 1990) as a massive effort to provide aid to more than two million southern Sudanese people under siege. Lifeline was made possible by an agreement negotiated by the UN with the government of the Sudan and the Sudan People's Liberation Movement & Army (SPLM/A) to allow humanitarian assistance to pass through certain "corridors of tranquillity" to civilians on either side of the southern Sudan civil war. Lifeline is the story of the testing of international law under fire, as agreed-upon international law gave way to political and military expediency. The sovereignty exercised by the Sudan government to allow Lifeline to be mounted was soon invoked to assert greater control over relief activities. Aid institutions failed to develop a common front for dealing with the authorities or to maintain an effective division of labor among themselves.[32]

Politics pervaded Lifeline from its inception. Lifeline was required because the Sudan's political institutions had failed to meet people's needs. Furthermore, political factors influenced decisions by governments, the UN, and NGOs concerning whether to help, when, how much, and through what channels. The aid agencies eventually found themselves caught up in the conflict. A humanitarian initiative, Lifeline's provision of relief aid proved a highly political act. According to the Sudan's Relief and Resettlement Commissioner, Ibrahim Abu Ouf, "Relief is not a value-free operation. It does not work in a vacuum. It is based on the interests of the countries involved, whether the Sudan or others. It has a cultural and a religious dimension. It is a network of sometimes conflicting interests and forces pushing toward different goals, though dressed up in the same garb."[33] The Lifeline experience demonstrates that humanitarian imperatives exercise no automatic legitimacy or compelling authority when political or military forces are otherwise inclined. Yet it also suggests that even where political and military agendas are dominant, humanitarian concerns can make their mark.[34]

The most critical interaction between politics and relief involved the decision of the warring parties (the Sudan government and the SPLM/A) to allow the establishment of Lifeline and to participate in it. Most observers agree that any "humanitarianism" displayed by either side was purely opportunistic to the extent that both sides embraced Lifeline at a time when, for political and military reasons, it was advantageous for them to do so, and then extricated themselves when Lifeline no longer served their interests. Eventually, both sides benefitted from the reprieve associated with Lifeline. They used the interlude to strengthen and consolidate their military positions and accused each other of doing so. Relief freed up resources to spend on preparing for, and fighting the war. A mixture of humanitarian and political interests affected the priority and timing of the involvement of foreign (or "donor") governments (individually and collectively) in relief activities in the Sudan. Foremost among them was the United States, from which many other governments have traditionally taken their cues in matters relating to humanitarian aid, refugees, and development.

Predominantly geopolitical considerations made the Sudan the largest recipient of U.S. aid in sub-Saharan Africa during the 1980s. Also strongly supportive of a major humanitarian initiative in the Sudan were the Dutch, Canadian, British, and Italian governments. A mixture of humanitarian and political considerations also figured in the heavy involvement of the European Union (EU) in Lifeline. Deferring to the UN's operational leadership, the EU contributed substantial amounts of funding and food to both UN and Sudanese government agencies, and to NGOs. The only African country that played a major role in relief assistance to the Sudan was Kenya. At the regional level, the OAU was conspicuous by its absence.[35]

Political considerations figured in the motivations of a few NGOs and influenced the operations of others. NGOs were also influenced by institutional politics of their own. The outcome of their humanitarian activities had political consequences. Most NGOs fall somewhere between the politicized humanitarianism of the Norwegian People's Aid (NPA) and the purportedly a-political approach of World Vision International. They seek to chart a course that does not choose sides yet acknowledges that humanitarian activities are circumscribed by political realities and have unavoidable political repercussions. Although caught up in the political crosscurrents of the civil war, NGOs did not become a very effective political force in their own right within the Sudan. For the most part, NGOs did not function as a community bound together by common purposes and proceeding according to agreed-upon rules. Most NGOs saw themselves as agencies with operational tasks to perform, not as organizations embodying a set of fundamental humanitarian principles. As a result, NGOs were unable to deal effectively with direct challenges to their integrity. More generally, heterogeneity among NGOs has traditionally been an obstacle to joint action, particularly in the area of the development of codes of professional conduct.

Finally, the interplay between politics and relief aid affected the involvement of the UN itself. Governments, the EU, and the OAU were quite willing to see the UN shoulder the lead responsibility. The nature of the UN as an intergovernmental body influenced its involvement in aid relief. Constituted of member states, the UN represented the political and humanitarian interests of governments. Lifeline's bias toward the political interests of sovereign states necessarily affected the UN's working relationships with NGOs. Over time, the perception of the UN's role as honest broker between competing political authorities suffered.[36]

The Rwanda Crisis in the Aftermath of the Events of April 6, 1994

The shooting down of a plane carrying Rwandan President Juvenal Habyarimana and Burundi President Cyprien Ntaryamira on its final approach into Kigali airport on April 6, 1994 unleashed one of the most brutal and systematic slaughter of civilians ever witnessed in

Africa. An estimated one million Rwandans (mostly women and children) were killed in the process. This genocide resulted within three months in the mass exodus of over two million Rwandan refugees to neighboring countries. A total of 1.3 million Rwandans fled as refugees to Zaire (including 850,000 in Goma and 450,000 in Bukavu-Uvira); about 387,000 sought refuge in Tanzania; some 310,000 fled from Rwanda into Burundi; and 15,000 took refuge in Uganda.[37] In addition, an estimated 2.2 million persons became displaced inside Rwanda.[38] In other words, over half of the country's total population (estimated at 8.1 million before the genocide began) has either been killed, decimated by epidemics, fled abroad, or become displaced inside Rwanda as a result of this brutal civil war.

The violence that erupted throughout Rwanda following the April 6 plane crash resulted in a devastating humanitarian crisis of almost unprecedented proportions. The extreme violence sparked the largest and swiftest mass exodus of people ever witnessed by UNHCR. In a period of less than 48 hours (between April 28-29), approximately a quarter of a million people streamed across the Rwandan border into Tanzania to seek refuge (137,000 more joined them later). The subsequent exodus of Rwandan refugees into Goma (eastern DRC) reached a half-million in a matter of days (rapidly increasing to 850,000).The magnitude of such population movements created one of the most challenging humanitarian crises in history. Yet, the initial response of the international community was less than enthusiastic. The delay by governments in spite of appeals by UN Secretary General Boutros Boutros-Ghali and UN High Commissioner for Refugees Sadako Ogata meant that international action was not taken that might have prevented the exodus or reduced its magnitude. As former U.S. envoy for Somalia Robert Oakley noted at the time, "At a minimum, an earlier response would have had many more relief workers and supplies on the ground to start work at once rather than after death and debilitation from disease and hunger had taken such a heavy toll".[39] Yet even before the first mass exodus of refugees to Tanzania, Boutros-Ghali was unsuccessfully urging the establishment of a UN peacekeeping force to prevent further politically inspired genocide inside Rwanda as well as to head off the outflow of refugees. The UN Assistance Mission in Rwanda (UNAMIR) was established in November 1993, following the signing of the Arusha Accords in August 1993. UNAMIR was given a broad mandate by the UN Security Council, including assistance in setting up the transitional government, demobilization, supervision of refugee repatriation, and humanitarian assistance. The Mission was 2,548-men strong, including 428 Belgian troops. As the scale of Rwandan horrors continued to rise and began to receive soul-searing television coverage, however, the international community slowly began to rally in a typical case of "too little, too late". After promptly evacuating their nationals under military escort on April 9-10, Belgium, France, and the U.S. adopted a passive attitude of "benign neglect" vis-à-vis the unfolding Rwanda crisis. Belgium's participation in UNAMIR was seriously jeopardized following the killing of 10 Belgian UNAMIR soldiers by Rwandan soldiers of the Presidential Guard on April 7. Following this incident, Belgium withdrew its UNAMIR contingent on April 20. On April 21, UN Security Council Resolution 912 reduced UNAMIR to a token level of 270 personnel and restricted its mandate to mediation and humanitarian aid.[40]

True to their unabashedly interventionist policy in Africa, the French launched, on June 23, a UN-authorized military intervention in western Rwanda from bases in eastern Zaire involving 2,300 marines and Foreign Legion soldiers and 300 Senegalese soldiers. Amid widespread national and international criticism, the French government justified its intervention as a purely humanitarian operation designed to protect threatened civilians. However, its close involvement with Rwanda's Hutu-dominated government—on whose side it had already intervened in October 1990—and its establishment of a security zone (or safe-haven) for displaced Hutus in southwestern Rwanda strongly suggests that geopolitical considerations pertaining to French presence and interests in central and eastern Africa were a more likely justification for intervention than their alleged humanitarian reasons. *Opération Turquoise* (as the French intervention was called), was unable to prevent the Tutsi-dominated rebel forces of the Rwandan Patriotic Front (RPF) from seizing the capital, Kigali, and constituting a new broad-based government headed by a moderate Hutu, Faustin Twagiramungu, on July 4-5. Claiming that it had fulfilled its duty, France rejected repeated and urgent appeals from the international community to prolong its military mission in Rwanda. All its troops left the country before the expiration of the UN mandate on August 21, after handing over control of a security zone sheltering some two million internally displaced Hutus to a UN peacekeeping force composed mainly of African units. It has now been established—including by a special French parliamentary committee—that France provided continued diplomatic, military, technical and financial support to the *génocidaires* extremists of *Hutu Power* (*Interahamwe* and *Forces armées rwandaises/* FAR) who planned and executed the genocide.[41]

After months of hesitation and benign neglect, the U.S. government launched on July 29 a massive emergency relief operation in favor of the Rwandan refugees and displaced persons. The operation involved the airlift of medicine, food and water and the dispatching of some 4,000 US military personnel (mostly logistics, transportation and communication experts), 200 of whom were deployed within Rwanda on July 31. On July 29, President Bill Clinton committed $470 million in U.S. emergency aid to Rwanda. Spurred by what he said could be "the world's worst humanitarian crisis in a generation," and stressing the essentially humanitarian character of this operation, President Clinton urged Americans to "reach out with their own private contribution to relief organizations" to help alleviate the suffering of the displaced Rwandans.[42]

Hampered by poor preparation and limited resources, aid agencies scrambled to cope with the enormous exodus of refugees from Rwanda. The violence forced almost all relief organizations to suspend their efforts in Rwanda and evacuate their staffs to neighboring countries. A few NGOs maintained a minimal staff in Nairobi (Kenya) on stand by and met regularly to coordinate relief efforts with the UN. Only a handful of international organizations maintained a limited presence in Rwanda throughout the crisis. Among them, the Swiss-based International Committee of the Red Cross (ICRC) and the French-based *Médecins sans Frontières* (MSF, or "Doctors Without Borders") both retained medical staffs and surgical teams in Kigali to provide medical treatment and emergency relief items to the victims. Their efforts, however, could not meet the massive needs of the affected population. Most of the Rwandan refugees and displaced persons suffered from a lack of shelter, medical treatment, and food supplies. It is estimated that between April and August 1994, at least 24,000 people died of cholera, dysentery and other diseases. Some of the U.S.-based humanitarian NGOs providing relief aid to Rwandan refugees in Burundi, Tanzania, Uganda, and Zaire are: AmeriCares, the American Red Cross (which provided $18 million in new support for Rwanda relief operations), CARE, Catholic Relief Services, Church World Service, Food for the Hungry, International Rescue Committee, the Salvation Army, Save the Children, World Concern, World Relief, and World Vision.

When all is said and done, one intriguing question—which echoes U.S. Ambassador Robert Oakley's concerns cited above—remains: why did no operational agency take appropriate preventive measures (such as pre-positioning food and water purification systems) when in became clear (back in May 1994) that the inevitable victory of the RPF would predictably trigger a mass exodus of Rwandan refugees toward DRC (Goma and Bukavu)? The answer to this troubling question has much do to with the fund-raising capacity of international humanitarian NGOs, which depends greatly on the international media exposure that African emergency situations receive. Typically, such media exposure usually occurs too late, when the situation has already reached a crisis point, with tens (if not hundreds) of thousands of deaths. These agencies are thus structurally condemned to intervene too late. [43]

When, on April 5, 1994, United Nations Security Council Resolution 909 extended the mandate of the UN Assistance Mission in Rwanda (UNAMIR) until July 29, 1994, some 2,500 UNAMIR troops from 23 countries were present. The resolution authorized UNAMIR to monitor the execution of the Arusha peace accord, between the Rwandan government and the RPF. In the aftermath of the April 6 plane crash, ten Belgian UNAMIR soldiers were killed by Rwandan soldiers, prompting the UN Security Council (through Resolution 912) to scale down UNAMIR's authorized strength to 270 troops and to change the Mission's mandate. UNAMIR was now to act as intermediary between forces and to assist in aid delivery, but has no authority to stop the killing of civilians. By May 3, fewer than 500 troops remained in Rwanda. Citing "strong evidence of preparations for further massacres of civilians," UN Secretary General Boutros Boutros-Ghali called on April 29 for an increase in UN presence that "would require a commitment of human and material resources on a scale which member states have so far proved reluctant to contemplate". Finally overcoming the resistance of the U.S. government, the UN Security Council adopted on May 17 Resolution 918 authorizing UNAMIR to increase its strength to 5,500 troops and expanding its mandate to include the security and protection of civilians. UN Security Council Resolution 925 extended UNAMIR's mandate until December 9, 1994. By June 20, 4,600 troops had been offered for UNAMIR from nine countries. On August 22, a 1,300-strong UNAMIR force (including 800 Ethiopians and 500 Ghanaian and other African nationals) replaced the departing French forces.[44]

In the months following the genocide, various high-level UN needs-assessment, human rights monitoring and evaluation missions were sent to Rwanda or to neighboring countries. On April 23, a UN Department of Humanitarian Affairs advance team entered Kigali to assess the needs of the region. On May 11, UN High Commissioner for Human Rights José Ayala Lasso reached Kigali after meeting RPF commander Paul Kagame in Byumba, Rwanda. On June 10, UN Human Rights Commission Special Rapporteur Bacre Wally Ndiaye began a visit to Rwanda. On July 1, the Security Council adopted Resolution 935 creating a Commission of Experts to analyze evidence of grave violations of international humanitarian law and possible acts of genocide in Rwanda Finally, speaking from Goma (Zaire), home to almost one million Rwandan refugees at the time, the UN High Commissioner for Refugees Sadako Ogata said that officials of the new Rwandan government in Kigali had assured her that they are committed to national reconciliation, but that it is too early to urge the refugees to return: "I'll never say they should go home until I'm absolutely convinced that everything is all right," she said. [45] Ogata's view on voluntary repatriation was at variance with that of her representatives in the field who, for days, had been encouraging the refugees to go home. The High Commissioner's remarks confused the debate over voluntary repatriation and highlighted a split within the UN refugee bureaucracy on this issue.

On April 25, Peter Hansen, Under Secretary General of the Department of Humanitarian Affairs, launched the UN interagency flash appeal for Rwanda to the international community. The appeal totaled $11.6 million for resources required by the UN and other IGOs to set up assistance programs for the internally displaced and refugees. In early May, the UNHCR issued an appeal of $56.7 million in funding to provide assistance for Burundian and Rwandan refugees in the region through July 15. In yet another case of burden-shifting, a UN-sponsored conference held in Geneva on August 2, 1994 which aimed at raising $435 million in favor of Rwandan refugees, only managed to obtain $137 million. This prompted the neighboring "first asylum" African countries, which hosted more than two million refugees but which are among the poorest in Africa, to call on the international community to share this unbearable burden through debt relief or financing of unplanned expenses. The Tanzanian delegate to the conference indicated that his country had to buy 200 metric tons of wood per day amounting to $12 million to accommodate the 387,000 refugees settled along the Tanzania-Rwanda border.[46]

On December 16, 1999, a UN-appointed independent commission of inquiry into the Rwanda genocide concluded that the United

Nations failed to predict, prevent, and stop it. Thus, the report reveals that on 11 January 1994, the Canadian general commanding UNAMIR, Roméo Dallaire, sent an urgent message to Kofi Annan (then head of the UN Department of Peace-Keeping Operations in which he reported an informant's claim that weapons were being stockpiled by Hutu extremist forces in preparation for mass killings of Tutsis. Dallaire requested authorization to try to seize the weapons, but his request was denied by DPKO. On 12 January, Dallaire shared this information with the ambassadors of Belgium, France and the United States., who could have acted to prevent the ensuing massacre, but chose not to do so. While Annan may be faulted for his "excessively cautious and perplexing attitude" in view of the gravity of the information received, the Secretary General is also guilty for "not having insisted with the Security Council that the UNAMIR contingent be reinforced."[47] As he himself acknowledges in his own recollection of the events, "Perhaps I had not been insistent enough with the Security Council."[48] Dallaire denounced the failure of the Security Council to act and pointed out that "...The ineffective reaction to meeting the critical needs of the Mission...has been nothing less than scandalous from the word go, and even bordering on the irresponsible and dangerous towards the personnel of the Mission here (...) an early and determined effort to get troops and resources on the ground under the UN's mandate could have avoided all this and already saved so many lives."[49]

International Humanitarian Intervention and Sovereignty

The end of the Cold War and the disintegration of the Soviet Empire have removed the saliency of the ideological factor (the struggle between East and West, capitalism and socialism) in international relations. These changes take place at a time when the 'Global Village" based on the revolution of instant communication is further shrinking the planet. Sacrosanct principles, such as sovereignty, territorial integrity and the sanctity of existing borders, are being challenged, while new ones, such as international humanitarian intervention, are emerging. The concepts of international solidarity and burden-sharing in assistance to African refugees must be reassessed in light of this new context.

As we noted earlier, non-interference in the internal affairs of states and respect for their sovereignty and territorial integrity are hallowed principles of both the UN and the OAU. On the other hand, universal humanitarian principles (i.e., a core humanitarian ethic) must be upheld. The essence of this dilemma is well captured by a former UN adviser on peacekeeping, F.T. Liu, when he states: "The concept of the sovereignty of states prevents the UN from intervening in their internal affairs without the consent of the recognized government. On the other hand, the organization is committed to upholding human rights and humanitarian principles and cannot remain indifferent to the plight of the civilian population affected by a civil war."[50] Indeed, the emerging consensus in the international community is that "the defense of the oppressed in the name of morality should prevail over frontiers and legal documents,"[51] and that "the principle of non-interference with the essential domestic jurisdiction of States cannot be regarded as a protective barrier behind which human beings could be massively or systematically violated with impunity."[52] In the same vein, Boutros Ghali remarked: "Respect for its [the State's] fundamental sovereignty and integrity are crucial to any common international progress. The time of absolute and exclusive sovereignty, however, has passed...It is the task of leaders of States today...to find a balance between the needs of good internal governance and the requirements of an ever interdependent world". And he concluded: "The sovercignty, territorial integrity and independence of States within the established international system, and the principle of self-determination for peoples...must not be permitted to work against each other in the period ahead."[53] In brief, in domestic situations where there is a breakdown of governance, massive abuse of human rights, or extensive violence to life, multilateral intervention may be necessary to restrain partisan violence, give protection and succor to the threatened, and help build new frameworks for governance.

This consensus culminated in UN Security Council Resolution 688 of April 5, 1991, which broke new ground in international law by approving "The right to interfere on humanitarian grounds" in the hitherto sacrosanct internal affairs of member states. Following the lead of Bernard Kouchner, founder of *Médecins sans Frontières* and one-time French Secretary of State for Humanitarian Affairs, some French legal experts and humanitarian NGO activists formulated a theory of an international right of victims to assistance, and of an international duty to assist them, culminating in an international right of international humanitarian intervention.[54]

In the same vein, John Steinbruner argues that in order to be endowed with international legitimacy, foreign intervention must be designed to protect fundamental human rights—i.e., those that have to do with life itself and its personal dimensions: food, clothing, shelter, physical protection, basic health services and family integrity. And Steinbruner concludes: "This implies...a new standard for organizing international relationships. Any government that fails to provide the most fundamental rights for major segments of its population can be said to have forfeited sovereignty and the international community can be said to have a duty in those instances to reestablish it. If the absence of functional sovereignty is declared in any situation, assertive measures to recreate it would be allowed..."[55] The protection of individual rights is thus emerging as an international norm which is at variance with the inviolability of international sovereignty. Indeed, it encourages intervention because the rights of individuals are often violated by their own governments.[56] Admittedly, the steady erosion of the concept of sovereignty is making it easier for international organizations, governments, and NGOs to intervene when governments refuse to meet the needs of their populations and substantial numbers of people are at risk.[57]

In this new world order, sovereignty no longer resides with states, but with the people within them. As Stedman suggests, "It may be...that the international community has begun to accept the proposition that interests of people come before the interests of states."[58] But the same author warns that the guiding principle of what he calls "the new interventionism," namely the international community's obligation to intervene whenever a state, or group within a state fails to meet the humanitarian needs of its people, cannot be enforced consistently.[59] What, then, should be the criteria for collective intervention? In this regard, Clark appropriately raises the question of a double standard. According to him, speedy humanitarian intervention in Iraq's internal affairs to protect Kurdish populations contrasts greatly with slow international action in Somalia (and, one might add, in Rwanda), and with non-intervention in Liberia and southern Sudan.[60] The same author suggests that the U.S. government should take the lead in proposing the creation of a UN Commission to review humanitarian assistance reform. According to him, such a commission should "identify which UN mandates and authorities require buttressing for collective involvement in internal conflicts, including the terms for asserting the right of survival over sovereignty."[61]

This line of reasoning ultimately raises a number of fundamental questions. Is the international community—including its African members—ready to adopt new international humanitarian norms blending universal humanitarian principles with traditional moral values that are the common heritage of mankind? Are world leaders ready to subject political acts to moral standards? Is the time ripe for the international community to identify a core humanitarian ethic and to observe a universally accepted minimum code of conduct in conflict situations?[62] There are indications that the thinking of influential African leaders of IGOs and NGOs is slowly moving in that direction.

The 1991 Kampala Document, adopted on the initiative of Nigerian president and Africa Leadership Forum founder Olusegun Obasanjo, acknowledges that there is a link between security, stability, development and cooperation in Africa, and that the security and stability of each African country is inseparably linked with the security of all African countries. While giving due recognition to the provisions of the UN and OAU charters with respect to the principles of good neighborliness and non-interference in the internal affairs of states, the Kampala Document goes on to note that "growing international concern for humanitarian causes and the experience in Africa of civil strife and acts of wanton repression, demonstrates an increasing concern over domestic conditions pertaining to threats to personal and collective security and gross violations of basic human rights." The proposed Conference on Security, Stability, Development and Cooperation in Africa must "aim at promoting and strengthening this welcome development to enable African countries to cooperate in ensuring the security of Africans at all levels."[63] Similarly, within the framework of his proposal for a Mechanism for Conflict Prevention and Resolution, OAU Secretary General Salim Ahmed Salim suggests that a consensus on widening the definition of the non-interference principle to include internal (in addition to inter-state) conflicts now exists among the member states and proposes that "within the context of general international law as well as humanitarian law, Africa should take the lead in developing the notion that sovereignty can legally be transcended, by the 'intervention' of 'outside forces',...particularly on humanitarian grounds." And he concludes: "Given that every African is his brother's keeper, and that our borders are at best artificial, we in Africa need to use our own cultural and social relationships to interpret the principle of non-intervention in such a way that we are enabled to apply it to our advantage in conflict prevention and resolution."[64] Pending a necessary (but still hypothetical) review of the OAU Charter along these lines, this would minimally imply a binding Declaration of the OAU Assembly of Heads of States and Government providing clear terms of reference for the Secretary General and the Bureau of the Assembly to act in this spirit.[65]

This begs the question of whether the African states are now ready to move beyond what Basil Davidson calls "nation-statism" (a narrow, negative and artificial form of post-colonial nationalism) toward some rational federalism that would accommodate the various African cultures. According to Davidson, a hopeful future for Africa "would have to be a federalizing future: a future of organic unities of sensible association across wide regions within which national cultures, far from seeking to destroy or maim each other, could evolve their diversities and find in them a mutual blessing."[66] In other words, African states should transcend the artificial sovereignty of the existing nation-states and create sub-regional federal structures within which the various national cultures would be granted sovereignty and the right to self-determination. This would remove one of the main sources of ethno-regional conflicts and create an enabling environment for peace and security, democratic governance and sustainable, participatory development in Africa, thus effectively reducing the number of refugees. Such is the challenge facing African leaders as they enter the new millennium.

Endnotes

1. *World Refugee Survey 1994* (Washington, DC: US Committee for Refugees, 1994), pp. 40-41, 46.
2. *Worldwide Refugee Information* [*Refugees and Asylum Seekers Worldwide; Principal Sources of Refugees, Refugees and Asylum Seekers Worldwide*] (Washington, DC: US Committee for Refugees, 1999); note that only the highest estimates of IDP in Angola and Algeria have been retained (the lowest estimates for these two countries being 1 million and 100,000, respectively).
3. 1951 *Geneva Convention Relating to the Status of Refugees*, Art. 1(A)(2); 1969 *OAU Convention Governing Specific Aspects of Refugee Problems in Africa*, Art. 1(2).
4. *OAU Convention*, Art. 3(2); Etienne R. Mbaya, "Political Asylum in the Charter of the OAU: Pretensions and Reality," *Law and State* vol. 35 (9 June 1987), pp.70-77.
5. Francis M. Deng, *Protecting the Dispossessed: A Challenge for the*

International Community (Washington, DC: The Brookings Institution, 1993), pp. 3-4.

6. J.P.L. Fonteyne, "Burden-Sharing: An Analysis of the Nature and Function of International Solidarity in Cases of Mass Influx of Refugees," *The Australian Year Book of International Law* vol. 8 (1983), pp. 167-9; Barry N. Stein, "The Nature of the Refugee Problem," *Conference on the International Protection of Refugees* (Montreal, Canada, 29 November-2 December 1987), pp. 15-16.

7. Fonteyne, "Burden-Sharing (...)," in *op. cit.*, pp. 172-5; David A. Martin, "New Developments in Refugee Law and Current Problems: Asylum Concept, Solidarity, and the Concept of Burden-Sharing," *Symposium on the Promotion, Dissemination & Teaching of Fundamental Human Rights of Refugees* (Tokyo, Japan, 7-11 December 1981).

8. Fonteyne, "Burden-Sharing (...)," in *op. cit.*, pp. 175-8.

9. Vitit Muntarbhom, "Refugee Problems and Developing Countries: Between Burden-Sharing and Burden-Shifting," *World Congress on Human Rights* (10-15 December 1990), pp. 5-6; J.N. Saxena, "Problems of Refugees in the Developing Countries and the Need for International Burden-Sharing," *World Congress on Human Rights* (10-15 December 1990), pp. 7-8.

10. Bill Frelick, "The Year in Review," in *World Refugee Survey 1994* (Washington, DC: US Committee for Refugees, 1994), pp. 2-3.

11. *World Refugee Survey 1994* (Washington, DC: US Committee for Refugees, 1994), table 6, p. 43).

12. Marc-Antoine Pérouse de Montclos, "L'Afrique rejette ses propres immigrés," *Le Monde diplomatique* (décembre 1999), p. 15.

13. *World Refugee Survey 1994*, table 5, p. 43.

14. Muntarbhom, "Refugee Problems in Developing Countries (....)," *op. cit.*; Stein, "The Nature of the Refugee Problem," *op. cit.*, pp. 3-4.

15. Andrew S. Natsios, "NGOs and the UN System in Complex Humanitarian Emergencies: Conflict or Cooperation?" in Thomas G. Weiss & Leon Gordenker (eds.), *NGOs, the UN, and*

Global Governance (Boulder: Lynne Rienner Publishers, 1996), p. 67.

16. Yves Beigbeder, *The Role and Status of International Humanitarian Volunteers and Organizations: The Right and Duty to Humanitarian Assistance* (Boston: Martinus Nijhoff Publishers, 1991), pp. 4-8.

17. A.S. Natsios, "NGOs and the UN System in Complex Humanitarian Emergencies," in *op. cit.*, pp. 67-81.

18. Y. Beigbeder, *op. cit.*, p. 10.

19. Natsios, "NGOs and the UN System in Complex Humanitarian Emergencies," in op. cit., pp. 67-8, 78-9.

20. Beigbeder, *op. cit.*, pp. 27-34.

21. *Ibidem*, pp. 31-33.

22. *World Refugee Survey 1994*, table 8, p. 43.

23. *OAU Charter*, Art. III(1, 2 & 3); Amadu Sesay, Olusola Ojo & Orobola Fasehun, *The OAU After Twenty Years* (Boulder: Westview Press, 1984), pp. 79-91.

24. Etienne R. Mbaya, "Political Asylum in the Charter of the OAU: Pretensions and Reality," *Law and State* vol. 35 (9 June 1987), pp. 73-4.

25. OAU, *African Charter on Human and People's Rights* [ACHPR] (Addis Ababa: OAU, 1981).

26. ACHPR, Art. 12(1,2,3 & 4).

27. ACHPR, Art. 12(5).

28. Beigbeder, op. cit., p. 80.

29. *Ibidem*, pp. 80-82.

30. *Ibidem*, p. 97.

31. Sadako Ogata, "Opening statement to the 44th Session of the Executive Committee of the High Commissioner's Programme," *PARinAC Information Note and Update* no. 1 (Geneva: UNHCR & ICVA, 1993), p. 1.

32. Larry Minear, et. al., *Humanitarianism under Siege: A Critical Review of Operation Lifeline Sudan* (Trenton, NJ & Washington, DC: The Red Sea Press/Bread for the World Institute on

Hunger and Development, 1991), pp. ix-xviii.

33. Quoted in Minear et. al., *op. cit.*, p. 65.

34. Minear et. al., *op. cit.*, pp. 65-6.

35. *Ibidem*, pp. 66-84.

36. *Ibidem*, pp. 84-98.

37. UNHCR estimates (18 August 1994).

38. *US-AID Situation Report # 5* (18 August 1994).

39. Robert B. Oakley, "A Slow Response on Rwanda," *The Washington Post* (27 July 1994), p. A27.

40. On UNAMIR and the role of the UN in Rwanda, see: Howard Adelmane Astri Suhrke (eds.), *The Path of a Genocide: The Rwanda Crisis from Vganda to Zaire* (New Brunswick: Transaction Publishers, 1999); Bruce D. Jones, *Peacemaking in Rwanda: The Dynamics of Failure* (Boulder: Lynne Rienner, 2001); Jean-Claude Willame, L'ONU au Rwanda (1993-1995) (Paris & Bruxelles: Editions Maisonneuve & Larose/Labor, 1996).

41. On French responsibility in the Rwanda genocide, see in particular: *Rapport de la Mission d'information parlementaire française sur le Rwanda* (15 décembre 1998) [Pierre Brana & Bernard Cazenave, Rapporteurs]; Colette Braeckman, *Rwanda: histoire d'un génocide* (Paris: Fayard, 1994); François-Xavier Verschave, *Complicité de génocide? La politique de la France au Rwanda* (Paris: La Découverte, 1994); Philippe Leymarie, "Litigieuse intervention française au Rwanda," *Le Monde diplomatique* (July 1994), p. 3; Gérard Prunier, *The Rwanda Crisis: History of a Genocide* (New York: Colombia University Press, 1995).

42. Bob Deans, "U.S. troops to lead massive Rwanda airlift," *The Atlanta Journal & Atlanta Constitution* (30 July 1994).

43. See in particular Paul Alexander, "Agencies scramble to help refugees," *The Atlanta Journal & Atlanta Constitution* (17 July 1994); and Geraldine Faes, "Rwanda: le suicide," in *Jeune Afrique* (28 July 1994), pp. 12-15.

44. On the role of UNAMIR in the months preceding the genocide in Rwanda, see in particular: Boutros Boutros-Ghali,

Unvanquisehed: A U.S.-U.N. Saga (New York: Random House, 1999), pp. 129-141; Bruce D. Jones, *Peacemaking in Rwanda: The Dynamics of Failure* (Boulder: Lynne Rienner Publishers, 2001); and Jean-Claude Willame, *L'ONU au Rwanda* (Paris: Maisonneuve & Larose, 1996).

45. reported by Keith B. Richburg, "U.N. Official Urges Caution on Repatriation," *The Washington Post* (2 August 1994), p. A18.
46. Msuya Waldi Mangachi, Minister-Counsellor in the Tanzanian Mission to the U.N. in Geneva, quoted in *Jeune Afrique* (11 août 1994), p. 79.
47. Afsané Bassir Pour, 'L'ONU est jugée responsable du génocide rwandais," *Le Monde* (17 décembre 1999); Fabrice Rousselot, "L'ONU devra présenter ses excuses au Rwanda," *Libération* (17 décembre 1999); Boutros Boutros-Ghali, *Unvanquished: A US-UN Saga* (New York: Random House, 1999), pp. 129-141.
48. B. Boutros-Ghali, *Unvanquished*, p. 140.
49. quoted in Boutros-Ghali, *Unvanquised*, p. 139.
50. quoted in Minear et. al., *op. cit.*, p. 107.
51. Speech by former UN Secretary General Javier Perez de Cuellar at the University of Bordeaux (France) on 24 April 1991; *UN Press Release* SG/SM/4560 (1991).
52. Javier Perez de Cuellar, *Report of the Secretary-General on the Work of the Organization* (New York: United Nations, 1991), p. 12.
53. Boutros Boutros-Ghali, *An Agenda for Peace: Preventive Diplomacy, Peacemaking and Peace-keeping* (New York: United Nations, 1992), pp. 9-10.
54. Beigbeder, *op. cit.*, pp. 353-384; Marie-Dominique Perrot (ed.), *Dérives humanitaires: États d'urgence et Droit d'ingérence* (Paris & Genève: Presses Universitaires de France/Nouveaux Cahiers de l'IUED, 1994).
55. quoted in F.M. Deng, *Protecting the Dispossessed*, p. 156.
56. Michael Mandelbaum, "The Reluctance to Intervene," *Foreign Policy* no. 95 (Summer 1994), p. 14.
57. Deng, *op. cit.*, p. 15.

58. Stephen J. Stedman, "The New Interventionists," *Foreign Affairs* vol. 72, no. 1 (1993), p. 16.
59. S.J. Stedman, *art. cit.*, p. 9.
60. Jeffrey Clark, "Debacle in Somalia," *Foreign Affairs* vol. 72, no. 1 (1993), p. 121.
61. J. Clark, *art. cit.*, p. 122.
62. Abdul Mohammed, in Minear et. al., *op. cit.*, p. vii.
63. *The Kampala Document,: Towards a Conference on Security, Stability, Development and Co-operation in Africa* (Abeokuta & New York: Africa Leadership Forum, 1991), pp. 1-3, 10.
64. OAU, *Report of the Secretary-General on Conflicts in Africa: Proposals for a Mechanism for Conflict Prevention and Resolution*; Report to the 56th Ordinary Session of the Council of Ministers, Dakar, Senegal (22-27 June 1992) [CM/1710(LVI)], pp. 11-12.
65. *Ibidem*, p. 13.
66. Basil Davidson, *The Black Man's Burden: Africa and the Curse of the Nation-State* (New York: Times Books, 1992), p. 286.

Chapter 9

The African Nation-State in Crisis:
Alternative Frameworks for Regional Governance

The end of the Cold War and the disintegration of the Soviet Empire offer both challenges and opportunities for Africa. According to the post-Cold War ideologues, in the post-Cold War international system, the ideological conflict between Western civilization and Islamic fundamentalism and the economic conflict between North and South have replaced the East-West conflict between capitalism and socialism. According to Samuel Huntington's civilizational paradigm, "...culture and cultural identities...are shaping the patterns of cohesion, disintegration and conflict in the post-Cold War world...In the post-Cold War world, the most important distinctions among peoples are not ideological, political or economic. They are cultural...The rivalry of the superpowers is replaced by the clash of civilizations...And the most dangerous cultural conflicts are those along the fault lines between (Western and Eastern) civilizations."[1] Is this really the case, and where does Africa actually stand in the new world order?

Principles such as sovereignty, territorial integrity, and the sanctity of existing borders are increasingly being challenged while new ones, such as international humanitarian intervention, regionalism, and federalism, are emerging. In Africa as elsewhere, the nation-state is coming under threat from above (regionalism and federalism) and below (ethnicity). Technological innovation is now helping to further undermine the nation-states as capital and information crisscross the world unfettered by national boundaries. While Afro-pessimists predict that the African state is in danger of imminent collapse, Afro-optimists caution that it would be unwise to ignore the signs of hope, which could be amplified over time to allow Africa to recover lost ground. After a brief overview of some of the most serious threats to the post-colonial African nation-states' sovereignty and integrity, this chapter will examine the opportunities available to these states as they attempt to improve their condition and status in the post-Cold War world through various subregional and regional strategies of economic and political development.

THE DOOMSDAY SCENARIOS OF THE AFRO-PESSIMISTS

Africa has of late become a political laboratory in which Western futurologists test various doomsday scenarios of the world's looming catastrophes. Robert Kaplan's much-quoted apocalyptic predictions—which, unfortunately, have gained credibility in the U.S. business and diplomatic communities—are a case in point: "West Africa is becoming *the* symbol of worldwide demographic, environmental, and societal stress, in which criminal anarchy emerges as the real 'strategic' danger." For Kaplan, Sierra Leone is a microcosm of what is occurring throughout Africa: "...the withering away of central governments, the rise of tribal and regional domains, the unchecked spread of disease, and the growing pervasiveness of war."[2] This pessimistic view is echoed by Jean-François Bayart's analysis of the grad-

ual process of "criminalization" of the African state through faction-
al struggle between various ethnically based armed groups over territory, mineral resources, and arms and drug trafficking networks.
According to Bayart and others, the historical process of mutation of
the African state from a "kleptocratic" to a "bandit" state has five
characteristic features:

(1) the diplomatic, economic and financial "devaluation" of black Africa;
(2) the failure of the democratic transitions initiated
in the early 1990s;
(3) the continuation and spread of armed conflicts;
(4) the restructuring of the subcontinent around new
foreign influences and axes of powers; and
(5) the increasing involvement of African economic
and political entrepreneurs in "illegal" or "criminal" types of activities.

As the authors remark, "...the multiplication of conflicts, the main
political logic of which is simple predation and which tend to be
accompanied by a growing insertion in the international economy of
illegality..., the spread of a culture of institutional neglect, systematic
plunder of the national economy and the uncontrolled privatization of
the state...all suggest that a slide towards criminalization throughout
the sub-continent is a strong probability." And they conclude:
"...informal and illicit trade, financial fraud, and the systematic evasion
of rules and international agreements could turn out to be a
means...by which certain Africans manage to survive and to stake their
place in the maelstrom of globalization."[3] Even the recent wave of
democratization that has spread throughout the continent since the
early 1990s has not tempered the gloomy predictions of staunch Afro-
pessimists, such as William Pfaff, who recently wrote (against all evidence) that "Most of Africa...lacks the crucial educated middle and
professional classes and the mediating private and public institutions

that compose a 'civil society'. Civil society makes democracy possible; without it, democracy has failed and will continue to fail in Africa."[4]

The intensity, scale and magnitude of the Rwanda tragedy of mid-1994 in which some one million innocent civilians were massacred, and which resulted in the mass exodus of over two million Rwandan refugees to neighboring countries while another one million became internally displaced, seemed to vindicate the Afro-pessimists' worst fears.[5] And it is true that the recent economic and social data from Africa is not very encouraging.

World Bank data shows that GNP per capita declined by -1.1 percent over the period 1985-1995. The average annual growth rate of GDP over the period 1990-95 was 1.4 percent in sub-Saharan Africa (SSA), as against 10.3 percent in East Asia and the Pacific. Global exports increased by 6 percent between 1990 and 1995, while global imports increased by 5.8 percent; during the same period, SSA's exports rose by a mere 0.9 percent while its imports rose by 1.9 percent. As a result, SSA's total external debt amounted to 226.5 billion dollars in 1995. According to the World Bank classification in terms of 1995 GNP per capita income, out of 133 countries listed, only 3 (Gabon, Mauritius, and South Africa) were classified as upper middle-income, 7 (Algeria, Botswana, Egypt, Lesotho, Morocco, Namibia, and Tunisia) as lower middle-income, and 30 as low-income.[6]

Africa is the most strife-torn region in the world. According to a Belgian study team, armed conflict occurred in 53 African countries—the exact membership of the OAU to date—between 1955 and 1995, with a total loss of life estimated at between 7 and 8 million (including one million in Rwanda and 2 million in Sudan).[7] At the end of 1998, there were 2,912,000 refugees and asylum seekers (in 19 countries) and 8,858,000 internally displaced persons (in 18 countries) in Africa, representing 22.8 and 47.1 percent of the world total, respectively. At that time, Angola, Burundi, Somalia, Sudan, Eritrea, Liberia and Sierra Leone accounted for 2,469,000 of these refugees and asylum seekers, and Angola, Congo, DRC, Burundi, Rwanda, Uganda, Somalia, Sudan, and Sierra Leone for 8 million of these internally displaced persons (including 4 million in Sudan and 1.5 million in Angola).[8] UNICEF estimates that 10 million children below 15 years of age have been abandoned in Africa. According to the UN Food and Agriculture Organization (FAO), 15 sub-Saharan African countries are facing exceptional food emergencies, and millions of people risk starvation and are in need of urgent food assistance. The food situation is particularly critical in the DRC (10 million people at risk), Somalia (1.6 million), Rwanda (900,000), Burundi (821,000), and Eritrea (500,000).[9]

UN statistics show that SSA has the highest incidence of human poverty (42 percent) and income poverty (39 percent) in the world, and both types of poverty are increasing both in proportion and in absolute numbers. SSA's human development index value stood at 0.380 in 1994, as against 0.911 for industrial countries (out of a maximum possible value of 1).[10] According to the World Health Organization (WHO), sub-Saharan Africa is home to two-thirds of the world's 33.4 million people living with AIDS, and the continent has 83 percent of the AIDS deaths and 95 percent of the world's AIDS orphans. . More than 5,000 people with AIDS die each day in Africa (13,000 by 2005), and economists estimate that as a result, the shrinking labor pool, added to other factors, will slow the continent's rate of economic growth by as much as 1.4 percentage points each year for the nest 20 years; in Africa's most industrialized states, the GDP could be 20 percent lower by 2005 than it otherwise would have been.[11] These glum economic and social statistics are a reflection of Africa's very real economic, social, and political crisis which, at bottom, is a crisis of the African nation-state.

THE AFRO-OPTIMISTIC VIEW

In a thought-provoking article, the Kenyan scholar Michael Chege leads the charge against the doomsayers' view of contemporary Africa: "...[this view] ignores the old homily that every cloud has a silver lining. And this includes the political storms in overcast tropical Africa...For within the contours of the silver lining may lie the policy lessons that might realistically be applied toward improving the political and economic conditions under whose shadow a substantial proportion of Africans now live."[12] This view is echoed by former U.S. Assistant Secretary of State for Africa Chester Crocker, when he says that "...it would be nice to hear more about the accomplishments and quiet successes of a vast region whose very diversity is one of its most striking features...There are signs of real vitality in a number of African economies...and there is inspiration and hope in the pragmatic miracle of South Africa's negotiated transition to democracy."[13]

In a resolutely upbeat address to Parliament in Cape Town during his State visit to South Africa (26-29 March 1998), U.S. President Bill Clinton declared: "Yes, Africa remains the world's greatest development challenge, still plagued in places by poverty, malnutrition, disease, illiteracy, and unemployment. Yes, terrible conflicts continue to tear at the heart of the continent...But from Cape Town to Kampala, from Dar-es-Salaam to Dakar, democracy is gaining strength, business is growing, peace is making progress. We are seeing...an African Renaissance."[14]

Since early 1990, the "winds of change" have swept throughout Africa, signalling the dawn of a new era, variously referred to as the "second independence," the "second liberation," or the "Springtime of Africa." After three decades of authoritarian one-party rule characterized by political repression, human rights abuses, economic mismanagement, nepotism and corruption, democracy is spreading like bush fire throughout Africa. A 1994 evaluation of the Carter Center's African Governance Program noted that 15 African countries could be described as "democratic", three were under a "direct democracy" regime, and 26 were in transition to democracy.[15] Admittedly, there have been some setbacks in a number of countries (such as Burundi, Cameroon, Côte d'Ivoire, Gabon, Guinea, Kenya, Niger, Nigeria, and Togo) where ruling autocrats have maintained or reinstated authoritarian rule. These states, as well as those still plagued by overt or latent ethnic conflict (such as Angola, Burundi, Congo, Ethiopia/Eritrea, DRC, Rwanda, Sierra Leone, and Sudan) are in a state of "political anomy" in which the governing elites cannot resolve their countries' complex security, economic, and political problems. On the positive side, there is inspiration and hope in the quiet revolution of South Africa's negotiated transition to democracy. The bold experiments in constitutional engineering of Ethiopia's cultural confederalism, and Uganda's no-party politics have the potential to produce better governance and political stability. And a new generation of African liberal constitutional reformers heading democratically elected governments has quietly assumed power in one African country after another (most notably in Cape Verde, Central African Republic, Gambia, Malawi, Mali, Niger, and Zambia).

THE RIGHT OF INTERNATIONAL HUMANITARIAN INTERVENTION

Non-interference in the internal affairs of states and respect for their sovereignty and territorial integrity are hallowed principles of both the United Nations and the Organization of African Unity. On the other hand, universal humanitarian principles must be upheld. Indeed, the emerging consensus in the international community is that "the defense of the oppressed in the name of morality should prevail over frontiers and legal documents,"[16] and that "the principle of non-interference with the essential domestic jurisdiction of States cannot be regarded as a protective barrier behind which human beings could be massively or systematically violated with impunity."[17] Or, as former UN Secretary-General Boutros Boutros-Ghali succinctly put it, "The time of absolute and exclusive sovereignty...has passed...The sovereignty, territorial integrity and independence of States within the established international system, and the principle of self-determination for peoples, both of great value and importance, must not be permitted to work against each other in the period ahead."[18] In brief, in domestic situations where there is a breakdown of governance, massive abuse of human rights, or extensive violence to life, multilateral intervention may be necessary to restrain partisan violence, give protection and succor to the threatened, and help build new frameworks of governance. In this spirit, French legal experts and humanitarian NGO activists have formulated a theory of an international right of victims to assistance, and of an international duty to assist them, culminating in a right of "international humanitarian intervention."[19] This right particularly applies in complex humanitarian emergencies which, according to Andrew Natsios, are defined by five common characteristics: the deterioration or complete collapse of central government authority; ethnic or religious conflict and widespread human rights abuses; episodic food insecurity, frequently deteriorating into mass starvation; macroeconomic collapse involving hyperinflation, massive unemployment and net decreases in GNP; and mass population movements of displaced persons and refugees escaping conflict or searching for food.[20]

Underpinning these political developments has been the African nation-state's progressive loss of effective territorial and economic sovereignty. Following Robert Jackson, Christopher Clapham describes contemporary African states as "quasi-states", that is "states which are recognized as sovereign and independent units by other states within the international system, but which cannot meet the demands of 'empirical' statehood, which requires the capacity to exercise effective power within their own territories, and be able to defend themselves against external attack." Such states, according to them, "have 'negative' or 'juridical' sovereignty, in that sovereignty is ascribed to them by other states, but do not possess the 'positive sovereignty' which derives from effective control." And Clapham argues that the end of the Cold War coincided with the failure of juridical statehood in Africa.[21]

As noted above, African states are becoming increasingly penetrated and undermined by the communication revolution as capital and information crisscross the world unhindered by national boundaries. In a number of countries (Angola, Congo, Liberia, DRC, Rwanda, Burundi, Sierra Leone, Somalia, and Sudan), the monopoly of power by one ethnic group/clan backed by foreign sponsors has led to government failure, then civil war.

Even in peaceful areas, few of the African governments are able to provide the basic amenities and minimal security required for functional sovereignty. As noted by Jeffrey Herbst, armies have challenged African governments (as in Rwanda, Burundi, Congo, DRC/Zaïre, Niger, Ethiopia, and Chad), and private security outfits such as the South African-based Executive Outcomes have helped governments such as Angola and Sierra Leone control their territory.[22] The only incorporated private mercenary army in the world that will contract to move in and wage full-scale war on behalf of its clients, Executive Outcomes views itself as a team of corporate troubleshooters, marketing a strategy of recovery to (mostly African) failing governments. This most unconventional outfit—staffed by former elite commandos of the apartheid regime and linked to British and South African corporate interests—is indicative of a new global trend: the "privatization of violence"—namely of defence and security—on the world scene.[23]

In Africa, the privatization of violence—or the delegitimization of public safety—go hand-in-hand with the liberalization and privatization of the state's economies prescribed by the omnipotent international financial institutions as part of their quasi-mandatory structural adjustment programs. This privatization process involves not only African parastatals, but also some strategic areas such as customs and public finance administration and other essential public services. As Béatrice Hibou has argued, the partial privatization of African public services, with its attendant fiscal and budgetary conditionalities, results in a dilution of sovereignty and reflects a minimalist conception of the state.[24]

African governments also appear powerless to control the much more threatening smuggling of drugs and weapons and the multiplying money-laundering operations. The involvement of senior government officials in these activities in some countries (Nigeria, Zambia, and South Africa) further undermines political and economic sovereignty. Environmental pressures combined with economic and political pressures further threaten the cohesion of African nation-states. Across the continent, southward migratory patterns (from the rural hinterlands to the coastal urban centers) resulting from relentless desertification and deforestation are leaving a trail of environmental damage. According to Achille Mbembe, new forms of non-state, trans-border sovereignty are emerging, and a new geopolitical reconfiguring of Africa is taking place. According to this scenario, four main geo-political areas are emerging in Africa: North Africa, which is progressively disconnected from the rest of the continent; a trans-continental, East-West Sahelian zone, characterized by migrations and de-territorialization; southern Africa, dominated by the South African giant, whose economies are becoming increasingly integrated with those of North America, Europe and Asia to the detriment of the rest of the African continent; and an "arc of conflict" including states in conflict in the Greater Horn and the Great Lakes region, in which the cycle of violence is fuelled by warlord politics and competition over control of mineral resources (such as diamonds in Angola and Sierra Leone). These competing and contradictory geopolitical dynamics—in which whole areas escape state sovereignty—significantly increase the risk of internal, inter-state, and subregional conflicts.[25]

This multi-pronged challenge to the African states' sovereignty and territorial integrity has naturally led to a crisis of the nation-state in Africa, the contours and implications of which are still taking shape. What is clear is that "the territorial division of Africa into nation-states based on colonial partition, with boundaries sanctified by the OAU as inviolable, is under the greatest pressure since independence."[26] African and other experts have proposed various solutions to this crisis, some more sensible and realistic than others, but all aiming at diluting sovereignty within existing or proposed subregional or regional political and economic entities.

NEW FRAMEWORKS FOR REGIONAL GOVERNANCE

The failure of the contemporary African state has its roots in Africa's colonial past. This failure can specifically be traced back to the Berlin Conference of 1884-85 during which the current map of Africa was drawn by the various European imperialist powers (notably Britain, France, and Germany) without regard to historical, geographic, and demographic variables, or pre-existing ethnic boundaries and political entities. Fearful of the potential disintegration of the newly created sovereign states, the framers of the OAU Charter of 25 May 1963 emphatically upheld the principles of sanctity of colonially inherited borders, sovereign equality and non-interference in internal affairs of states, and respect for sovereignty and territorial integrity. This, in hindsight, might have been their greatest mistake, whose legacy is still with us today. Admittedly, the founding fathers of the post colonial African states were faced with the intractable task of building nations within totally artificial states while in other parts of the world (particularly in Europe), states were erected on the bedrock of pre-existing nations. Thus, African nationalism naturally led to what Basil Davidson has called "nation-statism," namely a narrow, negative and artificial form of post colonial nationalism.[27]

European Re-colonization, Inter-African colonization, and Sub-regionalism

In a provocative article written in a distinctly Afro-pessimistic vein, William Pfaff laments the socio-political disintegration and economic collapse of the post colonial African state and calls for a "disinterested neo-colonialism," by which he means that the former European colonial powers (notably Britain, France, Italy, and Portugal) should reestablish a type of trusteeship authority over their respective former African colonies. In a proposal eerily reminiscent of the Berlin Conference, Pfaff seriously suggests the creation, within the European

Union, of a "Euro-African trust organization" to which African governments would irrevocably delegate extensive security, political, administrative, social, and economic powers for a half-century, perhaps a century.[28] In a similar vein, former U.S. assistant secretary of state for African affairs Herman Cohen recently suggested that the three (militarily powerful) members of NATO most familiar with the African military scene (Britain, France, and the United States) should consider the possibility of "adopting" Africa to help bring the continent up to fully operational status in the area of conflict management.[29] Besides their distinctly neo colonial and paternalistic overtones, such proposals blatantly disregard the African states' considerable intellectual and institutional capacity for political and economic recovery and, as such, should be dismissed as unfeasible.

An *habitué* of controversial proposals, the distinguished Kenyan scholar Ali Mazrui has recently come up with his own project for the salvation of Africa. He proposes a plan for inter-African colonization and annexation that in effect amounts to a kind of self-colonization. In a throw back to the UN Trusteeship system, Mazrui suggests that in the twenty-first century the governance of Somalia, Sudan, Angola, Rwanda/Burundi, and Zanzibar should be entrusted to Ethiopia, Egypt, South Africa, DRC, and Tanganyika, respectively. He also proposes that an African Security Council (on the UN model) should be set up with Egypt, Ethiopia, Nigeria, and South Africa as permanent members by virtue of their (actual or potential) regional power status.[30] This *Pax Africana* à la Mazrui is yet another version of the Pfaff proposal in which European powers are replaced by African ones. As such, this neo-sub-imperialist project should be rejected as incompatible with African cultural sub-nationalism and totally impractical.

Subregionalism usually refers to various types of economic and political integration schemes existing (or proposed) within the various African regions. Ever since they became independent in the early sixties, African states have consistently pursued policies of regional cooperation and integration as a means of promoting socio-economic development and of reducing their dependence on the West. While many institutions for regional cooperation and integration were created after independence in the various African subregions (north, west, central, east and southern Africa), progress toward integration has generally been slow. The regional integration schemes that have made substantial progress to date and that offer the best potential for future success are: in north Africa, the Arab Maghreb Union (AMU), created in 1989); in west Africa, the Economic Community of West African States (ECOWAS, 1975) and the (exclusively Francophone) West African Economic and Monetary Union (UEMOA, 1994); in central Africa, the Economic Community of Central African States (CEEAC, 1983); in eastern Africa the East African Community (1967-77; reconstituted in November 1999); in eastern and southern Africa, the Common Market for Eastern and Southern Africa (COMESA, ex-PTA, created in 1981, modified in 1991); and in southern Africa, the Southern African Development Community (SADC, created in 1980, modified in 1991).[31]

Faced with a growing number of internal ethnic conflicts that constitute a serious threat to regional security, African regional organizations have, since 1990, increasingly assumed security functions within the framework of their respective defence protocols. Thus, in August 1990, the ECOWAS Monitoring Group (ECOMOG) was set up as a peacekeeping force with a mandate to keep the peace, restore law and order, and ensure respect of the cease-fire in strife-torn Liberia. Composed of some 9,000 troops from five member-states under the dynamic leadership of Nigeria, ECOMOG has since been relatively successful in maintaining a precarious peace in that country, as well as in Sierra Leone. In west Africa, the exclusively francophone *Communauté Économique de l'Afrique de l'ouest* (CEAO) Defense Protocol, the *Accord de Non-agression et d'Assistance en Matière de Défense* (ANAD) was signed in 1977 by eight member-states and became operational in 1981. In addition to establishing an inter-allied command, a commission for the peaceful settlement of disputes, and a peacekeeping force, ANAD has set up a system of confidence-building measures to ensure that states are informed as to potential threats to their security. ANAD was able to establish a cease-fire in early 1986, following the "Christmas War" between Mali and Burkina Faso. In the Greater Horn, IGAD (Intergovernmental Authority on Development) has, starting in 1994, hosted and facilitated negotiating sessions between the Sudanese government and the southern Sudanese rebel forces to try to end that country's devastating war; it has also developed peace plans for Somalia and for the Ethiopian/Eritrean conflict.[32]

Beyond the Nation-State in Africa: Pan-Africanism, African Unity and Federalism

The severity of the crisis of the African nation-state calls for drastic solutions, possibly including redrafting frontiers according to the principle of self-determination. In Africa as elsewhere, history has a strange way of repeating itself. In 1990-1996 as in 1957-1963, the "Federal question" was very much at the center of the political debate among the African political and intellectual elite. And Kwame Nkrumah's much-maligned Pan-African blueprint—a political and economic union in the form of a Union Government of African States based on such mechanisms and institutions as an African Common Market and integrated monetary zone, with a common currency and central bank, a unified defence strategy with an African Military High Command; and a unified foreign policy and diplomacy—now almost 40 years old, is resurfacing in various forms.[33] The June 1991 summit meeting of the OAU (Abuja, Nigeria) adopted a treaty establishing an African Economic Community to be created in stages (via an African Common Market) by the year 2025.[34] Similarly, in May 1991, the Africa Leadership Forum of Nigerian president Olusegun Obasanjo launched the Kampala Document which acknowledges the link between security, stability, development, and cooperation in Africa. The Document's "Security Calabash" recommends: the constitution of a continental peacekeeping machinery; the adoption of a non-aggression treaty among all African countries; and the formation of an African Peace Council, composed of eminent African personalities and elder statesmen, charged with the task of creating and maintaining peace, harmony and tranquillity among African states.[35] Possibly the most ambitious and far-reaching recent peacemaking initiative is the OAU's Mechanism for Conflict Prevention, Management and Resolution adopted at the Cairo summit meeting of June 1993. It is noteworthy that the new OAU mechanism has a clear mandate to concern itself with internal conflicts; it is also charged with anticipating and preventing conflicts, as well as with peacekeeping and peace-building activities. The OAU mechanism started off with a U.S. contribution to its peacekeeping and peacemaking operations of $8.3 million for 1994-1995, and its eleven member-states Committee has, on average, met twice a year since 1994.[36]

Starting from the observation that "the consequences of the failed post colonial state are so destructive that radical solutions must now be contemplated to avert the wholesale destruction of groups of the African people," the Kenyan human rights activist-scholar Makau wa Mutua has proposed a redrawing of the map of Africa to construct only 15 viable states as opposed to the 54 existing today. The criteria for the creation of these new states include historical factors (such as pre colonial political systems and demographic patterns), ethnic similarities, and alliances based on cultural homogeneity and economic viability. Based on these criteria, Mutua's map of Africa creates new countries by abolishing some and combining others. Thus, the new Republic of Kusini (meaning "south" in Ki-Swahili), would include South Africa, Namibia, Zimbabwe, Mozambique, Lesotho, Swaziland, and Malawi. The new Egypt would combine Egypt and northern Sudan. Nubia would bring together Kenya, Uganda, Tanzania, and southern Sudan. Mali (an ancient west African empire) would include Mali, Senegal, Guinea, Sierra Leone, Liberia, Gambia, Guinea-Bissau, and Cape Verde. Somalia would absorb Djibouti, the

Ogaden province of Ethiopia and Kenya's north-eastern province. Congo would combine ethnically similar people of Central African Republic, Congo, DRC/Zaïre, Rwanda and Burundi, while Ghana would consist of Ghana, Côte d'Ivoire, Benin, Togo, Nigeria, Cameroon, Gabon, Equatorial Guinea, and Sao Tomé & Principe. Benin would take in Chad, Burkina Faso and Niger. Algeria and Angola remain the same, while Libya absorbs Tunisia. Morocco, Western Sahara, and Mauritania become Sahara. The new state of Kisiwani—which means "island" in Ki-Swahili—brings together Madagascar, Mauritius and the Comoros. Ethiopia and Eritrea would join in a federation.[37] While one may take issue with the historical, demographic, and ethno-regional logic of this plan, its urgency and relevance are undeniable.

As early as 1960, the Senegalese scholar Cheikh Anta Diop had proposed an ambitious and elaborate federal blueprint for Africa. Lamenting the relative failure of African regional organizations and of the OAU due to their member states' reluctance to relinquish any measure of sovereignty, Diop observed that Africa's security and development problems could only be resolved on a continental scale and within a federal framework. He argued that the rational development of Africa's tremendous energy and natural resources potential required a safe political and economic area that only a regional or subregional federated state could provide. Among his main policy recommendations are: the adoption of a single African working language for purposes of education, culture and administration; the immediate unification of francophone and anglophone Africa; the creation of a strong industrial infrastructure; and setting up a powerful modern army.[38] One wonders how many conflicts would have been avoided, how many lives would have been saved, and how much progress would have been achieved toward sustainable development had this plan been implemented.

CONCLUSION

One of the positive outcomes of the post-Cold War era has been to make African leaders realize that they must henceforth count first and foremost on themselves and develop appropriate strategies of collective self-reliance at the subregional and regional levels if they are to ever come out from underdevelopment. Recent changes in Franco-African relations point in that direction. In January 1994, the CFA franc was devalued by 50 per cent, signalling the demise of the Franco-African preferential monetary and trading area known as *la zone franc*. In this regard, as Albert Bourgi cogently remarked, "...the devaluation of the CFA franc will ultimately have a cathartic effect, that of mentally decolonizing the African leaders in their relations with France, thus finally cutting the umbilical cord which, for more that three decades, has tied them to their former *métropole*."[39] Significantly, a West African Economic and Monetary Union/WAEMU *(Union Économique et monétaire ouest-africaine)* including all seven Francophone countries of West Africa (plus Guinea-Bissau) was created at the same time, based on the European Union model. In central Africa, a similar regional organization, the Central African Economic and Monetary Union *(Communauté Économique et monétaire d'Afrique centrale/*CEMAC) was created in March 1994. Ultimately, all the major subregional economic groupings in Africa (AMU, WAEMU, ECOWAS, CEEAC, CEMAC, EAC, COMESA, and SADC) are expected to merge into a single, continent-wide African Common Market and African Economic Community by the year 2025 (see chapter 6 in this volume). In the area of peace and security, African states are now seriously contemplating the creation of an inter-African peacekeeping force under the aegis of the OAU, with French, British, American and Japanese financial and technical assistance and logistical support.

African scholars and policy makers have a duty to be bold and innovative in their constitutional and institutional engineering experiments. Having recognized the obvious shortcomings and dismal failure of the post colonial African nation-state, the challenge now facing them is to transcend the artificial sovereignty of the existing nation-states to create subregional and federal structures within which the various national cultures would have the right to self-determination and sovereignty. A new development model for Africa should integrate the concepts of security, development and democracy based on African historical, cultural and sociological realities and focussed on satisfying the basic (security, developmental, human, and political) needs of the African people at the national, subregional and regional levels. This would remove one of the main sources of ethnic-regional conflicts and create an enabling environment for peace and security, democratic governance and sustainable, participatory development in Africa.

Endnotes

1. Samuel P. Huntington, *The Clash of Civilizations and the Remaking of World Order* (New York: Simon & Schuster, 1996), pp. 20-21, 28.
2. Robert D. Kaplan, "The Coming Anarchy," *The Atlantic Monthly* vol. 273, no. 2 (February 1994), pp. 46, 48.
3. Jean-François Bayart, Stephen Ellis & Béatrice Hibou, *The Criminalization of the State in Africa* (Oxford & Bloomington: James Currey/Indiana University Press, 1999), pp. 1-13; quotes from pp. 30-31, 116.
4. William Pfaff, "A New Colonialism? Europe Must Go Back into Africa," *Foreign Affairs* vol. 74, no. 1 (January-February 1995), p. 3.
5. Howard Adelman & Astri Suhrke, *Early Warning and Conflict Management* [Study 2 of *The International Response to Conflict and Genocide: Lessons from the Rwanda Experience*]. Copenhagen: Steering Committee of the Joint Evaluation of Emergency Assistance to Rwanda, 1996, p. 5.

6. The World Bank, *World Development Report 1997* (New York: The World Bank/Oxford University Press, 1997), pp. 214ff.
7. GRIP, *Conflits en Afrique: Analyse des Crises et Pistes pour une Prévention* (Bruxelles: GRIP/Éditions Complexe, 1997), table 2, pp. 19-20.
8. *Worldwide Refugee Information* [*Principal Sources of Refugees, Principal Sources of Internally Displaced Persons*] (Washington, DC: U.S. Committee for Refugees, 1999).
9. Ruth Nabakwe, "FAO Blames Civil Strife for Food Shortage in Africa," *Panafrican News Agency* (16 December 1999).
10. United Nations Development Programme, *Human Development Report 1997* (New York: Oxford University Press, 1997), pp. 47, 148. The HDI is a composite index of achievements in basic human capabilities in three fundamental dimensions: life expectancy, educational attainment and income.
11. Jon Jeter, "AIDS Plants Crop of Death in Africa," *The Washington Post* (12 December 1999), pp. A1, A44.
12. Michael Chege, "What's Right with Africa?" *Current History* vol. 93, no. 583 (May 1994), p. 193.
13. Chester A. Crocker, "Stop the Pessimism about Africa," *USA Today* (12 September 1994), p. 13A.
14. Bill Clinton, *Address to the National Assembly and National Council of Provinces*, Cape Town (South Africa), 26 March 1998, reproduced in the *Cape Argus* (27 March 1998), p. 8.
15. *Africa Demos* vol. 3, no. 3 (September 1994), p. 27.
16. Speech by former UN Secretary-General Javier Perez de Cuellar at the University of Bordeaux (France) on 24 April 1991; *UN Press Release* SG/SM/4560 (1991).
17. Javier Perez de Cuellar, *Report of the Secretary-General on the Work of the Organization* (New York: United Nations, 1991), p. 12.
18. Boutros Boutros-Ghali, *An Agenda for Peace* (New York: United Nations, 1992), pp. 9-10.
19. Yves Beigbeder, *The Role and Status of International Humanitarian Volunteers and Organizations* (Boston: Martinus

Nijhoff, 1991), pp. 353-384; Marie-Dominique Perrot (ed.), *Dérives Humanitaires: États d'urgence et Droit d'ingérence* (Paris & Geneva: Presses Universitaires de France/Institut universitaire d'Études du développement, 1994).

20. Andrew S. Natsios, "NGOs and the UN System in Complex Humanitarian Emergencies: Conflict or Cooperation?" in Thomas G. Weiss & Leon Gordenker (eds.), *NGOs, the UN and Global Governance* (Boulder: Lynne Rienner Publishers, 1996), p. 67.

21. Christopher Clapham, *Africa and the International System: The Politics of State Survival* (New York: Cambridge University Press, 1996), pp. 15, 159; Robert H. Jackson, *Quasi-states: Sovereignty, International Relations and the Third World* (New York: Cambridge University Press, 1990).

22. Jeffrey Herbst, "Responding to State Failure in Africa", *International Security* vol. 21, no. 3 (Winter 1996/97), p. 124.

23. Elizabeth Rubin, "An Army of One's Own," *Harper's Magazine* (February 1997), pp. 44-55.

24. Béatrice Hibou, "The 'Social Capital' of the State as an Agent of Deception, or the Ruses of Economic Intelligence" in Bayart, Ellis & Hibou, *op. cit.*, pp. 69-113.

25. Achille Mbembe, "Les frontières mouvantes du continent africain," *Le Monde diplomatique* (novembre 1999), pp. 22-23.

26. *Ibidem.*

27. Basil Davidson, *The Black Man's Burden: Africa and the Curse of the Nation-State* (New York: Times Books, 1992).

28. William Pfaff, "A New Colonialism?", pp. 4,6.

29. Herman J. Cohen, "African Capabilities for Managing Conflict: The Role of the U.S.," in David R. Smock & Chester A. Crocker (eds.), *African Conflict Resolution: The U.S. Role in Peacemaking* (Washington, DC: U.S. Institute of Peace Press, 1995), p. 93.

30. Ali A. Mazrui, "The African State as a Political Refugee," in Smock and Crocker, (eds.), *op. cit.*, pp. 19-25.

31. On African regional integration, see African Development Bank,

African Development Report 2000: Regional Integration in Africa (New York: Oxford University Press, 2000); Ahmad A.H. Aly, *Economic Cooperation in Africa: in Search of Direction* (Boulder: Lynne Rienner Publishers, 1994); Peter Anyang' Nyong'o (ed.), *Regional Integration in Africa: Unfinished Agenda* (Nairobi: Academy Science Publishers, 1990); Daniel C. Bach (ed.), *Regionalisation in Africa: Integration & Disintegration* (Bloomington: Indiana University Press, 1999); and Réal Lavergne (ed.), *Regional Integration and Cooperation in West Africa: A Multidimensional Perspective* (Trenton: Africa World Press, 1997. See also chapter 6 in this volume.

32. On ECOMOG, see Robert A. Mortimer, "ECOMOG, Liberia and Regional Security in West Africa," in Edmond J. Keller & Donald Rothchild (eds.), *The End of the Cold War and the New African Political Order* (Boulder: Westview Press, 1995), pp. 149-64; R. Mortimer, "From ECOMOG to ECOMOG II:Intervention in Sierra Leone," in John W. Harbeson & Donald Rothchild (eds.), *Africa in World Politics* (Boulder: Westview Press, 3rd edition, 2000), pp. 188-207; and Margaret A. Vogt, "The Involvement of ECOWAS in Liberia's Peacekeeping" in Keller & Rothchild (eds), *op. cit.*, pp. 165-83; on ECOMOG and ANAD, see Guy Martin, "Francophone Africa in the Context of Franco-African Relations," in John W. Harbeson & Donald Rothchild (eds.), *Africa in World Politics: Post-Cold War Challenges* (Boulder: Westview Press, 2nd edn., 1995), pp.177-78; on the IGAD peace initiatives, see B.A. Kiplagat, "The African Role in Conflict Management and Resolution," in Smock and Crocker (eds.), *op. cit.*, pp. 34-37, and Samir Gharbi, "Djibouti: Un nouveau médiateur régional," *Jeune Afrique* (7-13 décembre 1999), p. 25. See also chapter 7 in this volume.

33. Nkrumah's Pan-African blueprint is contained in Kwame Nkrumah, *Africa Must Unite* (London: Panaf Books, 1963). On the contemporary relevance of the ideology of Pan-Africanism,

see also chapter one in this volume.

34. *Treaty Establishing The African Economic Community* (Addis Ababa, OAU, 1991).

35. *The Kampala Document: Towards a Conference on Security, Stability, Development and Cooperation in Africa* (Abeokuta & New York: Africa Leadership Forum, 1991), pp. 9-13.

36. D. Ocaya-Lakidi, rapporteur, *The OAU Mechanism for Conflict Prevention, Management and Resolution: Report of the Cairo Consultation* (New York:. International Peace Academy, 1996); OAU, *Resolving Conflicts in Africa: Implementation Options* (Addis Ababa: OAU Information Services Publication, Series [II] 1993). David R. Smock, "Introduction," in Smock and Crocker (eds.), *op. cit.*, pp. 6-7.

37. Makau wa Mutua, "Redrawing the map along African lines," *The Boston Globe* (22 September 1994), p. 17.

38. Cheikh Anta Diop, *Black Africa: The Economic and Cultural Basis for a Federated State* (Trenton & Chicago: Africa World Press/Lawrence Hill Books, 1987), foreword and pp. 88-9. [originally published in French as *Les Fondements économiques et culturels d'un État fédéral d'Afrique noire* (Paris: Présence Africaine, 1974)].

39. Albert Bourgi, "Dévaluation, Émancipation (...)," in *Jeune Afrique* (20-26 janvier 1994), pp. 46-7; on recent developments in Franco-African relations, see Guy Martin, "Francophone Africa in the Context of Franco-African Relations," in J.W. Harbeson & D. Rothchild (eds.), *op. cit.*, pp. 163-188; see also chapters 3 and 4 in this volume.

Chapter 10

Conclusion: The Continued Relevance of Pan-Africanism in the Twenty-first Century

THE AFRICAN PREDICAMENT AND THE DEMISE OF THE AFRICAN STATE

We conclude this book with an enquiry into the root causes, manifestations and possible solutions to the present African predicament, a term used by Andreski in the late 1960s to accurately describe the endemic African economic, social, and cultural crisis.[1] This enquiry starts with a fundamental question raised by Walter Rodney in 1972 and that still perplexes us almost thirty years later:

> In order to understand present economic conditions in Africa, one needs to know why it is that Africa has realized so little of its natural potential, and one also needs to know why so much of its present wealth goes to non-Africans who reside for the most part outside of the continent.[2]

Thirteen years later, a former secretary general of the OAU raises a similar question:

> ...one must ask why Africa remains powerless in today's
> world in spite of its rich historical heritage of brilliant civi-
> lizations, of its enormous economic potential, and of its
> 500 [now 766] million inhabitants.[3]

Why is a continent so richly endowed with natural resources and
minerals consistently rated as the poorest in the world? Why are
Africans, contrary to what pertains in the rest of the world, still strug-
gling for their basic human, political, economic and social rights?
Why is the African, 150 years after the abolition of slavery, every-
where still in bondage, a perpetual servant and beggar, hewer of
wood and drawer of water for the rest of the world? In short, why is
it that in spite of its enormous mineral wealth, energy resources and
agricultural potential, Africa is now, by any indicators, at a lower level
of economic and social development than it was at the time of independence in 1960, more than forty years ago?

Recent symptoms and manifestations of the African predicament
include war, ethnic/religious conflict, genocide (Rwanda), disease
(notably AIDS and Ebola), famine, and malnutrition. Economically,
Africa remains as underdeveloped (or *un*developed), indebted and
dependent as ever, a situation compounded by the negative impact of
the Structural Adjustment Programs imposed by the International
Monetary Fund and the World Bank on all African states. The crisis
of governance manifests itself in the current political decay. Thus, the
African state has variously been described by Africanists as soft, failed,
collapsed, warlord, criminalized, and predatory.

The nature and structure of the African state system has been
determined by successive exogenous processes of political domination
and economic exploitation, namely the trans-Atlantic slave trade, mercantilism, imperialism, colonialism and neocolonialism. In the post-
Cold War era, new and more sophisticated forms of Western domina-

tion and exploitation of Africa have emerged under the guise of "globalization". In fact, "globalization" is just another name for a neo-imperial order characterized by the dominance of a global culture based on Western political, economic and cultural values and institutions—parliamentary democracy and the market economy—leading to a progressive westernization of the world. In this new world economic system, the core geopolitical regions—North America, Western Europe and the Asia-Pacific area—are increasingly integrated via the trans-national corporations, while the countries of the South (particularly Africa) are increasingly impoverished and marginalized. In this neo-imperial order, only a dogmatic and ubiquitous "unified thought" (*pensée unique*) is allowed. This (purportedly universal) "unified thought" is the ideological expression of international capitalism. It is based on the key concepts of the primacy of the economic over the political; of the absolute and uncontested rule of the market; and of free trade, liberalization and privatization.[4]

Consider the sagacity and contemporary relevance of this observation, made by Leonard Barnes 33 years ago:

> While it is true that African independence has in many ways made a shockingly bad start, it has also to be remembered that the mini-states into which the continent has got itself fragmented are, as they stand, ungovernable...So the real failure of the new African rulers is not that they give bad government to meaningless units which cannot be governed well. It is rather that they insist on perpetuating the conditions that make good government impossible; in other words, *that they continually shy away from the closer political association with their neighbours which is the sole cure for the chronic unviability of all.*[5]

Writing 23 years later, Basil Davidson observes much the same situation:

...the frontiers of the colonial partition, however inappropriate to an independent Africa, became the sacred frontiers which it must be treason to question or deny...the nation-statist project—the attempt to turn colonially formed territories into nation-statist territories—looks increasingly like a mistake...Accepting the nation-state that was offered to them, the pioneering nationalists saw no useful alternative and asked no further questions about its credentials or potentials...[they]...should have understood that nation-states fashioned from the structures and relationships of colonial states, and thereby produced from European and not from African history, were bound to be heading for trouble...By the middle of the 1980s, the generalized collapse of the nation-statist project was widely perceived, whether inside or outside Africa...While the bureaucratic nation-state may still claim to exist in Africa...the thought that it may be near the end of its useful life is more advanced.[6]

Endowed with "juridical" sovereignty but devoid of the "positive" sovereignty which derives from effective control, "penetrated" as a result of technological advances and the communications revolution, subjected to the economic dictates—euphemistically called "conditionalities"—of the international financial institutions and to the political dictates of the major bilateral donors, challenged in its sovereignty by international humanitarian governmental and nongovernmental organizations, enjoined by the doctrine of the right and duty of humanitarian intervention to hand over the protection and assistance of its citizens to the international community, the African state, when it is not plagued by internal conflict and in danger of imminent collapse, is threatened with near-extinction. And — if we believe Barnes and Davidson—that may be just as well. Indeed the various historical exogenous processes described above, culminating with globalization, have cumulatively led to the creation of an African leviathan, a dysfunctional monster without any historical, cultural and ethnic substance and reality and whose main function is to exert political control and domination, and to maintain economic exploitation over the African people. As the late Claude Ake cogently observed, the state in Africa is not a public force but tends to be privatized in the sense that it is "appropriated to the service of private interests by the dominant faction of the elite." More interested in political survival than in development, African leaders give precedence to political domination over social transformation, and thus tend to be in conflict with the majority of their population.[7] At the end of his magisterial study of the African colonial state, Crawford Young concludes: "Stripped to its essentials, the heart of the African state crisis of the 1980s lies in this lethal combination of the colonial state heritage, the failed vision of the integral state, and the prebendal realities of political management." He then raises an intriguing and challenging question: "Can a new state be invented that sheds the debilitating traditions of the past?"[8]

Mueni Wa Muiu and this author take up the challenge as we sketch (in a work in progress) the contours of a new paradigm for the study of African politics and international relations, based on the concept of *Fundi wa Afrika*.[9] This ideal African state (*Fundi wa Afrika*) builds on the (still functional) remnants of the African indigenous institutions and draws ideological inspiration from the political thought of various African philosopher-kings. We argue that the building of such a democratic and developmental state as an instrument of people's power is a historical necessity if peace and security—as prerequisites of a genuine and thorough African reawakening and revival—are to prevail on the continent.[10]

Having recognized the obvious shortcomings and dismal failure of the post colonial African nation-state, the challenge now facing us is to transcend the artificial sovereignty of the existing nation-states to create subregional and federal structures within which the various national cultures would be recognized the right of self-determination and be granted sovereignty. As Davidson suggests, "A hopeful future...would have to be a federalizing future: a future of organic unities of sensible association across wide regions within which national cultures...could evolve their diversities and find in them a mutual blessing."[11] At this point, it might be useful to revisit some of the Pan-Africanist projects (both minimalists and maximalists) successively developed by Kwame Nkrumah in the early 1960s, Cheikh Anta Diop in the early 1970s, Edem Kodjo in the mid-1980s, and Makau wa Mutua and Olusegun Obasandjo in the early 1990s—most of which have been briefly examined in chapter 9— in order to assess their coherence and feasibility.

The Africa Leadership Forum's Kampala Document

In the early 1990s, African leaders began to think in innovative ways about adopting new principles and creating new institutions to manage the continent's problems and challenges. The most ambitious and far-reaching proposals are contained in the *Kampala Document*. Subtitled "Towards a Conference on Security, Stability, Development & Cooperation in Africa" (CSSDCA), it was adopted at a meeting convened on May 19-22, 1991 by a non-governmental organization and African think-tank, the Africa Leadership Forum, created and led by Nigerian president Olusegun Obasanjo. Constructed around four "calabashes"—security, stability, development and cooperation –, the Kampala Document calls for the adoption of "binding principles" for action. Of particular relevance to the Pan-African project is the cooperation calabash, which advocates inter-African cooperation, using existing subregional groupings as building blocks towards the achievement of an African Economic Community (AEC). The Document urges African states to intensify the various subregional processes of integration and to agree upon a shortened timetable for the AEC. It also points out that these states need to devolve key responsibilities to continental institutions endowed with supranational authority. Finally, the Document advocates the rationalization of the numerous intergovernmental regional African organizations now in existence, by reducing their numbers and making the remaining ones leaner and more efficient.[12] The OAU considered the Document at its June 1992 summit in Dakar (Senegal), but the proposal to adopt it was tabled for further consideration in the face of opposition from some member states concerned, in particular, by potential restraints on their sovereignty posed by the "supranationality" clause. The gap between the principles put forth in the Document and states' actual behavior was made painfully clear when its intellectual mentor, Olusegun Obasanjo, was jailed by the Nigerian military regime of Sani Abacha for advocating more democratic governance. Since reassuming the presidency in May 1999 following democratic elections, Obasanjo has indicated his resolve to reactivate the CSSDCA process.

Kwame Nkrumah's Union of African States

By 1961, the newly-independent states of Africa were divided into two rival politico-ideological blocs: the Brazzaville-Monrovia Group, constituted by 20 moderate, pro-Western (and predominantly Francophone) African states; and the Casablanca Group, constituted by seven, predominantly radical nationalist/socialist African states (see introduction). Convened as a Conference of Independent African States at the head of state level, the Addis Ababa summit meeting (May 22-26, 1963) resulted in the adoption of the charter of the Organization of African Unity (OAU). While ostensibly the result of a cooperative venture between the Brazzaville-Monrovia and Casablanca groups—which were then disbanded — the OAU Charter in fact reflected the views of the former, more numerous and better organized group. This explains why such principles as respect for the sovereign equality of all states, non-interference in the internal affairs of other states, and respect of sovereignty and territorial integrity became the cornerstone of the charter, and effectively rendered the OAU weak, ineffectual and powerless.

As the undisputed leader of the Casablanca Group and a leading Pan-Africanist in his own right, Ghana's first president Kwame Nkrumah had his own plan for the unity of Africa, outlined in his book *Africa Must Unite* which was distributed at the Addis Ababa summit as the Pan-Africanists' manifesto.[13] Nkrumah saw the total and immediate political and economic union of Africa as the only appropriate response to the policies of balkanization and "divide-and-rule" pursued by the then-European Community (EC) and France through such neo-colonial schemes as the Franco-African Community and the Yaoundé Convention. As he succinctly put it "We are Africans first and last, and as Africans our best interests can only be served by uniting within an African Community."[14] Consequently, Nkrumah called for a continental government for Africa in the form of a Union of African States (UAS), loosely modeled on the United States of America (which he greatly admired). This UAS would have a central government (the Union Government of African States), and an elaborate institutional structure reflecting unified policies in the areas of economic planning, military and defence strategy, and foreign policy and diplomacy, including an African Common Market and integrated monetary zone, with a common currency and central bank, and a Military High Command.[15]

Interestingly, Nkrumah's elaborate Pan-African blueprint—which never had a chance at the Addis Ababa summit and which is now almost 40 years old—is resurfacing in various forms and in a variety of forums. Thus the June 1991 summit meeting of the OAU (Abuja, Nigeria) adopted a treaty establishing an African Economic Community to be created in stages (via an African Common Market) by the year 2025. Similarly, the Kampala Document's 'security calabash' recommends, inter alia, the creation of a continental peace keeping machinery; the adoption of a non-aggression treaty among all African countries; and the formation of an African Peace Council composed of eminent African personalities and elder statesmen, and charged with the task of ensuring that peace, harmony and tranquility is created and maintained among African states.[16] Possibly the most ambitious and far-reaching recent peacemaking initiative is the OAU's Mechanism for Conflict Prevention, Management and Resolution adopted at the Cairo summit meeting of June 1993, which—though underfunded and understaffed—is currently engaged in early warning, preventive diplomacy, and conflict prevention.[17]

Cheikh Anta Diop's Federal African State

In just over 100 dense pages, Cheikh Anta Diop—arguably one of Africa's greatest scientists, most original thinkers and prolific writers—outlines the economic and cultural bases of a Federal African State.[18] Building on earlier research documenting the essential historical, cultural and linguistic unity of Africa,[19] Diop advocates the adoption of a single African language for official, educational and cultural use throughout the continent.[20] Warning against the dangers of the 'South Americanization'—the proliferation of small, dictatorial states afflicted by chronic instability—of Africa, and calling for a break with "fake institutions" (Franco-African Community, Commonwealth, EurAfrica), Diop recommends the creation of a strong African army and notes that sub-Saharan Africa's abundant natural, energy and food resources can easily sustain a larger population than the present one.[21] According to Diop, the Federal African State would extend from the Tropic of Cancer to the Cape, and from the Indian Ocean to the Atlantic, thus uniting Francophone, Anglophone and Lusophone Africa (but excluding North Africa). Sub-Saharan Africa's hydro-electric potential, he argues, is one of the greatest in the world. The Congo Basin alone (with the Inga and Kisangani dams) could provide electricity to the whole continent. Africa's abundant solar and uranium resources could sustain an elaborate solar and nuclear industry. All of these resources should be har-

nessed toward the processing of the continent's raw materials. Diop
further argues that Africa's import dependence could be drastically
reduced if three key industries were developed: food processing
(rice), clothing (cotton), and housing (cement and concrete). In the
area of transport and communication, Diop suggests that priority be
given to the construction of tarmacked roads and the development o
civil aviation, then maritime transport and last, railways.

According to Diop, the constituent economic and cultural ele
ments of a Federal African State would be: a single African language
based on the essential historic, cultural and linguistic unity of Africa
the immediate political and economic unification of Francophone
Anglophone and Lusophone Africa, and the creation of a strong Pan
African army; an elaborate industrial infrastructure (heavy industr
and manufacturing) using Africa's abundant hydro-electric, solar an
uranium resources in order to process the continent's raw materi
als;.an elaborate transport network; and a policy encouraging popu
lation growth.[22]

It is noteworthy that the two blueprints of Nkrumah and Dio
are infused by the same Pan-Africanist ideal, but differ in emphasi
in a complementary fashion. Nkrumah provides a broad canvas an
elaborate political, economic and military institutional infrastructure
while Diop fills in the policy details in terms of language and culture
population, energy, industry, agriculture, transport and communica
tion. The fact that Nkrumah was first and foremost a political mar
and Diop essentially an academic and scientist, probably explair
their different approaches.

Edem Kodjo's Rationalized Pan-Africanism

A Togolese national and former secretary general of the OAU (1978
1983), Edem Kodjo offers a modernized (but essentially similar) ve
sion of Nkrumah's and Diop's Pan-Africanist blueprints in his boc
Et Demain l'Afrique.[23] Starting from the observation that Africa

marginalized and powerless, a passive subject rather than a major actor in the contemporary international system, Kodjo notes that Africa is a continent of contradictions and paradoxes: it is where humanity began and boasts a rich historical heritage, yet today it is at the bottom of the world hierarchy; it is threatened by famine, yet uncultivated arable land is plentiful; it is endowed with an incredible abundance and variety of minerals, yet it boasts the largest number of least-developed countries.[24] Should one despair of its fate and give up on it? According to Kodjo, the way out of this predicament lies in the adoption of what he calls a "rationalized Pan-Africanism." As Nkrumah and Diop did before him, Kodjo observes that most of Africa's current problems have their origin in its arbitrary and artificial borders agreed upon at the Berlin Conference of 1884-85 and sanctified by the 1963 OAU Charter, which created territorial units devoid of any geographical, historical, political, cultural, linguistic and ethnic substance or reality: ",,, under these circumstances, one must admit that because they destroy the unity of the African people, artificial boundaries constitute a major obstacle to the development of their creative potential." It logically follows that "Africa's best hope for the future requires that Africans resolutely fight against the preservation of the artificial boundaries that divide them, and in favor of African unity within broad subregional economic frameworks." More specifically, Kodjo advocates the creation, within each of the five African subregions—north, west, central, eastern and southern—of common markets (through the usual stages of customs unions and free-trade areas) that would eventually merge into a single African Common Market (ACM) and lead to an African Economic Community (AEC). Furthermore, Kodjo points out that political integration must be pursued simultaneously with economic integration. To that aim, he suggests that the present, non viable state structures be reformed and that new politico-economic federations be set up in their place. Each of these politico-economic federations should be endowed with political, economic, administrative, military, educational, university, scientific, technical, artistic and cultural institutions promoting African people's integration and unity. According to Kodjo, only such politico-economic federations, each led by one or several "leader-state" (État pilote), have a real unification potential at the continental level. Kodjo then goes on to identify five "leader-states"—or "federating units" (pôles fédétateurs)—responsible for moving forward the process of integration in their respective geographical areas/subregions: Egypt/Algeria, Nigeria, Congo/Zaïre, Ethiopia, and South Africa. As Nkrumah did before him, Kodjo truly believes that this process of political and economic integration will eventually lead to the creation of the United States of Africa.[25]

Overall, Kodjo's approach is gradualist and functionalist in that he advocates the creation of subregional politico-economic federations which are eventually to merge, in stages, into continental politico-economic organizations (AEC and U.S. of Africa). Note that since his book was published, the ACM and AEC have become a reality following a decision of the June 1991 OAU summit meeting. Kodjo's perspective, however, is distinctly Pan-Africanist.

Makau wa Mutua's New Map of Africa

Starting from the observation that the "consequences of the failed postcolonial state are so destructive that radical solutions must now be contemplated to avert the wholesale destruction of groups of the African people," the Kenyan human rights activist-scholar Makau wa Mutua proposed in 1994 a redrawing of the map of Africa to construct only 15 viable states as opposed to the 54 existing today. The criteria for the creation of these new states include historical factors (such as pre-colonial political systems and demographic patterns) ethnic similarities, and alliances based on cultural homogeneity and economic viability.

Based on these criteria, Mutua's map of Africa creates new countries by abolishing some and combining others. Thus, the new Republic of Kusini (meaning 'south' in Ki-Swahili), would include

South Africa, Namibia, Zimbabwe, Mozambique, Lesotho, Swaziland and Malawi. The new *Egypt* would combine Egypt and northern Sudan. *Nubia* would bring together Kenya, Uganda, Tanzania and southern Sudan. *Mali* (an ancient west African empire) would include Mali, Senegal, Guinea, Sierra Leone, Liberia, Gambia, Guinea-Bissau and Cape Verde. *Somalia* would absorb Djibouti, the Ogaden province of Ethiopia and Kenya's north eastern province. *Congo* would combine ethnically similar people of the Central African Republic, Congo, Congo/Zaïre, Rwanda and Burundi, while *Ghana* would consist of Ghana, Côte d'Ivoire, Benin, Togo, Nigeria, Cameroon, Gabon, Equatorial Guinea and Sao Tomé & Principe. *Benin* would take in Chad, Burkina Faso and Niger. *Algeria* and *Angola* remain the same, while *Libya* absorbs Tunisia. Morocco, Western Sahara and Mauritania become *Sahara*. The new state of *Kisiwani* (which means 'island' in Ki-Swahili) brings together Madagascar, Mauritius and the Comoros. Ethiopia and Eritrea constitute a federation.[26]

The Maximalist Pan-African Blueprints: An Assessment

What is common to all the maximalist Pan-African projects (Nkrumah, Diop, Kodjo and Mutua) is that they are all infused by the Pan-African ideal. All of them stress the need and urgency of the political, economic and cultural unification of the African continent as the only viable counter-strategy to the various neo-colonial policies of balkanization and "divide-and-rule" pursued by the Western powers under the guise of "globalization." The most elaborate and ambitious project is that of Nkrumah, on which Kodjo's is based. While elements of these projects are progressively being put in place (e.g., the AEC and ACM), the mode and pace of African regional integration, as well as the conflicts which continue to plague many African countries and subregions, do not bode well for the realistic attainment of these goals in the foreseeable future (even by the 2025 deadline set for the achievement of the AEC).

The 37th summit of the OAU's heads of states and government meeting in Lusaka, Zambia (June 2001) decided to formally transform (within one year) the OAU into an African Union (AU). The AU is based on the New African Initiative (NAI), itself a merger of the Millennium Partnership for the African Recovery Program (sponsored by Algeria, Nigeria and South Africa) and the OMEGA Plan (sponsored by Senegal). In essence, the NAI is a neo-liberal plan based on the accelerated liberalization and privatization of the African economies, with Western economic and financial assistance. As for the United States of Africa's project originally conceived by Nkrumah and proposed by Lybia's leader Muammar Qaddafi at the Lusaka summit, it was rejected by the African leaders in attendance as "unrealistic" and "utopian."

If one accepts that the African state as it presently exists must be abolished, then a redrawing of the African map along new subregional lines as suggested by Mutua could be envisaged, each with its own leader-state as suggested by Kodjo (a project facilitated by the advent of majority rule in South Africa). Once this new African map has been drawn, the elaborate economic, politico-diplomatic and military institutional set-up envisaged by Nkrumah could be put in place, and the linguistic, cultural, population, energy, industrial, agricultural and transport policies devised by Diop implemented. The prophets of doom (Afropessimists) who are inclined to dismiss this project as utopian should ask themselves: how many more African men, women and children must die of disease, AIDS, hunger, malnutrition and war before we finally wake up to the fact that the severity of the African crisis calls for drastic solutions? Indeed, the United States of Africa is an idea whose time has come.

Endnotes

1. Stanislav Andreski, *The African Predicament: A Study in the Pathology of Mondernization* (New York: Atherton Press, 1968)

2. Walter Rodney, *How Europe Underdeveloped Africa* (Washington, DC: Howard University Press, 1982), p. 20.
3. Edem Kodjo, *Et Demain l'Afrique* (Paris: Éditions Stock, 1985), p. 12.
4. This argument is cogently and eloquently put forward by Ignacio Ramonet in *Géopolitique du Chaos* (Paris: Éditions Galilée, 1997).
5. Leonard Barnes, *African Renaissance* (Indianapolis: The Bobbs-Merrill Company, 1969), p. 11 (emphasis added).
6. Basil Davidson, *The Black Man's Burden: Africa and the Curse of the Nation-State* (New York: Times Books, 1992), pp. 114-5, 168, 181-2, 252 , 288.
7. Claude Ake, *Democracy and Development in Africa* (Washington, DC: The Brookings Institution, 1996) (the quote is from p. 42); see also Guy Martin, "Reflections on Democracy and Development in Africa: The Intellectual Legacy of Claude Ake," *Ufahamu* vol. 26, no. 1 (Winter 1998), pp. 102-109.
8. Crawford Young, *The African Colonial State in Comparative Perspective* (New Haven: Yale University Press, 1994), p. 292.
9. *Fundi wa Afrika* means 'builder of Africa' or ' tailor of Africa' in the Ki-Swahili language.
10. Mueni Wa Muiu & Guy Martin, *"Fundi Wa Afrika: Toward a New Paradigm of the African State* (Peterborough: Broadview Press, forthcoming). The African political thinkers we draw inspiration from are: Claude Ake, Steve Biko, Amilcar Cabral, Cheikh Anta Diop, Frantz Fanon, Kwame Nkrumah, Anton Muziwakhe Lembede, Samora Machel, Julius Nyerere, Thomas Sankara and Ahmed Sékou Touré.
11. Basil Davidson, *The Black Man's Burden*, p. 286.
12. Africa Leadership Forum, *The Kampala Document: Towards a Conference on Security, Stability, Development & Cooperation in Africa* (Abeokuta & New York: Africa Leadership Forum, 1991), pp. 32-37.
13. Kwame Nkrumah, *Africa Must Unite* (London: Panaf Books, 1963).

14. K. Nkrumah, *op. cit.*, p. 217.

15. Nkrumah, *op. cit.*, pp. 216-222.

16. *The Kampala Document*, pp. 9-13.

17. See D. Ocaya-Lakidi (rapporteur), *The OAU Mechanism for Conflict Prevention, Management and Resolution: Report of the Cairo Consultation* (New York: International Peace Academy, 1996); OAU, *Resolving Conflicts in Africa: Implementation Options* (Addis Ababa: OAU Information Services Publication, Series [II], 1993); Terrence Lyons, "Can Neighbors Help? Regional Actors and African Conflict Management," in Francis M. Deng & Terrence Lyons (eds.), *African Reckoning: A Quest for Good Governance* (Washington, DC: Brookings Institution Press, 1998), pp. 67-99.

18. Cheikh Anta Diop, *Les Fondements économiques et culturels d'un État fédéral d'Afrique noire* (Paris: Présence Africaine, 2ème édition, 1974); translated as *Black Africa: The Economic and Cultural Basis for a Federated State* (Chicago & Trenton: Lawrence Hill Books/Africa World Press, 1987).

19. Cheikh Anta Diop, *L'Afrique noire pré-coloniale* (Paris: Présence Africaine, 1960); C.A. Diop, *L'Unité culturelle de l'Afrique noire* (Paris: Présence Africaine, 1960).

20. C.A. Diop, *Les Fondements* (...), pp.11-29.

21. *Ibidem*, pp. 30-37.

22. *Ibidem*, pp. 46-52, 56-80 and 110-122.

23. Edem Kodjo, *Et Demain l'Afrique* (Paris: Éditions Stock, 1985) translated as *Africa Today* (Accra: Ghana Universities Press, 1989).

24. E. Kodjo, *op. cit.*, pp. 11-56.

25. *Ibidem*, pp. 245-276; the quotes are from pp. 248 & 260 respectively.

26. Makau wa Mutua, "Redrawing the map along African lines," *The Boston Globe* (22 September 1994), p. 17.

Bibliography

Abrahamsen, Rita. *Disciplining Democracy: Development Discourse and Good Governance in Africa.* London & New York: Zed Books, 2000.

Adebajo, Adekeye. *Building Peace in West Africa: Liberia, Sierra Leone, and Guinea-Bissau.* Boulder & New York: Lynne Rienner/International Peace Academy, 2002.

Adedeji, Adebayo, ed. *Africa within the World: Beyond Dispossession and Dependence.* Atlantic Highlands: Zed Books, 1993.

Africa Leadership Forum. *The Kampala Document: Towards a Conference on Security, Stability, Development & Cooperation in Africa.* Abeokuta & New York: Africa Leadership Forum, 1991.

Ake, Claude. *Democracy and Development in Africa.* Washington, DC: The Brookings Institution, 1996.

————. *The Feasibility of Democracy in Africa.* Dakar: Council for the Development of Social Science Research in Africa/CODESRIA, 2000.

Akinrinade, Sola & Amadu Sesay, eds. *Africa in the Post-Cold War International System.* London & Washington, DC: Pinter, 1998.

Aldeman, Howard & Astri Suhrke, eds. *The Path of a Genocide: The Rwanda Crisis from Uganda to Zaire.* Piscataway: Transaction Publishers, 1998.

Aluko, Olajide, ed. *Africa and the Great Powers in the 1980s*. Lanham: University Press of America, 1987.

Aly, Ahmad A.H.M. *Economic Cooperation in Africa: In Search of Direction*. Boulder: Lynne Rienner, 1994.

Amate, C.O.C. *Inside the OAU: Pan-Africanism in Practice*. London: Macmillan, 1986.

Anda, Michael O. *International Relations in Contemporary Africa*. Lanham: University Press of America, 2000.

Andreski, Stanislav. *The African Predicament: A Study in the Pathology of Modernization*. New York: Atherton Press, 1968.

Anyang' Nyong'o, Peter, ed. *Regional Integration in Africa: Unfinished Agenda*. Nairobi: Academy Science Publishers, 1990.

Attah-Poku, Agyeman. *African Stability and Integration: Regional, Continental and Diasporic Pan-African Realities*. Lanham: University Press of America, 2000.

Ayittey, George B.N. *Africa in Chaos*. New York: St. Martin's Press, 1998.

Bach, Daniel C., ed. *Regionalisation in Africa: Integration & Disintegration*. Oxford & Bloomington: James Currey/Indiana University Press, 1999.

Barnes, Leonard. *African Renaissance*. Indianapolis: The Bobbs Merrill Co., 1969.

Barry, Mamadou Aliou. *La Prévention des Conflits en Afrique de l'Ouest: Mythes ou réalités?* Paris: Éditions Karthala, 1997.

Bassey Ibok, S. & William G. Nhara, eds. *OAU Early Warning System on Conflict Situations in Africa*. Addis Ababa: Organization of African Unity/OAU, 1996.

Baulin, Jacques. *La Politique africaine d'Houphouët-Boigny*. Paris: Éditions Eurafor-Press, 1980.

Bayart, Jean-François. *The State in Africa: The politics of the belly*. New York: Longman, 1993.

Bayart, Jean-François. Stephen Ellis & Béatrice Hibou, *The Criminalization of the State in Africa*. Oxford & Bloomington: James Currey/Indiana University Press, 1999.

Birmingham, David. *The Decolonization of Africa*. Athens: Ohio University Press, 1995.

Braeckman, Colette, *Rwanda: Histoire d'un génocide*. Paris: Fayard, 1994.

―――. *Terreur Africaine: Burundi, Rwanda, Zaire: Les racines de la violence*. Paris: Fayard, 1996.

―――. *L'Enjeu Congolais: L'Afrique centrale après Mobutu*. Paris: Fayard, 1999.

Brüne, Stefan, Joachim Betz & Winrich Kühne, eds. *Africa and Europe: Relations of Two Continents in Transition*. Münster & Hamburg: Lit Verlag, 1994.

Callaghy, Thomas M. & John Ravenhill, eds. *Hemmed In: Responses to Africa's Economic Decline*. New York: Columbia University Press, 1993.

Cervenka, Zdenek. *The Organization of African Unity and its Charter*. New York: Praeger Publishers, 1969.

Cervenka, Zdenek. *The Unfinished Quest for Unity: Africa and the OAU*. New York: Africana Publishing Co., 1977.

Chazan, Naomi, Peter Lewis, Robert Mortimer, Donald Rothchild & Stephen J. Stedman. *Politics and Society in Contemporary Africa*. Boulder: Lynne Rienner, 3rd edition, 1999.

Chinweizu. *The West and the Rest of Us: White Predators, Black Slavers and the African Elite*. New York: Vintage Books, 1975.

Chipman, John. *French Power in Africa*. Oxford: Basil Blackwell, 1989.

Cilliers, Jakkie & Greg Mills, eds. *Peacekeeping in Africa*. Johannesburg: Institute for Defence Policy/South African Institute of International Affairs, 1995.

Clapham, Christopher. *Africa and the International System: The Politics of State Survival*. New York: Cambridge University Press, 1996.

Clark, John F. & David E. Gardinier, eds. *Political Reform in Francophone Africa*. Boulder: Westview Press, 1997.

Clough, Michael. *Free at Last? U.S. Policy Toward Africa and the End of the Cold War*. New York: Council on Foreign Relations Press, 1992.

Cohen, Herman J. *Intervening in Africa: Superpower Peacemaking in a Troubled Continent*. New York: Palgrave, 2000.

Crocker, Chester A. *High Noon in Southern Africa: Making Peace in a Rough Neighborhood.* New York: W.W. Norton, 1992.

Davidson, Basil. *The Black Man's Burden: Africa and the Curse of the Nation-State.* New York: Times Books, 1992.

DeLancey, Mark W., ed. *Aspects of International Relations in Africa.* Bloomington: Indiana University Press, 1979.

DeLancey, Mark W., Wm. C. Reed, R. Spyke & P. Steen. *African International Relations: An Annotated Bibliography.* Boulder: Westview Press, 2nd edition, 1997.

Deng, Francis M. & I. William Zartman, eds. *Conflict Resolution in Africa.* Washington, DC: The Brookings Institution, 1991.

Deng, Francis M., Sadikiel Kimaro, Terrence Lyons, Donald Rothchild & I. William Zartman. *Sovereignty as Responsibility: Conflict Management in Africa.* Washington, DC: The Brookings Institution, 1996.

Deng, Francis M. & Terrence Lyons, eds. *African Reckoning: A Quest for Good Governance.* Washington, DC: Brookings Institution Press, 1998.

Diop, Cheikh Anta. *Les Fondements Économiques et culturels d'un État fédéral d'Afrique noire.* Paris: Présence Africaine, 2ème édition, 1974.

———. *Black Africa: The Economic and Cultural Basis for a Federated State.* Chicago & Trenton: Lawrence Hill Books/Africa World Press, 1987.

Dumoulin, André. *La France militaire et l'Afrique. Coopération et *interventions: un État des lieux.* Bruxelles: GRIP/Éditions Complexe, 1997.

El-Ayouty, Yassin & I. William Zartman, eds. *The OAU After Twenty Years.* New York: Praeger Publishers, 1984.

El Ayouty, Yassin, ed. *The OAU After Thirty Years.* New York: Praeger Publishers, 1994

Englebert, Pierre. *State Legitimacy and Development in Africa.* Boulder: Lynne Rienner, 2000.

Esedebe, P. Olisanwuche. *Pan-Africanism: The Idea and Movement, 1776-1991.* Washington, DC: Howard University Press, 2nd edition, 1994.

Furley, Oliver & Roy May, eds. *African Interventionist States: The New Conflict Resolution Brokers.* Aldershot & Brookfield: Ashgate Publishing, 2001.

Gaillard, Philippe (entretiens avec). *Foccart Parle 1.* Paris: Fayard/Jeune Afrique, 1995.

Gaillard, Philippe (entretiens avec). *Foccart Parle 2.* Paris: Fayard/Jeune Afrique, 1997.

Glaser, Antoine & Stephen Smith. *Ces Messieurs Afrique: Le Paris-Village du continent noir.* Paris: Calmann-Lévy, 1992.

———. *Ces Messieurs Afrique 2: des réseaux aux lobbies.* Paris: Calmann-Lévy, 1997.

———. *L'Afrique sans Africains: Le rêve blanc du continent noir* Paris: Stock, 1994.

Gouteux, Jean-Paul. *Un génocide secret d'État: La France et le Rwanda, 1990-1997.* Paris: Éditions sociales, 1998.

GRIP. *Conflits en Afrique: Analyse des Crises et Pistes pour une Prévention.* Bruxelles: GRIP/Éditions Complexe, 1997.

Hansen, Emmanuel, ed. *Africa: Perspectives on Peace and Development.* London & Tokyo: Zed Books/The United Nations University, 1987.

Harbeson, John W. & Donald Rothchild, eds. *Africa in World Politics: The African State System in Flux.* Boulder: Westview Press, 3rd edition, 2000.

Harris, Gordon. *Organization of African Unity: An Annotated Bibliography.* New Brunswick: Transaction Publishers, 1994.

Herbst, Jeffrey. *States and Power in Africa: Comparative Lessons in Authority and Control.* Princeton: Princeton University Press, 2000.

Howe, Herbert M. *Ambiguous Order: Military Forces in African States.* Boulder: Lynne Rienner, 2001.

Hugon, Philippe. *La zone franc à l'heure de l'euro.* Paris: Karthala, 1999.

Ihonvbere, Julius O. *Africa and the New World Order.* New York: Peter Lang, 2000.

Imobighe, T.A. *The OAU, African Defence and Security.* Benin City: Adena Publishers, 1989.

Jinadu, L. Adele & Ibbo Mandaza, eds. *African Perspectives on the Non-Aligned Movement.* Harare: African Association of Political Science, 1986.

Jones, Bruce D. *Peacemaking in Rwanda: The Dynamics of Failure.* Boulder & New York: Lynne Rienner/International Peace Academy, 2001.

Joseph, Richard, ed. *State, Conflict, and Democracy in Africa.* Boulder: Lynne Rienner, 1999.

Kamto, Maurice, J.E. Pondi & Laurent Zang, eds. *L'Organisation de l'Unité Africaine: Rétrospective et Perspectives Africaines.* Paris: Économica, 1990.

Khadiagala, Gilbert M. *Allies in Adversity: The Frontline States in Southern African Security, 1975-1993.* Athens: Ohio University Press, 1994.

Khadiagala, Gilbert M. & Terrence Lyons, eds. *African Foreign Policies: Power and Process.* Boulder: Lynne Rienner, 2001.

Keller, Edmond J. & Donald Rothchild, eds. *Africa in the New International Order: Rethinking State Sovereignty and Regional Security.* Boulder: Lynne Rienner, 1996.

Kieh, George Klay & Ida Rousseau Mukenge, eds. *Zones of Conflict in Africa: Theories and Cases.* New York: Praeger Publishers, 2002.

Kodjo, Edem. *Et Demain l'Afrique.* Paris: Stock, 1985.

Kodjo, Edem. *Africa Today.* Accra: Ghana Universities Press, 1989.

Laïdi, Zaki. *The Superpowers and Africa: The Constraints of a Rivalry* Chicago: The University of Chicago Press, 1990.

Lara, Oruno D. *La Naissance du Panafricanisme: Les racines caraïbes*

américaines et africaines du mouvement au 19ème siècle. Paris: Maisonneuve & Larose, 2000.

Laremont, Ricardo René, ed. *The Causes of War and the Consequences of Peacekeeping in Africa.* Westport: Heinemann, 2001.

Lavergne, Réal, ed. *Regional Integration and Cooperation in West Africa: A Multidimensional Perspective.* Trenton & Ottawa: Africa World Press/International Development Research Centre, 1997.

Legum, Colin. *Africa since Independence.* Bloomington: Indiana University Press, 1999.

Lumumba-Kasongo, Tukumbi. *Political Re-Mapping of Africa: Transnational Ideology and the Re-Definition of Africa in World Politics.* Lanham: University Press of America, 1994.

———. *The Dynamics of Economic and Political Relations Between Africa and Foreign Powers: A Study in International Relations.* New York: Praeger Publishers, 1999.

Madsen, Wayne. *Genocide and Covert Operations in Africa, 1993-1999.* Lewiston: The Edwin Mellen Press, 1999.

Makgoba, Malegapuru William, ed. *African Renaissance: The New Struggle.* Sandton & Cape Town: Mafube/Tafelberg, 1999.

Mamdani, Mahmood. *Citizen and Subject: Contemporary Africa and the Legacy of Late Colonialism.* Princeton: Princeton University Press, 1996.

Manning, Patrick. *Francophone Sub-Saharan Africa, 1880-1995.* New York: Cambridge University Press, 2nd edition, 1998.

Martin, Guy. *African Regional Integration: Lessons from the West and*

Central African Experiences. Lagos: Nigerian Institute of International Affairs [Lecture Series no. 50], 1989.

Martin, Guy. "France and Africa." In *France in World Politics.* Edited by Robert Aldrich & John Connell. London & New York: Routledge, 1989: pp. 101-126.

————. "The Preferential Trade Area for Eastern & Southern Africa: Achievements, Problems & Prospects." In *Regional Integration in Africa: Unfinished Agenda.* Edited by Peter Anyang' Nyong'o. Nairobi: Academy Science Publishers, 1990: pp. 157-179.

————. "Security and Conflict Management in Chad." *Bulletin of Peace Proposals* 21, no. 1 (March 1990): pp. 37-47.

————. "African Regional Cooperation and Integration: Achievements, Problems and Prospects." In *21st Century Africa: Towards a New Vision of Self-Sutainable Development.* Edited by Ann Seidman & Frederick Anang. Trenton & Atlanta: Africa World Press/African Studies Association Press, 1992, pp. 69-99.

————. "Francophone Africa in the Context of Franco-African Relations." In *Africa in World Politics: Post-Cold War Challenges.* Edited by John W. Harbeson & Donald Rothchild. Boulder: Westview Press, 2nd edition, 1995: pp. 163-188.

————. "The Re-marginalization of Africa in the New World Order." *Ufahamu* 23, no. 3 (Fall 1995): pp. 149-152.

————. "Continuité et changement dans les relations franco-africaines." *Afrique 2000: Revue africaine de politique internationale* no. 26 (janvier-mars 1997): pp. 7-18.

————. "Conflict Resolution in Africa." *African Journal on Conflict Prevention, Management & Resolution* 1, no. 2 (May-August 1997).

pp. 14-18.

Martin, Guy. "Reflections on Democracy and Development in Africa: The Intellectual Legacy of Claude Ake." *Ufahamu* 26, no. 1 (Winter 1998): pp. 102-109.

————. *The African Nation-State in Crisis: Alternative Frameworks for Regional Governance.* Bellville: Centre for Southern African Studies/University of the Western Cape [Southern African Perspectives no. 76], 1999.

————. "The African Nation-State in Crisis: An Alternative Framework for Regional Governance," in *Globalisation and the Post-Colonial African State.* Edited by Dani W. Nabudere. Harare: AAPS Books, 2000, pp. 155-168.

————. "Lomé Convention/Cotonou Agreement," in *The Oxford Companion to Politics of the World.* Edited by Joel Krieger. New York: Oxford University Press, 2nd edition, 2001, pp. 506-8.

————. "France's African Policy in Transition: Disengagement and Redeployment." In *Mélanges Euro-Africains offerts au Professeur Max Liniger-Goumaz.* Edited by Luis Ondo Ayang *et. al.* Madrid: Editorial Claves para el Futuro, 2001, vol. 1, pp. 373-388.

Mazrui, Ali A. *Towards a Pax Africana: A Study of Ideology and Ambition.* Chicago: The University of Chicago Press, 1967.

————. *Africa's International Relations: The Diplomacy of Dependency and Change.* London: Heinemann, 1977.

Mazzeo, Domenico, ed. *African Regional Organizations.* New York: Cambridge University Press, 1984.

Melvern, Linda. *A People Betrayed: The Role of the West in Rwanda's Genocide.* London & New York: Zed Books, 2000.

Michailof, Serge, ed. *La France et l'Afrique: Vade-mecum pour un nouveau voyage.* Paris: Karthala, 1993.

Mshomba, Richard E. *Africa in the Global Economy.* Boulder: Lynne Rienner, 2000.

Nabudere, Dani W., ed. *Globalisation and the Post-Colonial African State.* Harare: African Association of Political Science/AAPS Books, 2000.

Nkrumah, Kwame. *Africa Must Unite.* London: Panaf Books, 1963.

Nzongola-Ntalaja, Georges. *Revolution and Counter-Revolution in Africa.* London: Zed Books, 1987.

Ojo, Olajedi O., ed. *Africa and Europe: The Changing Economic Relationship.* London: Zed Books, 1996.

Ojo, Olatunde J.C.B., D. Katete Orwa & C.M.B. Utete. *African International Relations.* New York: Longman, 1985.

Okolo, Julius E. & Timothy M. Shaw, eds. *The Political Economy of Foreign Policy in ECOWAS.* New York: St. Martin's Press, 1994.

Olukoshi, Adebayo O. & Liisa Laakso, eds. *Challenges to the Nation-State in Africa.* Uppsala: Nordiska Afrikainstitutet, 1996.

Onwuka, Ralph I. & Amadu Sesay, eds. *The Future of Regionalism in Africa.* New York: St. Martin's Press, 1985.

Onwuka, Ralph I. & Timothy M. Shaw, eds. *Africa in World Politics: Into the 1990s.* New York: St. Martin's Press, 1989.

Osabu-Kle, Daniel T. *Compatible Cultural Democracy: The Key to Development in Africa*. Peterborough: Broadview Press, 2000.

Oyebade, Adebayo & Abiodun Alao, eds. *Africa After the Cold War: The Changing Perspectives on Security*. Trenton: Africa World Press, 1998.

Péan, Pierre. *Affaires Africaines*. Paris: Fayard, 1983.

———. *L'Argent Noir: Corruption et sous-développement*. Paris: Fayard, 1988.

Pondi, Jean-Emmanuel. *Relations Internationales Africaines: Bibliographie annotée de 20 années de recherche à l'Institut des Relations Internationales du Cameroun/IRIC*. Berne: Peter Lang, 1993.

Prah, Kwesi K. *Beyond the Color Line: Pan-Africanist Disputations*. Trenton: Africa World Press, 1998.

Prendergast, John. *Frontline Diplomacy: Humanitarian Aid and Conflict in Africa*. Boulder: Lynne Rienner, 1996.

Prunier, Gérard. *The Rwanda Crisis: History of a Genocide*. New York: Columbia University Press, 1995.

Ramonet, Ignacio. *Géopolitique du chaos*. Paris: Éditions Galilée, 1997.

Rodney, Walter. *How Europe Underdeveloped Africa*. Washington, DC: Howard University Press, 1982.

Ropivia, Marc-Louis. *Géopolitique de l'Intégration en Afrique noire.* Paris: L'Harmattan, 1994.

Rotberg, Robert I., ed. *Peacekeeping and Peace Enforcement in Africa: Methods of Conflict Prevention.* Washington, DC: Brookings Institution Press, 2000.

Roy, Jean-Louis. *Une nouvelle Afrique: À l'aube du XXIème siècle.* Montréal: Éditions Hurtubise HMH, 1999.

Sandbrook, Richard. *Closing the Circle: Democratization and Development in Africa.* Toronto & New York: Between the Lines/Zed Books, 2000.

Sangaré, Louis. *Les fondements économiques d'un État confédéral en Afrique de l'Ouest: Les étapes africaines de l'intégration multisectorielle sous-régionale.* Paris: L'Harmattan, 1998.

Schraeder, Peter J. *U.S. Foreign Policy Toward Africa: Incrementalism, Crisis and Change.* New York: Cambridge University Press, 1994.

———. *African Politics and Society: A Mosaic in Transformation.* Boston & New York: Bedford/St. Martin's, 2000.

———. "African International Relations." In *Understanding Contemporary Africa.* Edited by April A. Gordon & Donald L. Gordon. Boulder: Lynne Rienner, 3rd edition, 2001, pp. 143-187.

Schwab, Peter. *Africa: A Continent Self-Destructs.* New York: Palgrave, 2001.

Sesay, Amadu, ed. *Africa and Europe: From Partition to Interdependence or Dependence?* Dover: Croom-Helm, 1986.

———, ed. *The OAU After Twenty-five Years.* Cambridge, U.K.: St.

Martin's Press, 1990. .

Shaw, Timothy M. & S. Ojo, eds. *Africa in the International Political System*. Lanham: University Press of America, 1982.

Smock, David R., ed. *Making War and Waging Peace: Foreign Intervention in Africa*. Washington, DC: U.S. Institute of Peace Press, 1993.

Smock, David R. & Chester A. Crocker, eds. *African Conflict Resolution: The U.S. Role in Peacemaking*. Washington, DC: U.S. Institute of Peace Press, 1995.

Sorbo, Gunnar M. & Peter Vale, eds. *Out of Conflict: From War to Peace in Africa*. Uppsala: Nordiska Afrikainstitutet, 1997.

Thiam, Doudou. *The Foreign Policy of African States: Ideological Bases, Present Realities and Future Prospects*. Westport: Greenwood Press, 1977.

Thomson, Alex. *An Introduction to African Politics*. London & New York: Routledge, 2000.

Thompson, Vincent Bakpetu. *Africa and Unity: The Evolution of Pan-Africanism*. London: Longman, 1969.

Verschave, François-Xavier. *Complicité de génocide? La politique de la France au Rwanda*. Paris: La Découverte, 1994.

———. *La Françafrique: le plus long scandale de la République*. Paris: Stock, 1998.

———. *Noir Silence: Qui arrêtera la Françafrique?* Paris: Les Arènes, 2000.

Wallerstein, Immanuel. *Africa: The Politics of Unity*. New York: Vintage Books, 1969.

Wallerstein, Immanuel. *Africa and the Modern World*. Trenton: Africa World Press, 1990.

Walraven, Klaas van. *Dreams of Power: The Role of the Organization of African Unity in the Politics of Africa*. Aldershot & Leiden: Ashgate/African Studies Centre, 1999.

Wolfers, Michael. *Politics in the Organization of African Unity*. London: Methuen, 1976.

Wright, Stephen, ed. *African Foreign Policies*. Boulder: Westview Press, 1999.

Zartman, I. William. *International Relations in the New Africa*. Lanham: University Press of America, 1987.

———. *Ripe for Resolution: Conflict and Intervention in Africa*. New York: Oxford University Press, updated edition, 1989.

———. ed. *Europe and Africa: The New Phase*. Boulder: Lynne Rienner, 1993.

———. ed. *Collapsed States: The Disintegration and Restoration of Legitimate Authority*. Boulder: Lynne Rienner, 1995.

———. ed. *Traditional Cures for Modern Conflicts: African Conflict "Medicine"*. Boulder: Lynne Rienner, 2000.

Zeleza, Paul Tiyambe. *A Modern Economic History of Africa. Volume*

1: The Nineteenth Century. Dakar: CODESRIA Book Series, 1993.

————. *Manufacturing African Studies and Crises.* Dakar: CODESRIA Book Series, 1997.

Index